DEATH BY CHOICE

DEATH BY CHOICE

DANIEL C. MAGUIRE

DOUBLEDAY & COMPANY, INC.
GARDEN CITY, NEW YORK
1974

ISBN: 0-385-07642-8
Library of Congress Catalog Card Number 73–81441
Copyright © 1973, 1974 by Daniel C. Maguire

To my son, whose birth occurred during the writing of this book on death to remind me powerfully and anew of the miracle and the sanctity of life, and to his mother, whose affirmation of life is exuberant and communicable.

Acknowledgments

Acknowledgments will be brief or unread. So be it. My cordial thanks go to Elizabeth Bartelme, Doubleday editor who suggested this book and then, with cruel and unusual insistence on a deadline, pressed me to complete it; to James O'Gara, editor of *Commonweal*, who first invited me to address this subject in print; to Arthur Turner, M.D., for answering many importunate questions; to Dennis Doherty, my Marquette University colleague in ethics, for good criticism; to Denise McHugh, who exemplifies the potential of the underestimated nursing profession, for suggestions born of experience; to Regina Hall for invaluable research assistance; to David Stoughton for straight answers to many questions concerning the law; to Karen Gritzmacher, Lorna Rixmann, and Mary Beth Zannoni, who deciphered and then typed my manuscript; to Margie, my wife, for ideas and criticism offered in spite of the demands of new maternity; and to my parents and the countless others who gave me a love for life, which is the indispensable prerequisite for any attempt at a humane evaluation of death and our moral dominion over it.

Contents

DEATH BY CHOICE

PART ONE

A New Climate for Death

About two million people die each year in the United States, and the American culture has finally decided to take note of this fact. Death in our day is having its belated due. It is slipping out from under denials and disguises and bursting into explicit, obsessional, and, at times, pornographic recognition. Harvard professor Edwin Schneidman goes so far as to dub this "the age of death." "In the Western world," he writes, "we are probably more death-oriented today than we have been since the days of the Black Plague in the 14th century."[1] There is a thanatology boom in colleges and in print and there are random reports from the lecture circuits that death is now outdrawing the perennials—sex and politics.

Though there are many levels and facets to this revolutionary shift in death-consciousness, the overall meaning is probably one of gain and health and not of decadence and morbidity. Only in a mature culture can death come of age and be received and accepted as a natural companion of life. The death preoccupation we are witnessing is probably a clumsy but significant rite of passage. At the very least, it might exonerate Americans of the British historian Arnold Toynbee's charge that, for Americans, death is un-American and an affront to every citizen's inalienable right to life, liberty, and the pursuit of happiness.[2] But, more than that, it affects and may well have epochal meaning for Western Culture. Western civilization is Faustian in the sense that it is impatient with limits. It is a *can do* and *will do* civilization. Its paramount accents are on action and power. Small wonder that it has been so slow to come to grips with death, which is, after all, the very ultimate in passivity, impotence, and limit.

Whatever the long-term cultural significance of our current concern with death, however, there are shorter-term questions which are now urgently addressing the moral consciences of mortal men. Some of these questions are old and some are new welling out of the qualitative changes that technology has made. Basically, they arise from the fact that man is the only animal who knows he is going to die and who also knows he can bring about his own death. Only man can be troubled, like Hamlet, about the relative advantages of death over continued living. Before the prospect of death, man is, in the most poignant sense of Sartre's phrase, "condemned to freedom." He may allocate his own death or passively await its arrival. He may have death by chance or death by choice. He may also, in a reflective way, allocate death for others when he judges that certain values outweigh the need or right of others to remain alive. Indeed, history shows that men have chosen death for other men with a rather formidable liberality. Men have also chosen to bring their own lives to a voluntary close. But it is no gentle irony that humans have traditionally been much quicker to justify the killing of others than the killing of self. Historically, and even into our day, suicide is more morally repugnant than slaughter.

At any rate, if the problem of willful death-dealing is as old as man, what and whence are the new problems and urgencies?

The problems have taken on new urgency because of a) revolutionary developments in medical science; b) the laggardly state of the law; and c) important shifts in moral outlook.

FOOTNOTES—PART ONE

1. Edwin Schneidman, "The Enemy," *Psychology Today* 4, no. 3 (August 1970): 37.

2. For a study of the changing American attitudes toward death, cf. *Social Research* no. 3 (Autumn 1972), an issue devoted to the topic "Death in American Experience." Also, in a popular vein, cf. Kenneth L. Woodward, "Death in America," *U.S. Catholic/Jubilee*, January 1971, pp. 6–11.

CHAPTER 1

Medicine: Powers and Problems

There are promising changes that are also troubling in the medicine of this day. Medical science has acquired dramatic new powers over life and death. As the French physician J. Hamburger says: "It is clear that the enormous increase in the power of the doctor raises many questions which have never previously been posed—'Science has made us gods before we are even worthy of being man.'"[1] Science, which once basked in the illusion that it was somehow "value-free" is suddenly up to its neck in value-loaded questions.[2] Medicine becomes more and more implicated with ethics as it is repeatedly forced to ask itself if it *may* do what it suddenly and often surprisingly *can* do.

And, speaking of the surprising, medicine, which has been making all these quantum leaps in our century, suddenly finds itself bereft of an agreed-upon definition of death, which, by any standard, is a very fundamental problem. "When you are dead, you are dead," is no longer a meaningful truism since death is now seen, not as a "moment" but as a process and indeed as a very manipulable process. The current terms "brain death" and "heart death" suggest an unsettling distinction, especially since you can have one without the other. Furthermore, in days of primitive medicine, death was often the solution for many of "nature's mistakes" and tragedies. Now medical technology can forestall the solution that death once would have brought in those cases where death would have been thought a blessing. As Sir Theodore Fox told the Royal College of Physicians in 1965, "though cures are getting commoner, so too are half-cures, in which death is averted but disability remains."[3] The inability to define death and the ability to create situations where death would appear to be preferable, is part of the perplexing yield of scientific medical progress.

In this chapter, I will trace out some of the revolutionary advances in medicine and show the questions raised by this progress. This chapter will seek to give the questions that modern medicine presents to morality and to law and to see the medical climate in which questions of death by choice are being faced.

What are some of the problem-making powers of modern medicine? Perhaps the most obvious achievement of medical science is the mounting longevity of the species. For most of his history, man has been a rather short-lived creature, especially when compared with some of the other warm-blooded creatures.[4] Scholars can only estimate the average length of life for our prehistoric ancestors by studying fragmentary data and by observation of contemporary groups whose conditions probably approximate those of prehistory. According to these estimates, prehistoric man lived on the average about eighteen years.[5] In those medically and socially brutish days survival beyond forty was a rare achievement. Longevity mounted, however, but slowly. Professor Monroe Lerner of Johns Hopkins University writes:

> With the rise of the early civilizations and the consequent improvements in living conditions, longevity must surely have risen, reaching perhaps 20 years in ancient Greece and perhaps 22 in ancient Rome. Life expectancy is estimated to have been about 33 years in England during the Middle Ages, about 35 in the Massachusetts Bay Colony of North America, about 41 in England and Wales during the nineteenth century, and 47.3 in the death registration states of the United States in 1900.[6]

Since 1900, many of the communicable diseases have been conquered and life has lengthened. We have thus entered the gerontological era. E. Fuller Torrey, M.D., of the Stanford University Medical Center writes: "Since 1900 the average life expectancy has increased from 47 to 70 years. . . . It has been estimated that about one-quarter of all human beings who have ever reached age 65 are alive today."[7] Those over sixty-five are expected to increase from 18.5 million in 1966 to 24.5 million in 1980—which will be something like one out of every eight persons.[8] What is even more striking is that the principal causes of death are now diseases of the heart and malignant neoplasms (cancer). As of 1966 it was estimated that heart disease accounted for 39.3 per cent of all deaths and cancer for 16.2 per cent.[9] Now, if one speculates—and one may, given the track record of medicine—that these two killers can be brought under substantive control, we would have mastered the causes of nearly half our current deaths. With an imaginative eye on the future, Sir George Thompson in his book *The Foreseeable Future* entertained the possibility that if all the causes of senility are conquered, all death will be by accident or by intent.[10] Sir George is not alone in his speculations. Dr. Torrey reports that research is progressing toward elucidating the mystery of aging:

> Why must cells and organisms grow old at all? A frog's egg has been injected with a protein that arrests its growth; it apparently does not grow old. And a "juvenile hormone" that apparently stops aging in caterpillars is being explored. Besides this, there is the possibility of "preventive surgery" being developed, replacing organs before they age and wear out.[11]

Some people are so sure of the medical wonderland of the future that they are attempting to insure themselves a share in it. In January of 1967, Dr. James H. Bedford of Glendale, California, was dying of lung cancer. Before he died he made provisions for having his body frozen and put into cold storage in the hope that when a cure for lung cancer was found, he could be revived and cured.[12] This freezing away for a better day approach is known as cryonics. In existence are the Cryonics Societies of California and New York, the Society for Biosis, and the Life Extension Society. Dr. Torrey is willing to say that "with further study it becomes apparent that their theories are far from absurd."[13] Hamsters have been frozen to −5°C and reanimated. A cat's brain was frozen for 203 days in Japan and reanimated. And it is common practice to freeze human skin, corneas, blood, sperm, nerves, and bone and use them later. Bone has been frozen for as long as eleven years. And hypothermia, lowering the body's temperature to slow metabolic processes, is an acknowledged medical procedure.[14]

The quest for immortality marches on. An important ethical

question, however, is asked by physician J. Russell Elkinton: "When Adam and Eve ate of the fruit of the Tree of Knowledge, they lost their immortality. Do we really want it back?"[15] What would be the quality and meaning that people would find in protracted life?

As law professor Bayless Manning writes about the day when people can be kept alive for 150 to 200 years:

> Somewhere along the way, consciously or unconsciously, explicitly or implicitly, society will have to make some basic decisions about the allocation of economic resources as between human beings of advanced years and those who are younger. . . . We have not begun to consider the violent social dislocation that would be brought about if a large fraction of the population were to be kept alive for significantly longer periods of time.[16]

Is it not possible that people will sense that there is truly a time for living and a time for dying and that future man will have the decision of death taken off his organism and put onto his will? Are not the pressures for shaping a moral position on death by choice mounting with every medical advance? Medical advance has helped to give us the population problem. Will it not intensify that problem until men realize that individual death is a service to the life of the species since, if death continues to recede, we may find ourselves medically ingenious but beleaguered by a lack of room and resources? Could a moral obligation then arise to terminate one's life responsibly? Will not this problem grow with our technical control over life so that our debt to the species will more and more have to be voluntarily and not involuntarily rendered? And while indulging in these futuristics, what if people do not have the compliance and social consciousness of the Eskimo elders who departed this life on an ice floe? Would compliance have to be enforced? By whom, and with what distinctions? Would a utilitarian calculus weigh the worth to society of Mr. Jones as opposed to Dr. Einstein? Could we not also expect that as infant mortality goes down and disease is further vanquished, and population pressures on the earth's resources increase, there will be special challenges to the right to life of defective children? Lest we appear to have stretched our futurism to the point of implausibility, let us note the words of Millard S. Everett in his book *Ideals of Life:*

> My personal feeling—and I don't ask anyone to agree with me—is that eventually, when public opinion is prepared for it, no child shall be admitted into the society of the living who would be certain to suffer any social handicap—for example, any physical or mental defect that would prevent marriage or would make others tolerate his company only from a sense of mercy. . . . Life in early infancy is very close to non-existence, and admitting a child into our society is almost like admitting one from potential to actual existence, and viewed in this way only normal life should be accepted.[17]

The British jurist Glanville Williams also discusses the program of "involuntary euthanasia" for defective infants. Noting that the Euthanasia Society of America included this idea in its original program, he observes that "the legalization of euthanasia for handicapped children would bring the law into closer relation to its practical administration, because juries do not regard parental mercy-killing as murder."[18] He also notes: "The proposal certainly escapes the chief objection to the similar proposal for senile dementia: it does not create a sense of insecurity in society, because infants cannot, like adults, feel anticipatory dread of being done to death if their condition should worsen."[19] Thus what to some is unthinkable, has been thought and written. Medical power with every victory over disease creates conditions that stir up moral questions about death by choice and will continue to do so.

DEATH AS FRIEND OR ENEMY

Some of the other problems presented by the new medical capabilities are quite close to home and are not related to population stress. They arise from the fact that medicine cannot distinguish between good death and bad death. As medicine has developed, it is geared to promoting life under all circumstances. Death is the natural enemy of the healing science.

Death, however, can at times be a friend. It can at times be a welcome deliverance from a situation that had ceased to be bearable. Pneumonia has been referred to as "an old man's friend" since it often served, in days of simpler science, to shorten the old man's final agony. Actually, it was death that was the friend; pneumonia merely gave access to it. Now, of course, pneumonia usually can be contained and the old man lingers on in agony.

Dr. Eliot Slater, Editor-in-Chief of the *British Journal of Psychiatry*, puts it in blunt language: "Death performs for us the inestimable office of clearing up a mess too big to mend; if we are going to intervene, then we must have at least some hope of doing this ourselves."[20] What Dr. Slater is unambiguously saying is, if diseases like pneumonia, etc., can be a friend, why can we not be? Is it not within man's inherent moral freedom to recognize instances when death would be a blessing and to bring it about in ways that would be even more merciful than a bout of pneumonia? (Pneumonia is, by no reckoning, a pleasant friend.)

Let us look at another example of the inverse side of medical progress. Sometimes patients with a terminal illness will be unable to take nourishment by mouth. In these cases they are now fed intravenously. Sometimes, the intravenous feeding is not a friend. Consider this case:

> A cancer patient is in extreme pain and his system has gradually established what physicians call "toleration" of any drug, so that even increased doses give only brief respites from the ever-recurring pain. The attending physician knows that the disease is incurable and that the person is slowly dying, but because of a good heart, it is possible that this agony will continue for several weeks. The physician then remembers that there is one thing he can do to end the suffering. He can cut off intravenous feeding and the patient will surely die. He does this and before the next day the patient is dead.[21]

Many of the older theologians approved of discontinuing the intravenous feeding in this kind of case.

Or what of the obligation to maintain the use of an oxygen tent? Ethicists have long since granted that it is moral to discontinue the use of oxygen in certain circumstances where death will inevitably follow. Thus Charles McFadden, a conservative moralist, writes: ". . . if one were to think of recourse to oxygen as a *permanent* means of surviving I feel certain it should be classified as an *extraordinary* measure, which would not be morally binding."[22]

There are other cases where nature taking its own course would seem to be the best doctor. Consider the case of a diabetic patient who has been using insulin for years and who develops an inoperable and very painful kind of cancer. By continuing with the insulin, she may live many months in agony. By discontinuing the insulin she would lapse into coma and die painlessly. Here is a case where diabetes would appear to be a friend.[23]

Interestingly, this case was considered by Catholic moralists some years ago—in a very conservative period of Catholic moral theology—and reasons were found that might justify this action. There was a stern view that the patient would have to continue using the insulin since it was a normal medicament. However, Gerald Kelly, was not so sure. He noted that ordinary means to preserve life must be taken when there is "a reasonable hope of success." Regarding the rigorous opinion, Kelly said: ". . . I no longer consider this solution as certain because I am not sure we are justified in stating that the patient must prescind from the cancer in determining her obligation of using the insulin."[24]

The obvious question, then, is: what of the patient suffering from a similar cancer who does not have the "blessing" of diabetes? Is she to be friendless in the absence of an accommodating disease? Cases like this press on us the question: must mortal man await the good pleasure of biochemical and organic factors and allow these to determine the time and the manner of his demise? Putting it in religious language, can the will of God regarding a person's death be manifested only through disease or the collapse of sick or wounded organs, or could it also be discovered through the sensitive appreciations and reasonings of moral men?

There is, of course, a big difference between not using insulin or not treating pneumonia and overdosing a patient to accelerate the death process. An evaluation of that difference will be part of our subsequent moral evaluation of the distinction between omission and commission. While looking at the questions posed by the current state of medical science, however, we can see that the failure to use ordinary means (antibiotics, insulin, oxygen) when they are available and necessary for life, and when death results from their deliberate non-use, does give new vigor to the old question of whether the prohibition against all direct action to terminate life is hermetically closed. Though omission and commission are different realities with a potential for radically different moral meaning, they have a suggestive similarity in that in both cases, someone is dead who would have been alive if a different decision (to act or not act) had been made. Without offering moral judgment at this moment, it is enough here to note the moral case for omission is raising the question of the moral case for commission with increasing insistency in our day.

Some of the most difficult cases which medical progress has thrown at us involve children. Moralist Paul Ramsey of Princeton University presents one of the questions that medicine is putting to morals: "Should cardiac surgery be performed to remove the lesions that are part of the picture in cases of mongolism, from which many mercifully died before the brilliant developments of recent years?"[25] Obviously, this is a very real question for many persons. At Johns Hopkins University Hospital, the parents of a mongoloid baby requiring surgery for survival, refused to give permission. This case is not, by any means, unique but it received national attention in the fall of 1971. The baby was ordered to have nothing by mouth. It took the baby fifteen days to succumb, during which time the hospital staff had to watch the infant struggle unsuccessfully for life. Many moral and legal questions were raised by this one incident. Should the parents have been made to take the child home and bear the pain of standing the death watch that their decision inaugurated? Should the state have taken legal charge of the baby away from the parents and then authorized the operation, or should a court order have overruled the parents' decision? If it was thought that the child's death would indeed have been a mercy, could it not have been accelerated by increasingly large doses of morphine? In other words, should a certain amount of commission be added to the fundamental omission of the operation.

Though the death of this child *may* have been a mercy, the dying was not. In fact, is this not a case where the omission might have been immoral without the act of overdosing to shorten the final fifteen days of torture? In other words, maybe omission was harder to justify in this case than commission. Or is the entire question of opting for this baby's death morally repugnant? Professor Arthur J. Dyck of Harvard Divinity would seem to think so, since he refers to this very incident to show that those who reject out of hand any comparison of what happened in Nazi Germany with what we could expect here, had better take heed.[26] Dyck sees the Johns Hopkins case as "murder." Is he correct?

Dr. Warren Reich, a senior research associate at the Kennedy Center for Bioethics at Georgetown University, posed a difficult case at the meeting of the International Congress of Learned Societies in the Field of Religion in September 1972.[27] The case involved a girl (Missy) who was born with spina bifida with meningomyelocele of the lumbar spine. Spina bifida refers to an opening in the spine and meningomyelocele is a condition in which portions of the spinal cord, as well as meninges and spinal fluid, have slipped out through the spinal opening and are enclosed in a sac. The child lacked reflex activity in both legs and could not control her anal or urinary sphincters. She had club feet.

Hydrocephalus, "water on the brain," develops in 90 per cent of these cases. To treat that, a "shunt" has to be surgically inserted to drain the cerebrospinal fluid from the brain into the heart or peritoneum. Even with a shunt, the child would have a fifty-fifty chance of being mentally retarded. Missy's complications might eventually require a surgical procedure which would allow her urine to drain into a bag which she would wear on her abdomen permanently. Bowel control would be a lifelong problem for her. Kidney failure is a constant danger and the most common cause of death for children with this affliction. Broken bones and burns are the frequent lot of such children also, due to problems in mobility and sensation.

In the panel discussion of this case, Dr. Harmon Smith of Duke University Divinity School noted that until ten years ago, about 80 per cent of such babies died and that today 75 per cent survive. Thus again, medical advance brings on troubling new moral questions. Should this baby have been allowed to die from the meningitis that would normally ensue in such cases? Or should the medics have begun at once what would be for the child a lifetime of extraordinary care? The panel at the congress (which, along with Reich and Smith, included Dr. Eric Cassell of Cornell University Medical College) considered only these two options.

In the discussion, it was suggested to the panel that there were other options, such as the direct termination of life. This was an option that no member of the panel would even consider. "I find it is absolutely incredible, even in a mere debate, to consider this a serious alternative in a group of moralists and theologians," said Professor Smith. The other panelists agreed that this line should never be crossed. A very fair question, of course, is, why? Why is it so clear that these two alternatives exhaust the moral possibilities of the described case and that the path of direct termination is beyond the pale?

First of all, it is not clear that meningitis would be an efficient "friend." As Dr. Reich pointed out, babies have been known to survive the meningitis and live a number of years without being aware of anything and requiring a great amount of physical care. Thus the problem could be intensified by mere omission and reliance on the disease to achieve the desired results. Furthermore, as one of the doctors in the audience pointed out in this discussion, death by meningitis in such cases is not normally serene. It is not really a neat solution. Disease in this instance may not come to the aid of ethics.

There can be good reasons offered to keep a child like this alive. Advances are being made in the treatment of nearly all the symptoms of this affliction. It may even be argued that if people do not take a chance on life for such children, medicine will not be able to learn all that it needs to conquer and prevent this disorder. It may be further argued that we should be extremely cautious about opting for death for a child.[28] Caution is further indicated by the basic fact that a decision is being made for another person.

Given the realities of the case as described, however, it is possible that death might be seen as preferable to the kind of life this child could have. The moral question then is whether the death should be entrusted to the imminent disease or whether it could be brought on by the administration of drugs or whether a compromise could be found whereby the drugs are used to comfort and to weaken in co-ordination with the meningitis. In the present state of legal and moral debate, the latter possibility would offer the advantage of protective ambiguity. There is no precise way of knowing whether a drug is accelerating death as it relieves discomfort since the unrelieved discomfort might accelerate death too and since the degree of immunity to the drug is a variable. Still, this flight to ambiguity would represent a retreat from the question to be explored in this book, viz., can it be moral and should it be legal to take direct action to terminate life in certain circumstances?

Another of the terrible new powers of medicine is its ability to prolong life at a vegetative level. Take the case of a patient whose spontaneous brain activities are limited to those arising from the brainstem, which controls breathing and circulation. Such a creature can be kept alive with stimulants and nourishment for a long period of time. Does it make good sense to do so?

In fact, patients with hopelessly damaged brains can be kept alive for indefinite periods through the use of respirators which keep the heart and lungs pumping. In these cases, the brain may, by any definition, be dead. Cases have been known where autopsy later revealed that the brain had even liquefied.[29] A California doctor reports the case of a patient with irreversible brain damage who was maintained for eight years. Tubes for feeding and release of wastes kept the body going in a state of no mental response. "You could have taken a lighted match and held it against his eye and he still wouldn't have known you were there," the doctor said.[30] His eight-year expenses came to $300,000. If the tubes had been taken away, he would have died completely within seventy-two hours.

The moral questions that arise out of such bizarre cases are these: is merely physical, vegetative life sacred, or is it life that is actually or potentially personal that is sacred? In cases like this, is the burden of proof not on those who would keep such life going rather than on those who would end it? What could justify prolonging life like this unless the body was being sustained in this way in anticipation of organ transplantation? What are the moral presuppositions of persons responsible for such life-extending feats?

Another problem arising from the previous case and from other less extreme situations is the moral significance of cost. How should one weigh the potential cost of treatment in determining whether to live or die? Dr. Robert Glaser, Dean of the School of Medicine at Stanford University, takes note of the cost of heroic procedures. He cites the case of Mike Kasperak, a heart transplant patient, who spent the last sixteen days of his life in a hospital at a cost of $28,845.83. This cost was mitigated by the fact that the surgical team were salaried, full-time academicians who submitted no fee.[31] The National Heart Institute estimates the minimum cost of a heart transplant at $20,000, plus several hundred dollars a day for the postoperative period when rejection is an enduring problem. Insurance, of course, is a major relief. In Kasperak's case hospital insurance paid most of the bill but did not cover the $7,200 worth of blood he needed. How should patients and families of patients weigh these costs? Or should this unseemly calculus be removed by an enlightened government picking up the tab for all extraordinary expenses associated with specified kinds of illness?

The use of the kidney machine (hemodialysis) is another miracle of modern medicine. Yet, again, progress poses questions. Remarkable as it is, dialysis does not always produce a healthful and tolerable existence for all renal patients. What then is the right of a patient to go off dialysis and face certain death? One patient went off dialysis because he thought "that he was dying slowly, without dignity, and leaving an unpleasant memory for his teen-age children as well as making intemperate demands on their sympathy, attention, and devotion."[32]

Pacemakers are another marvel of modern medicine. They stimulate the heart for persons who have no spontaneous rhythmical function of the heart. Thousands of persons are alive today because of these. Here again, a new blessing leads to new questions. In March 1972, New York City's Cornell Medical Center got court permission to install new batteries in the pacemaker of an incompetent seventy-nine-year-old man over his wife's objections. State Supreme Court Justice Gerald P. Culkin declared the patient incompetent, and named the hospital director his guardian.[33] Here both medicine and the law stood in the way of what the woman perceived to be a good death.

And so the questions mount. Should we try to cure a severely brain-damaged child or adult who contracts pneumonia or appendicitis? Does a man have a right to give a paired organ such as a kidney for transplant if there is a possibility that he may need that organ some day and die if the remaining kidney should fail? Should a seriously defective child be stimulated to breathe at birth? How much blood should be given to terminal patients? May a dying person offer one of his healthy organs even though this will weaken him and speed up his death? Or could he do even more than this?

The British attorney Mary Barrington writes: "Death taken in one's own time, and with a sense of purpose, may in fact be far more bearable than the process of waiting to be arbitrarily extinguished. A patient near the end of his life who arranged his death so as, for example, to permit an immediate transfer of a vital organ to a younger person, might well feel that he was converting his death into a creative act instead of waiting passively to be suppressed."[34]

What is Death?

One last problem deriving from the flow of medical achievement is a most pressing one. It concerns the detection of death. Obviously this is a problem when we address the termination of life. If you terminate the life of a patient whose brain is dead, are you terminating a person's life, or merely terminating the vestigial vital processes of an oxygenated corpse?

The determination of death twenty-five years ago was not a very difficult job. If the patient's heart stopped beating and he stopped breathing, he was pronounced dead. Sometimes death was verified by electrocardiogram. Sometimes too there was an injection of a drug like epinephrine (adrenaline) to produce a few more heartbeats. But death was a rather definitive and definable moment.

Today, the old criteria have been robbed of their simplicity. Prompt cardiac resuscitation can restore a normal heartbeat in many cases, and mechanical assistance can keep a heart going that has lost all spontaneous capacity to pump. In some cases, as we mentioned, the brain could be quite dead and yet respirators could keep cardiovascular and respiratory functions going.

In some cases where the cerebral cortex has been destroyed, the brainstem continues for a time to regulate heart and lung functioning. The question that arises is, can a "man" with a beating heart (maintained by lingering brainstem control) be declared dead if the cerebral cortex is clearly dead? Should we, in a word, move to brain death as opposed to heart death as the real death? The unique importance of the brain would seem to support this view. "The brain only gives man his reality; where it has disappeared, man no longer is."[35]

An agreement on brain death might present itself as the obvious solution, but here, as anywhere, facile solutions are suspect. There is the practical problem of how to determine that a person is dead of brain and therefore dead. The most promising means for discovering brain life or its absence, could appear to be the use of the electroencephalogram (EEG). A flat EEG might seem to be a clear-cut criterion for brain death. It is not. Persons with flat EEGs for several hours have been known to recover.[36] Furthermore, persons with flat EEGs have been observed to continue breathing for up to six hours.[37] Lower body temperatures and other factors can also affect the readings of the EEG. There are, however, other ways of supporting the judgment that death has overtaken the brain, which medical science is exploring at this time.

Dr. Julius Korein, Professor of Neurology at the New York University School of Medicine, states the problem this way: "Basic to the definition of the death of an individual is identification of the irreversible destruction of that critical component of the system which represents the essence of the person and which cannot be replaced with man-made devices which may serve as auxiliary support systems."[38] Korein distinguishes between brain death (death of the entire brain including brainstem) and cerebral death. He concludes that when cerebral death has been determined, the physician should pronounce the patient cerebrally dead and suggest the discontinuation of cardiovascular and pulmonary support systems.[39] In other words, cerebral death is death. It is his opinion that "Advances in medicine have accelerated development of techniques that will allow the physician to define and diagnose cerebral death with accuracy and rapidity in an appropriate hospital setting."[40] If this is true, the concept of cerebral death may be the best that can be done by way of updating the detection of death.[41]

Perhaps a case could best illustrate the need and the nature of a new definition of death. It concerns a twenty-year-old man who suffered a complete shattering of his cerebral cortex in an automobile accident four years previously.

> Since then only the brain stem has sustained life. All thought and feeling have been erased, and he has not moved a single muscle of his body since the accident. But he is in "excellent health", although he feels no stimulus of any kind, from within or without. Once an angular blond youth of sixteen, he is now a baby-faced "brunette" seemingly ten years old. He is fed through an indwelling nasal tube.[42]

It would seem obvious that such a situation requires a declaration of death. Death, in other words, should be declared even before the breathing stops, and even if a respirator is going to keep the body oxygenated for purposes of organ donation. The problem of whether or not we would bury a breathing corpse or whether or not a funeral parlor would receive one, is not a practical difficulty. Even if the brainstem has some life in it, the withdrawal of all support will quickly silence the lingering signs of life.

But what of the organs of the cerebrally dead? If we pull the plugs and allow the patient to die fully—heart, lungs, and even brainstem—we might also have waited so long that asphyxia has damaged all organs for potential transplant. Dr. Henry Beecher asks about the situation in which a decision has been made to turn off the respirator while the heart is, with this mechanical aid, still beating. His question is, ". . . what difference does it make whether the heart is stopped by inexorable asphyxia or by removal?"[43]

The question can also be asked about a case in which the heart is still beating by reason of brainstem functioning although cortical activity is entirely extinguished. Could this patient be declared dead so as to make it possible to keep him (it) breathing for purposes of transfer of tissue? Beecher is worried about the waste of needed organs due to timid and passé definitions of death. By his calculations, there could be made available in the United States each year over 10,600 kidneys for approximately 7,600 needy kidney recipients and 6,000 livers for 4,000 potential liver recipients. In this situation he believes that what is radical is not redefining death in a way that these tissues can be saved, but rather it is the waste of these organs that is clearly questionable.[44] Beecher, however, is willing to grant that he is proposing something that is not yet generally digestible. "Although the issues seem clear, it is doubtful whether we as a medical society have yet achieved enough emotional and sociologic maturity to handle this question boldly. Nevertheless, to fail to do so verges on the unethical."[45]

The problem of defining death in the presence of continuing heartbeat, however, is more than sociologic and emotional. There are also serious moral and legal considerations. To tie the definition of death to the organ needs of others, might build in a conflict of interest situation in the medical profession which is not in the best interests of the departing patient. The specter of organ privacy might come to dwell over the deathbed. If, however, it can be seen that the cortically brain dead patient is departed, not departing, it should not be impossible to devise sufficient safeguards to ensure that organ needs do not befoul the declaration of death.

In concluding this overview of the problem-laden world of medical progress, it can be said that lawyers and moralists and all who face death must be grateful to medicine, for it has given them the prospect of fewer ills and greater length of days. It has also given us perplexing questions that will take a length of days to ponder.

FOOTNOTES—CHAPTER 1

1. *Ethics in Medical Progress* (Ciba Foundation Symposium), ed. G. E. W. Wolstenholme and Maeve O'Connor (Boston: Little, Brown & Company, 1966), p. 134. Hamburger's quotation is from J. Rostand, *Pensees d'un Biologiste* (Paris: Stock, 1939).
    2. For comment on this, cf. *The Dying Patient*, ed. Orville G. Brim, Jr., Howard E. Freeman, Sol Levine, and Norman A. Scotch (New York: Russell Sage Foundation, 1970), p. ix.
    3. Quoted in *Euthanasia and the Right to Death: The Case for Voluntary Euthanasia*, ed. A. B. Downing (London: Peter Owen, 1969), p. 14.
    4. *Length of Life of [Some] Mammals and Birds* (After A. I. Lansing)

Animal	Usual Length of Life (in years)
Bear	40–50
Camel	25–45
Hippopotamus	40
Rhinoceros	40–45
Horse	40–50
Elephant	70
Fin whale	Several hundred?
Vulture	118
Eagle	104
Goose	80
Ostrich	50

Alvin I. Goldfarb, M.D., *Death and Dying: Attitudes of Patient and Doctor*, Symposium no. 11, Group for the Advancement of Psychiatry Publication, 104 E. 25th St., New York, New York 10010, 1965, p. 604.
    5. Brim et al., op. cit., p. 7; also see *The Facts of Life—From Birth to Death*, (New York: Macmillan Co., 1951).
    6. "When, Why, and Where People Die," in Brim et al., p. 8.
    7. *Ethical Issues in Medicine: The Role of the Physician in Today's Society*, ed. E. Fuller Torrey (Boston: Little, Brown & Company, 1968), p. 389.
    8. Joseph Fletcher, "Elective Death," in ibid., p. 143.
    9. Monroe Lerner, in Brim et al., op. cit., p. 14.
    10. Cited by Glanville Williams, *The Sanctity of Life and the Criminal Law* (New York: Alfred A. Knopf, 1970), p. 348.

20 A NEW CLIMATE FOR DEATH

11. Torrey, op. cit., pp. 389–90.
12. Ibid., p. 390.
13. Ibid.
14. Ibid., pp. 390–91.
15. "The Dying Patient, The Doctor, and The Law," Villanova Law Review 13 (1968): 732.
16. "Legal and Policy Issues in the Allocation of Death," in Brim et al., op. cit., pp. 269–70.
17. Quoted in Williams, op. cit., pp. 349–50.
18. Ibid., p. 349.
19. Ibid.
20. In Downing, op. cit., p. 51.
21. Gerald Kelly, S.J., "The Duty of Using Artificial Means of Preserving Life," Theological Studies 11 (1950): 210. Kelly is quoting here from Josephy V. Sullivan's dissertation at The Catholic University of America, Catholic Teaching on the Morality of Euthanasia, p. 72. Sullivan concludes that the action of the physician here is morally defensible if the patient is spiritually prepared for death.
22. Medical Ethics, 6th ed. (Philadelphia: F. A. Davies Company, 1967), p. 250. See also Edwin Healy, S.J., Medical Ethics (Chicago: Loyola University Press, 1956), pp. 70–72.
23. Pain can be almost completely controlled in an up-to-date hospital setting. However, there are other factors to be considered: there can be undesirable effects of pain management; some hospitals are not up-to-date; and some patients do not wish to die in a hospital.
24. Kelly, op. cit., p. 216.
25. Paul Ramsey, The Patient as Person (New Haven and London: Yale University Press, 1970), p. 115.
26. "An Alternative to the Ethic of Euthanasia," in To Live or To Die: When, How, and Why?, ed. Robert H. Williams (New York, Heidelberg, Berlin: Springer-Verlag, 1973), p. 108.
27. Cf. Internal Medicine News, November 1, 1972, for an account of the session where Dr. Reich's case was discussed.
28. Dr. Reich argued for this at the congress meeting. He said that means that may be considered extraordinary for the aged might be seen as ordinary for neonates.
29. Hannibal Hamlin, "Life or Death by EEG," Journal of the American Medical Association 190, no. 2 (October 12, 1964): pp. 112–13.
30. The National Observer, March 4, 1972.
31. In Brim et al., op. cit., p. 119.
32. George E. Schreiner and John F. Maher, "Hemodialysis for Chronic Renal Failure: III. Medical, Moral and Ethical, and Socio-Economic Problems," Annals of Internal Medicine 62 (March 1965): 553–54.
33. The National Observer, March 4, 1972.
34. "Apologia for Suicide," in Downing, op. cit., p. 161.
35. M. Goulon and P. Babinet, "Le coma depassé," Cahiers Laennec, September, 1970, p. 18.
36. "At least two cases in Paris were observed to have a flat EEG for several hours, followed by complete recovery; in both cases the coma was due to severe barbiturate poisoning." Downing, op. cit., p. 69.
37. "Refinements in Criteria for the Determination of Death: An Appraisal," A Report by the Task Force on Death and Dying of the Institute of Society, Ethics, and the Life Sciences, Journal of the American Medical Association 221, no. 1 (July 3, 1972): 53.
38. "On Cerebral, Brain, and Systemic Death," in Current Concepts of Cerebrovascular Disease: Stroke, A Publication of the American Heart Association, Inc.,

8, no. 3 (May–June 1973): 9. Of the distinction between cerebral death and brain death, Korein says: "The former describes irreversible destruction of the supratentorial structures of the cerebrum bilaterally, including cortex, white matter, basal ganglia, and thalamus; the latter implies destruction of the entire cerebrum and *also* of brain stem and cerebellum."

39. Ibid., p. 10.

40. Ibid., p. 14.

41. Cf. "A Definition of Irreversible Coma; Report of the Ad Hoc Committee of the Harvard Medical School to Examine the Definition of Brain Death," *Journal of the American Medical Association* 205, no. 6 (August 5, 1968): 85–88; "Ethical Problems Created by the Hopelessly Unconscious Patient," *New England Journal of Medicine* 278, no. 26 (June 27, 1968): 1425–30. The criteria offered by the Ad Hoc Committee are a refinement of a clinical detection of death. They include these conditions: unreceptivity and unresponsivity, no movements or breathing, no reflexes, and a flat EEG. The report recommends that all these tests be repeated at least twenty-four hours later with no change before death can be pronounced. The tests are most useful for deciding when it is truly hopeless to keep a person on a respirator. Some criteria of the report, however, would be useful for a determination that the cerebral cortex is extinguished in its operations.

42. Reported by Joseph Fletcher, in Downing, op. cit., p. 61.

43. "After the 'Definition of Irreversible Coma,'" *New England Journal of Medicine* 281, no. 19 (1969): 1071.

44. "Scarce Resources and Medical Advancement," *Daedalus*, Spring 1969.

45. "After the 'Definition of Irreversible Coma,'" p. 1071.

CHAPTER 2

The Laggardly State of the Law

If medicine is in a turmoil because of too much change, law is in trouble because of too little. Law, as now constituted in most nations, and certainly in the United States, is not equipped to make distinctions where there are real differences. It plods along encumbered by faded and inadequate categories that do no justice to the moral and medical facts of life and death. Summarily, there are several major problems unmet in our legal structures.

Writing as a moralist who is not a lawyer, I will nevertheless dare to make the following allegations: 1) criminal law, in life-taking situations, does not appreciate the essential difference that motive makes. At the present time, motive is significant in only two extrinsic respects: a more benign motive may mitigate the punishment to a degree; and motive may be evidence as to who did the deed. Thus if someone has a motive, he may be tied to a particular killing; the motive will be part of the evidence. 2) In addition to the neglect of motive and, indeed, related to it, the law is functioning with an artificial and nominalistic notion of malice in cases of mercy killing. 3) The law does not make the distinctions that should be made (because there are real differences) in death-producing situations. Because of all of this, law is guilty of turning its eyes from the ongoing practices of physicians and other citizens and of putting juries in the clumsy position of finding implausible technical reasons for rendering milder judgments than the law allows. 4) Finally, in the words of Thomas A. Wassmer, S.J., writing in the *Villanova Law Review*: "There is no legal definition of death based on 20th century facts."[1] All of the above discussion on the medical quandary about when a person is dead is generally unattended by the law. Some moves have been made, as we shall see, to redefine the legal understanding of death, and some good writing has been done suggesting new legal approaches to dying situations in a medical context, but the legal establishment (if one may speak of it in monolithic terms) is not rising to the occasion. The legal mind is understandably conservative and slow to change, but in a matter as fundamental as the understanding of death, and given the rush of events, law does not have time for indefinite contemplation.

Perhaps some cases will illustrate the problems of the law. On August 9, 1967, Robert Waskins, a twenty-three-year-old college student, killed his mother by shooting her three times in the head. When the police arrived and advised him of his rights to silence, he simply replied: "It's obvious, I killed her." He was arrested and charged with murder.

Waskins' mother had been suffering from leukemia. She had at the most several more days to live. She was, however, in extreme pain and wanted to die. In fact she had begged her son to kill her. Three days previously, she had tried to commit suicide by taking an overdose of sleeping pills. Both her husband and the doctors witnessed to the fact that she was in deep pain at the time she was shot.

The case went to court. The letter of the law had little to offer Waskins. Motive, however benevolent, is no defense in a case of intentional and premeditated killing. Motive can influence the judge in sentencing, but the most lenient sentence in Waskins' case would be fourteen years in prison with no hope of probation.

On January 24, 1969, a jury deliberated for only forty minutes and with instant psychoanalysis found Waskins not guilty by reason of insanity. They further found that he was no longer insane, and he was released! There is no psychiatric evidence that Waskins was ever insane, but thus the case was resolved.[2]

In a famous case in New Hampshire in 1950, Dr. Herman Sander was charged with the murder of his cancer-stricken patient.[3] Dr. Sander had given the patient ten cc. of air intravenously four times and she died within ten minutes. The patient had asked the doctor to put her out of her misery.[4] The doctor noted on the patient's chart that he had given her these air injections.

The defense offered for Sander at his trial was that the patient was already dead at the time of the injections. The jury acquitted the doctor apparently on the grounds that there was no proof that his action had caused the patient's death. Thus ended what appears to be the first case in which a doctor in this country was tried on the charge of euthanasia.[5] Jurists who had hoped that the case would be a precedent setter on the legality of euthanasia, however pleased they might have been for Dr. Sander, were understandably disappointed in the rationale of the verdict.[6] The jury, it would seem, can scarcely be faulted. The judge had instructed them at the very outset of the trial that the question of mercy killing could not legally be an issue at the trial. One wonders what could be the issue?

Sometimes, in cases of mercy killing, the evidence is simply brushed aside. In the Illinois case of *People* v. *Werner*, the defendant pleaded guilty to a manslaughter charge for having suffocated his wife, who was a hopelessly crippled arthritic and had begged her husband to put her out of her misery.[7] After hearing testimony from the family of the defendant regarding his devotion to his wife and after the doctor testified to the excruciating pain and mental despair of the woman, the defendant was allowed to change his plea to not guilty. The court then acquitted him on the grounds that a jury would not be inclined to convict in such cases. The judge also observed that in this case, there was no likelihood of recidivism, i.e., of repeating this kind of activity.

Resorting to reasons of insanity for acquittal in mercy killing cases is a common tactic. This tactic would seem to constitute a commentary on the state of the law. What is happening in these instances is that there is a flight to psychiatry when there is no help from the law. Such cases are not rare. Carol Paight, a Connecticut college girl was indicted for second-degree murder for killing her hospitalized father who was dying of cancer. She was acquitted for temporary insanity at the time of the commission of the act.[8] And, in Michigan, Eugene Braunsdorf won the same merciful judgment after killing his crippled adult daughter, who was spastic and incapable of speech, and who had required hospitalization all of her life.[9]

On June 20, 1973, Lester Zygmaniak shot and killed his brother George in his hospital bed. George had been paralyzed from the neck down in a motorcycle accident. The paralysis appeared to be permanent. George had begged his brother to kill him. On November 5, 1973, Lester Zygmaniak was acquitted on grounds of temporary insanity. It was found that he was no longer insane and he was released.

Here again, the court offers a diagnosis in place of a verdict. And a remarkable diagnosis it is, pretending as it does to psychiatric competence in three tenses. First of all it was determined that Zygmaniak was so insane in the past that his condition excused him from guilt in an otherwise criminal act of homicide. Then it was decided that he was completely cured, and, since he was released from custody, the court was apparently convinced that his psychiatric disability would never recur.

The wheels of justice do not grind evenly, here, however. In the same year in which Paight and Braunsdorf were so acquitted, Harold Mohr in Pennsylvania was convicted of voluntary manslaughter for the killing of his blind, cancer-stricken brother. He was sentenced to from three to six years in prison and a $500 fine even though he also pleaded temporary insanity, and even though, in contrast to the other two cases, there was in the Mohr case evidence that the accused had acted upon his brother's urgent and repeated requests. Ironically, the judge, in sentencing Mohr, described the defendant as a martyr who must suffer the price of martyrdom![10]

Consider also the case of John Noxon, a well-to-do lawyer, who was convicted of first-degree murder for killing his six-month-old mongoloid son. Although his sentence was eventually reduced and Noxon was paroled after five years, the Massachusetts Supreme Court affirmed the trial court's decision and denied Noxon's request for a new trial.[11]

As a final example of the uncertain state of the law, it is interesting to note the Texas case of *Sanders* v. *State*.[12] Here the act of assisting someone to kill himself by furnishing the means of death is considered to be innocent of any criminality. Then the Texan Court of Criminal Appeals went even further, saying that someone who "administered" poison was guilty of no offense if the poison was taken voluntarily. This would seem to give an open road to some forms of euthanasia in the state of Texas. However, in another case, the Texas court went on to say that anyone who administered poison by placing it in the "victim's" mouth was guilty of murder. In other jurisdictions, however, persons who mixed poison and made it available to incurably ill persons who wanted it and took it, were found to be guilty of murder.[13]

Beyond all theoretical questions of what the legal situation ought to be, two things are painfully obvious about the way it is. The current situation is inherently unfair by reason of the unevenness in the judgments reached. Verdicts range from murder in the first degree to acquittal. Prosecutors, judges, and juries generally approach cases of mercy killing in a way that contradicts the law as given. Devious means to circumvent the rigor of the law are the order of the day. But devious means are unregulated and, in some cases, the law in all of its conceptual rigor will be enforced. Thus the evenhandedness that a rule of law should ensure to create a sense of justice in society, is not in evidence.

Secondly, the way in which the law has to be circumvented would appear to merit the epithet *hypocritical*. Judges and juries, sensing that the law as it stands is deficient, and being unable to do anything about it, declare the defendant deficient, i.e., insane. Pleasing as acquittal may be to the defendant, there is some inequity in his having to get the verdict he and the jury want and believe to be just by the loss of his claim to mental health. The situation is all the more macabre since it is often clear that the defense of insanity is only a gimmick used to make it possible to slip out from under the harshness commanded by the law but not by the facts.

A CRITIQUE OF THE LAW

A moralist who has never been admitted to the bar should, perhaps, tred lightly in criticizing the law. This moralist, as might already have been noticed, intends to do no such thing. By way of defense for this trans-disciplinary aggression, it should be stressed that the subject of death by choice cannot be handled within the precincts of any one discipline. Thus, for example, the lawyer Glanville Williams on the very first page of his book *The Sanctity of Life and the Criminal Law* confesses that he will be involved in his book in "many risky trespasses outside the lawyer's proper sphere." He justifies the trespass into ethics and other such areas by acknowledging that the law is often doubtful and that thus one's attitude on morality and other matters will ultimately shape the solution to matters before the law.[14] He then proceeds throughout much of his book to do ethics as well as law.

Likewise, any moralist who addresses this subject finds himself enmeshed in the legalities of the case. For one thing, he may find himself reaching conclusions which he sees as moral but which the law sees as felonious. Thus what he sees as good, the law may see as murder. This obviously demands dialogue. Furthermore, the law is replete with moral assumptions and presuppositions.

In fact, law is inextricably bound to the work of ethics and lawyer Williams need not have apologized for overtly doing what theoreticians and practitioners of law are always doing. In a true sense, law is a species of applied ethics. Ethics is the science which seeks to know what is moral or what is immoral, what is befitting man as man and what is not. Lawmakers face the same challenge. Ethics begins with certain anthropological assumptions, or, more simply, certain estimates of what man is, so that it can pursue its work of seeing what does or does not befit him. Law does this too. Every law that is passed and every constitution that is drafted is chock-full of moral and religious presupposition about the nature of man and what is good for him in the light of that nature. To see the morals of a society, start with its laws.

Very often lawmakers are unaware of the fact that they are steeped in and functioning out of very particular moral assumptions that they have never examined or exposed to the light of criticism. It is one of the tasks of ethics to point out those as-

sumptions and show how to assess them. The dialogue between
ethics and law is a sore need of our society. There is no area of
society that is more involved in values than the law and thus
the science of values (ethics) should be a part of every lawyer's
training and equipment. All of this, then, to assert that when a
moralist addresses and criticizes the law, it is not a trespass, but
a natural dialogue. No apologies are needed.

Senator Edward Gurney favors us with a trenchant summary
of the law today regarding death by choice. (Gurney uses the
term "euthanasia," a term which I will later argue is quite ambiguous.) Gurney says: "Generally, it can be said that euthanasia, whether voluntary or involuntary, and whether by
affirmative act or by omission, is a violation of existing criminal
law."[15]

Law professor Arval A. Morris confirms this. Arguing for the
desirability of "permitting each man's last act to be an excer-
cise of his free choice between a tortured, hideous death and a
painless, dignified one," Morris concludes: "This choice is not
available under current law. Today, if a physician motivated
solely by mercy, consciously and deliberately kills his suffering
patient in a painless manner at the request of the patient, his
act is considered to be murder—probably in the first degree."[16]

Though Gurney's statement is more chaste, both the above
citations are, in substance, charges against the present state of
things in American law. The charges require some detailed but
hopefully not too tedious analysis. The first point to be pressed
here is this: the present categories of the law do not encompass
the realities involved in death by choice, i.e., cases in which by
omission or by commission one's own death or the death of another is opted for in preference to continued living. The kinds
of death spoken of here are those usually referred to as mercy
killing or euthanasia in popular parlance. The motives for these
deaths is compassion and an unselfish desire to bring on death
when continued living is unbearable due to physical and/or
mental suffering in a medical context. What we wish to do is to
show that mercy killings thus described do not fit into any of
the categories of unjustifiable homicide available in American

law. They are not murder in the first or second degree, nor are they a form of criminal manslaughter.

MURDER IN THE FIRST DEGREE

Murder is the killing of one human being by another with malice aforethought, either express or implied.[17] "First degree murder is distinguished from other grades of homicide primarily by the mental element known as 'malice aforethought' or 'express' malice, and the unique characteristic of this degree of murder is deliberation or premeditation—a design to take life."[18] Thus first-degree murder is not something unplanned or impulsive or the product of sudden and overwhelming passion. Its hallmarks are express malice, deliberateness, and premeditation.

In a mercy killing case, there is usually obvious deliberateness and premeditation. The mercy killer has to plan to get the poison or shotgun or whatever means he may use. The immensely serious action, normally involving a loved one, will have been mulled over for a long time during the progressive course of illness. Mercy killings are usually clearly planned events. There is deliberation and premeditation aplenty. But what about the business of "express malice"?

Here the court often turns to the classical definition of Blackstone: "express malice is, when one with a sedate and deliberate mind, and formed design, doth kill another; which formed design is evidenced by external circumstances discovering that inward intention, as lying in wait, antecedent menaces, former grudges, and concerted schemes to do him some bodily harm."[19]

Blackstone's revered definition is suggestive of problems for the case at hand. Blackstone alludes to motive here and implies (what should be obvious) that malice imports some sinister overtones in the agent's reason for acting.[20] Thus the idea of ambush, menacings, and grudges. The conclusion would seem to be, then, that the mercy killer is certainly not eligible for the charge of first-degree murder since his motives, be they right, wrong, or misguided, do not at all manifest Blackstone's or anyone else's "express malice."

However, Blackstone and the nature of malice to the contrary not withstanding, efforts are made to describe mercy killing as first-degree murder. How do the courts achieve this? How do they describe the "malice" of the mercy killer? In the California Supreme Court case of *People* v. *Conley*, Chief Justice Traynor shows how it is done. He observes that ". . . one who commits euthanasia bears no ill will toward his victim and believes his act is morally justified, but he nonetheless acts with malice if he is able to comprehend that society prohibits his act regardless of his belief."[21] What this remarkable description amounts to is a non-malicious sort of malice! Blackstone stresses the quality of ill will in explaining malice. The courts which allege malice in mercy killings admit that there is no ill will. Indeed, in the case of Harold Mohr we noted that the judge sent the mercy killer off to jail with the expressed and almost admiring recognition that the man was a martyr. One wonders just what he was a martyr to. Could it, perchance, be to the inadequacy of the laws? Are there malicious martyrs?

At this point, there is no attempt to prove that some of the killings grouped under the umbrella term "mercy killing" may indeed be good acts which should also be made legal acts. (That will be argued later.) The point here is that there seems to be a *prima facie* case for wonderment as to whether the law has lapsed into a surd when it says that malice involves ill will toward the victim except when it is the malice of a mercy killer, in which case there is no ill will toward the "victim" but there is malice all the same. What seems to be happening here is that the law is trying to overrule the logical principle of non-contradiction which it is not within the jurisdiction of the law to do. This attempt deserves further analysis.

When the law imputes malice to mercy killings it is making two mistakes: first, it has locked itself into inadequate categories by indulging in the Anglo-Saxon penchant to confuse reality with legality. Happily for the human race, legality and reality do not coincide. That is why wise judges are needed to temper the shortcoming of the written law. That is also why the Greeks insisted on the virtue of *epikeia*, the virtue by which one sensed that the law is too general to cover every particular case and that therefore there are valid exceptions which epikeia discovers. Epikeia discerns the primacy of the spirit over the letter of the law. It is the virtue which knows that the spirit gives life whereas the letter can be lethal.

Anglo-Saxon literalism needs constant reminders of this ancient wisdom. It is, however, understandable that American law, touched as it is by this literalism and by unrealistic expectations of the law, could come to the conclusion that one need not look beyond the broken letter of the law to indict and convict. Anglo-Saxon literalists (and, therefore, American legalists) could take a good lesson from the quite different attitude toward law found in many Latin nations. Here there is an ingrained sense that though law is an essential underpinning of society, it is by no means the measure of the real. Thus Latins would be much less likely to say "there ought to be a law" when they think of something desirable for society, whereas this would be a reflex reaction for us. They are less likely to think, when there is a law, that it does justice to the intricacies of the infinitely variegated real world. While Latins may sin by excessive detachment from the law, Anglo-Saxon literalists sin by excessive and naïve confidence in the adequacy of the letter of the law.[22]

There can be no doubt that the mercy killer, by hastening or causing death, has broken the letter of the law. But the letter may not do justice to the full reality of the case or to the meaning and spirit of the law. The letter of the law exists in the realm of the generic, the abstract, and the normally true, whereas the deeds of men exist in the concrete. They are individual and differentiated.

The error, then, is reducible to this: to say that mercy killing is first-degree murder because it is premeditated and malicious, and that it is malicious because it is against the law, is a non sequitur. It ignores the possibility that this case is not covered by the law as it now stands. It also lumps together all kinds of disparate cases. By not observing the distinction between illegality and malice, it puts Dr. Sander, who dispatched his patient at her request to put her out of terrible misery, in a class with a rapist who kills his victim to destroy the evidence. Both are, on the face of it, murderers in the first degree. Obviously, common sense, to which the law is not immune, protests. And, of course, the judges and juries who wiggle out of such judgments by gymnastic contortions, are also protesting.

The second mistake the law makes when it attributes malice to the mercy killer, is that it is unfaithful to the normal legal usage of the term malice. As was indicated in Blackstone's description of "express malice," the law does see malice as malicious. In explaining the malice appropriate to murder in the first degree, the language of the statutes and the courts makes it clear what things would show malice. They list such things as "lying in wait" (concealment in ambush for purposes of catching the victim unaware), torture, extreme cruelty, or committing the killing during the commission of some other felony, such as killing someone after forcibly entering his home, or in the act of arson, or rape. It is said, further, that malice involves "malignant recklessness of the lives and safety of others." It imports "particular ill will," "hardness of heart," "cruelty," "a mind regardless of social duty," "wicked disposition," "callous disregard," and the like.[23] The terms "grudges," "revenge," "menaces," and "malignant heart" all appear in the realistic definition of malice.

The problem here is not between a popular and a technical-legal use of the term malice. The point is that the law does use the terms malice and malicious in ways that correspond substantially with common usage. Thus "malicious abandonment" refers to the desertion of a spouse without just cause; a "malicious act" is done with intent to injure; "malicious injury" involves spite, wantonness, fraud, or violence; and "malicious mischief" involves ill will and resentment.[24]

Clearly these expressions imply that the malice necessary for murder and other malicious crimes is not just a knowledge of illegality but is rather constituted by very malevolent dispositions of mind and intent. In cases of assisted death or mercy killing, however, the law does not stay with this realistic understanding of malice. Courts may and often do find extenuating psychological reasons for lesser charges than first-degree murder in "mercy killing" cases, but at the conceptual level deliberate mercy killing is first-degree murder if it is done with intent and knowledge of its illegality.

Again, mercy killings may be wrong and because of this maybe they should be classified as illegal and felonious. They do not, however, qualify under the essential requirement of first-degree murder—"malice aforethought." If they are wrong, another category and rationale must be found for them.[25] Non-malicious malice will not do, especially since it is a cover for an ethically unnuanced view of mercy killing inherent in current law.

MURDER IN THE SECOND DEGREE

Murder in the second degree is characterized by "implied malice," which is present, for example, where death is caused by recklessness, but where willful design is absent.[26] Thus a murder charge goes from first to second degree when there is no deliberately and explicitly formed plan to take life or where the action is not part of another felonious action, which other felony would, the law thinks, show enough malice to make the murder first degree.

The key then to second-degree murder is "implied malice," as opposed to malice that is "aforethought" or "express." Some statutes define second-degree murder as a killing "perpetrated by any act imminently dangerous to others and evincing a depraved mind regardless of human life, although without any premeditated design to effect the death of any particular individual."[27] Sometimes verbal provocation will be enough to change the charge from first to second degree. An example of this may be illuminating and may help show whether we are in a category suitable for acts of mercy killing.

> Where the deceased refused to withdraw the remark that defendant was a "son of a bitch," by continued repetition of the remark in the face of the defendant's stern warning not to continue with the name-calling, there was sufficient provocation to merit a reduction of the charge from first to second degree murder.[28]

Similarly, the intoxication of the killer at the time of the act may have the effect of reducing the crime to second-degree murder.[29]

The first and obvious difficulty with fitting mercy killing into the second degree of murder, is that we are still dealing with malice, albeit implied. Everything we said about malice above also applies here. The term means something that mercy killing does not mean if one uses the term the way the law usually does. Mercy killings are not caused by recklessness. They will be marked by considerable emotional strain, but they are caused by willful design. They are not the result of provocation to anger, or intoxication, or of a depraved, thoughtless mind.

Suppose, however, we were to grant for the sake of argument that there is some kind of legal malice involved in mercy killing. Would it be correct to say that it was of the "implied" kind? On the contrary, if it is artificial to say there is express malice in these cases, it is also artificial to say that the malice is of the implied variety. The word "implied" points to diminished premeditation. It is difficult to imagine one killing out of compassion with diminished premeditation. The motivating compassion which leads the mercy killer to act would also lead him to act only after extensive premeditation. Angry killings may be uni-motivational, but not compassionate killings.

The differences between anger and compassion are important here. Anger tends to swallow up all competing forces and feelings. It is a peculiarly blinding passion. As an old saying has it: "No angry man ever thought his anger unjust." The compassion of a mercy killing situation is a very different emotion. It would normally involve an excruciating conflict of motives. Compassion is a work of love and love is a unitive force which resists separation. The motive of releasing the beloved from pain has to engage that other unitive force of love and win out over it. Notice that in the cases given above, the dying persons who asked to have their lives ended, had to ask repeatedly for this to be done. This is a common and significant fact in such cases.

The emotions of a mercy killer are competing emotions and the act of the mercy killer is a very willful act which ends an inner conflict with a strong decision.

Another reason why the mercy killer is to be presumed a willful and premeditative agent, is that usually this is the first time that a person will have done such a thing. The action is utterly discontinuous with the person's past life and this would increase the likelihood that the person would not slide lightly into it. Also, mercy killing is usually done for a relative or dear one. Such a decision is not likely to be a spur-of-the-moment decision.

When the action is done for someone who is not a relative or close friend, there is still ample cause for keen premeditation. The natural feeling that someone else ought to do it has to be overcome. A doctor doing it has to counter all the pressures within his profession to resist the medical failure which is death. In a word, the presumption in these cases is in favor of willful action with premeditation. If there is malice, it is express and aforethought.

On these two counts, therefore, mercy killing does not fit into the category of second-degree murder: there is no malice in the accepted sense of the term, and even if there were, it could not be characterized as implied. Mercy killing is not murder in the second degree.

MANSLAUGHTER

Manslaughter is a distinct offense, not a degree of murder. It is an unlawful killing of a human being done without malice, express or implied, either in a sudden quarrel or unintentionally while in the commission of an unlawful act.[30]

If this sounds a lot like second-degree murder to the astute reader, let him be consoled in knowing that many distinguished juries have been baffled by the way in which the law in word and in practice distinguishes the various degrees and classes of homicide. Voluntary manslaughter is that which is done in the heat of passion caused by a *sudden* provocation. (Involuntary manslaughter is a killing which results from the commission of certain non-felonious but unlawful acts without the intention of taking life. Obviously, mercy killing does not fit into the involuntary category since it is entirely geared to taking life.) What then of voluntary manslaughter?

Voluntary manslaughter is usually a consequence of quarrels and combats. It occurs suddenly, without reflection or prearranged plan to kill. The killer acts "in the heat of blood." The things which would usually provoke this heat are assault, trespass, epithets, insults, gestures, and threats. The emotion provoked may be anger, resentment, or it may be fear, terror, extreme excitement, or nervousness. For this charge to stick, and not be upped to murder in some degree, the courts seem to agree that the passion must not have had time to cool. The manslayer acts with all reason obliterated by the sudden provocation.[31] There is no premeditation and no malice. Manslaughter is like an angry strike of retaliatory, unanticipated lightning.

There are two reasons why voluntary manslaughter is not a suitable classification for mercy killings. First, this charge requires that the agent be impelled by uncontrollable passion arising from a sudden provocation. The passions of the mercy killer, on the contrary, tend to arise out of a long, intensifying agony, involving conflicting emotions, during which, barring insanity, reason will have some say. Manslaughter is incompatible with "lots of time." The courts presume that if there was "an appreciable length of time," there was premeditation.[32] There is, it would seem, always "an appreciable amount of time" in mercy killing. People do not usually gun down a relative upon the first news that he has a terminal illness.

All of the emotions cited in manslaughter cases are self-defensive in character. This is a psychological element that both anger and fear have in common. The emotions and motive of the mercy killer are of another nature. They are marked by sympathy, concern, and anxiety for another generated usually over a long period of time in a context that is likely to generate strong and mixed emotions with the consequent need for adjudicating reason. In any other kind of case, I do not believe that all of these things could be present and that a manslaughter charge could be sustained. No, those who would put mercy killing into the first-degree murder class are on better ground, and, as we have argued, their better ground is not sufficient.

In the second place, manslaughter, though it does not involve malice in the sense that murder does, is an action where death is dealt without reason or just cause. It is a lesser crime than murder only because of the distraction of the killer. There is, presumably, no just cause for ending a life.

Mercy killing is based on the position that there may be a just cause for ending life. This is the fundamental reason why mercy killing does not fit into any of the categories of unlawful killing. Of course, there are apparent mercy killings which are immoral and should be unlawful. The patient may be done in for reasons that have nothing to do with mercy. This is why, even if our law were reformed to permit some kinds of mercy killing, the mercy killer would still have to prove his mercy.

MOTIVE

One need not be a trained jurist to see the importance of *motive* in human actions. Suppose someone enters a home in the absence of the owner and begins to remove property. What is his motive, his reason for acting? If the motive is to keep this property, the crime is theft. If the motive is to remove it because the house is on fire and the fire fighters have not yet arrived, it is an act of heroic friendship. The essential difference in the two actions is the motive.[33]

A layman looking at the law might be surprised to learn that under the system of laws prevalent in the United States at this time, motive is not an essential element in a charge of murder in mercy killing cases. *That* you killed is all that matters; *why* you killed is irrelevant.[34] As the lawyer Philip Small puts it: "Euthanasia, 'the merciful extinction of life' is closely akin to murder in the first degree in that both are the product of wilfull, deliberate, and premeditated acts or omissions. The major, and, indeed, only distinction between the two rests in the actor's motive in perpetrating the crime."[35] Motive may mitigate the punishment, but it does not constitute a defense for the mercy killer against the charge of murder as the law stands today.

This situation makes neither good sense nor good law. Motive, in the real world, is not just the trimmings on a human action; it is normally a major constitutive cause of the meaning of that action. It might be well to look at one human situation and let common sense pronounce on the significance of motive and the deficiency of a system of law which does not allow for it universally.[36]

A recent case in the Netherlands has been widely reported.[37] Mrs. Geertruida Postma, a physician, injected 200 mg of morphine into a vein of her mother, inducing death. Her mother had had a breast removed, had suffered a cerebral hemorrhage, was partially paralyzed, could scarcely speak, had pneumonia, and was deaf. She had repeatedly told her daughter of her desire to die and had made an unsuccessful suicide attempt. One day in November 1971, Mrs. Postma visited the old-age home and found her mother propped in a chair, tied by her arms, and in extreme misery.

Mrs. Postma explained how this became for her the decisive moment. "When I watched my mother, a human wreck, hanging in that chair, I couldn't stand it any more. So I shouted in her ear. 'It's all right, Mother! I will take care of you.' The next day I gave her the fatal shot."

Mrs. Postma probably could have allowed the death to appear unassisted but chose not to. Instead, she went to the director of the old-age home and explained what had happened. He summoned the police; Mrs. Postma's utter honesty throughout was remarkable. Even for purposes of defense, she would not distort the truth of the case. She admitted during the trial that her mother's physical suffering was not really unbearable. "Her physical suffering was serious, no more. But the mental suffering had become 'unbearable.' "

She also noted that she was convinced that she should have acted sooner. The court found her guilty but gave her only a one-week suspended sentence and a year's probation.

Even those who decide that Mrs. Postma's action was morally wrong would probably grant that her action is not the same *kind* of action as that of a person who kills in order to rob. Both actions issue into death but they are substantially different actions because the motives are substantially different.

Motive is too important and too controlling a factor to be down-played in any area of the law. Let me give here a mercifully brief analysis of the ways in which motive makes a difference. If the reader begins to feel that the writer is clobbering a dead horse by stressing the basic importance of motive, the writer reminds him that the horse lives! Common sense may proclaim from the rooftops the significance of motive in the meaning of human action but, when it comes to mercy killing, the criminal law of homicide has not heard. It is in the hope that analysis will have a better hearing that the next few words are written. Here, then, are the ways in which the motive of the mercy killer and the motive of the murderer vary:

1. The effects on the agent are different. Law has to weigh whether an action is likely to be repeated and in need of deterrence. Mercy killing is usually a once-in-a-lifetime experience. A doctor, of course, would have more opportunities, and good law would have checks so that a doctor could not misuse his obvious opportunity to dictate death. The individual doctor should not normally have the decision to make about inducing death and law could make sure that he does not.

2. The effects on others are different. Any action promoting a disrespect for life must be checked by law. Actions like that of Mrs. Postma do not have this effect. There are, of course, many disagreements about the moral right to induce death in such cases, but the argument is not between those who respect life and those who do not; rather, it is between those who feel that the respect for life requires the right to hasten or bring on death in certain circumstances and those who insist that life must not be shortened, at least by any positive action. Thus it is a debate within the context of respect for life. There is no such debate about the right to kill while robbing.[38]

3. The attitude toward law is different in the motivational context of mercy killing. The mercy killing act is usually not a part of a pattern of disregard of law. In the cases of Dr. Sander and Dr. Postma, the deed was duly reported. In other cases, most persons submit limply to the legal consequences of an act they deemed necessary. If anything, the mercy killer seems to feel that his action is preter-legal more than illegal. Public reaction indicates a good deal of this same attitude.

4. The motive of the mercy killer is further distinguished by the constraining absence of alternatives. This is not the case with the killer-robber. The robber's life-style is a ruthless one to which there are innumerable humane alternatives. The mercy

killer judges that in the conflict situation before him, there are no other alternatives. Continued living is insupportable and death will not come quickly enough. The mercy killer acts in a bind. The true murderer makes a brutal, utterly arbitrary, and needless option.

5. Popular support for mercy killers (or at least popular hesitations to indict) is another factor to consider in assessing the motive and thus the act of mercy killing. Outside of a criminal subculture, there is no popular support for murder. There is, however, very often general identification with the mercy killer in publicized cases and a sense of relief if the defendant is acquitted or receives a light sentence. A remarkable example of this is found in the case of Suzanne van de Put, who was put on trial in 1962 in Liége for killing her radically deformed eight-day-old daughter. The child had been a victim of thalidomide. Madame van de Put was acquitted at the end of a six-day trial. The thousand people in the courtroom erupted with joy at the announcement. The word spread to the waiting crowds outside, where a traffic-stopping celebration began. Trams rang their bells and drivers sounded their horns in approval.

Uproar, of course, is a dubious moral index. Probably more revealing is the lack of disapproval and the quiet relief that greets benign judicial solutions to these cases. At such times, the motive and hence the act of the mercy killer wins a kind of non-condemnation or even endorsement.

6. Finally, and this is really a summation and conclusion, moralists in all ages have always stressed the crucial importance of motive in evaluating human behavior. Medieval moralists called it the "causa principalissima," the most significant cause of the moral meaning of human actions. It is not the only meaningful factor. All kinds of other things have to be weighed, such as the effects, the alternatives, the manner of execution, etc., but the motive is a prime factor in making an action mean what it means humanly and morally.

Human actions are not like diamonds or other stones that have their value regardless of their setting. The circumstances make the action what it is. In the words of Thomas Aquinas:

"human actions are good or bad according to their circumstances."[39] This sounds like Thomas was serving up a dish of this nebulous thing called "situation ethics"; in fact he was merely repeating a traditional doctrine which observed that a change in circumstances (including motive as a primary circumstance) could change the moral quality of the act. American law does not recognize this in any systematic or consistent way in its view of homicide. Until it does, juries will have to squirm and be devious in mercy killing cases.

What the law must recognize is that you cannot repeal the real, and motive is real and determinative of the quality of human behavior to a considerable extent. It is the hallmark of humane law to be discriminating in its judgments and in its use of punishment. Medieval law is criticized because it did not mete out punishment in proportion to the gravity of the offense. Instead, a whole series of very different acts were listed together as capital offenses.[40] Largely because American law does not recognize the essential meaning of motive in all homicides, it ends up in a mischievous muddle, putting mercy killing and heinous murder in the same bag. The conceptual error here is of enormous magnitude.

MERCY KILLING IN OTHER LANDS

Law is always interested in precedents, and the legal systems of other nations offer us a few striking ones. There have been a variety of modern reforms in various countries, most of them stressing, in mercy killing situations, the significance of motive and the character of the action. The reform which went furthest is that of Uruguay. This law provides for the complete exoneration in a homicide case where the act was motivated by compassion and performed upon the "victim's" own request. As it was promulgated in 1933 it reads: "The judges are authorized to forego punishment of a person whose previous life has been honorable where he commits a homicide motivated by compassion, induced by repeated requests of the victim."[41] This provision is understood to be a conferral of power on the judges to offer pardon in these circumstances.

Germany does not go as far as Uruguay in this regard, but its laws are an enlightened move in the direction of reform. The German law follows the trend of modern European reform by stressing not the type of act so much as the type of actor. Thus they are concerned not with a type of action like killing, considered in the abstract, but with the psychological state of the actor, the killer. They want to know the actor's character, his dangerousness or lack of it, the probability that he will repeat his act, his motives. To get it out of the abstract and into the concrete, German law even replaced the conventional terms "murder" and "manslaughter" with the personal terms "murderer" and "manslayer."[42] Premeditation and deliberation are not looked on as significant since both compassion and villainy can be premeditated, and the law sensibly recognizes that compassion and villainy are not the same reality. Motive is seen as of the utmost importance.

The German definition of a murderer shows the paramount importance of motive. Notice what a far cry it is from the confusion of "malice aforethought" of American law. "A person is a murderer if he kills a human being out of lust for killing; for the satisfaction of sexual desire; out of greed, or any other base motives; in a treacherous or cruel manner or by means causing common danger; or in order to make possible or to conceal another crime."[43] Mercy killings are in the separate category of "homicide upon request." These are indeed punishable, but with lighter sentences.

The Swiss Penal Code provides that the judge "may mitigate the punishment . . . where the actor was induced to commit the act (acted) by honorable motives . . ." This, in cases of compassion, may lead to total exoneration.[44]

Also, Swiss law provides that whoever "from selfish motives" assists someone to commit suicide shall be punishable unless the motives are not selfish; then there will be no punishment.[45] This means that a physician who, motivated by compassion, assists his patient to commit suicide is not subject to punishment.

ON NOT WAITING FOR THE LAW

As noted above, mercy killing, whether by affirmative act or by omission, is a violation of existing criminal laws, although, as I have argued, the law has no existent category to classify them realistically as criminal.[46] The situation in life, however, does not reflect the situation on the books. It might seem to do so with regard to omission, since there has never been a prosecution of a person for an act of omission.[47] There are indications, however, that the facts and the laws are worlds apart. In a survey of 250 Chicago internists and surgeons, 156 responded to a questionnaire asking: "In your opinion do physicians actually practice euthanasia in instances of incurable adult sufferers?" Sixty-one per cent affirmed that physicians actually practice it, at least by omission, or what is sometimes called passive euthanasia. What is most revealing, however, of the American dilemma here is that 72 per cent said the practice should not be legalized.[48] Thus, although it occurs, they think, in the practice of a majority of their colleagues, it should not be permitted.

Professor Diane Crane of Johns Hopkins University asserts that "Some doctors resort to 'invisible acts' in which patients' lives are deliberately shortened by manipulating dosages of pain-killing drugs."[49] Most doctors who do this are at great pains to maintain the invisibility of their actions. There are some instances of high visibility, however. Dr. Walter W. Sackett, a Miami general practitioner, admits publicly that he has allowed patients to die "hundreds of times" during his thirty years of medical practice. What is more, the outspoken Dr. Sackett estimates that 75 per cent of all doctors have made similar allowances on one or more occasions. For this reason, Sackett, who is also a member of Florida's state legislature, has been trying to push a "death with dignity" bill through the legislature. He has had no success so far. He claims that he finds major support for his bill among the elderly. "They fear the prolongation of dying," he says, "more than death itself."[50]

Perhaps Sackett is drawing the long bow in estimating the incidence of at least passive euthanasia. The statistics of bill-pushers are always worth a second check. But then again there might be no exaggeration in his figures. Dr. Louis Lasagna, M.D., argues that decisions on lengthening or shortening life are unavoidable for doctors. "There is no place for the physician to hide," he says.[51] He will constantly run into situations where he will have to choose between a treatment that provides less physical and mental stress but shortens life, and one that will surely prolong life, but at the cost of much suffering. Lasagna mentions a survey that shows that about a third of all doctors feel that mercy killing is justified in the case of a terminal patient who is in great pain without hope of relief or recovery. (He notes that the figure is close to 40 per cent for Protestants and Jews and 7 per cent for Roman Catholics.) He adds that many physicians covertly practice euthanasia in the case of children born with gross congenital anomalies by not resuscitating the child at birth.[52]

Dr. Lasagna comes out in favor of "euthanasia," suggesting the possibility of committees made up of medical and non-medical members, including "perhaps" (!) representatives of the patient's family. He concedes that the taking of life is an awesome business but that safeguards are conceivable which could prevent abuse of the procedure.[53]

Dr. Earl Babbie, in his book *Science and Morality in Medicine*, reports the attitudes of teaching physicians on allowing deformed babies to die. The following hypothetical situation was presented:

> During the recent thalidomide alarm, many prospective mothers reportedly asked their physicians to allow their babies to die at birth if any bizarre deformities were present. If a physician had complied with such a request and was being tried for murder, do you think you would be sympathetic to his case or not?

The responses offered for selection were: definitely sympathetic; probably sympathetic; probably non-sympathetic; definitely not sympathetic. Overall, two thirds of the respondents were sympathetic to the physician. One third were "definitely sympathetic."[54]

In summary, Professor Bayless Manning is probably accurate

when he says that the topic has been too long subterranean "and decisions are predominantly being made by thousands of doctors in millions of different situations and by undefined, particularized, *ad hoc* criteria."[55] This state of affairs is not something desirable under law, for it leaves things to the vagaries of a "rule of man" instead of providing for the fairness and consistency of a "rule of law."

The Legality of Doing Nothing at All

In 1957, Pope Pius XII addressed the question of whether a respirator can be turned off if the patient is in a final and hopeless state of unconsciousness. The Pope reasoned that the respirator in these circumstances is not morally obligatory, and, therefore, it can be turned off. He recognized that this action causes "the arrest of circulation," but he said it is nonetheless, licit.[56]

Many American physicians feel that this position is reasonable and permissible under American law. Many more are not so sure, and one can sympathize with their uncertainty. Lawyer William Cannon considers the matter of "pulling the plug" under American law and comes up with this conclusion: ". . . if it is concluded to be an omission, the law is murky at best. If, however, it is concluded to be an affirmative act, the law has a ready charge: Murder in the first degree."[57] In other words, "pulling the plug" might be murder in Cannon's opinion. The area of omission in the law then is, as Cannon allows, "murky," to say the least.

In general, in our law, there is no obligation to be a good Samaritan. (On this issue, too, some European law has moved imaginatively ahead of us.)[58] But what of a physician who does not bring aid? For some omissions, physicians are liable in much the same way they would be for unpermitted operations or positive malpractice. If a doctor is out wining and dining and gets a call that a patient has suddenly become critically ill from pneumonia, the doctor must drop everything and go, or see that another doctor does go. If he does not respond to the call, he is liable criminally and civilly should death ensue.[59] In this case, omission is punishable. And, since motive does not matter in this criminal law, if the doctor arriving at the bedside failed to give the needed aid because he knew that his old patient would be better off out of his misery and because he knew further that the patient had been longing and praying for death —it is the same as if he had stayed out on the town and not answered the call. Or is it?

The question that boggles the law is whether actions such as stopping cardiac resuscitation, turning off a respirator or a kidney machine are omissions or commissions. If they are commissions, the charge is murder. "If turning off the respirator is an 'act' under the law, then it is unequivocally forbidden: it is on a par with injecting air into the patient's veins," writes law professor George P. Fletcher.[60] If it is an "omission," the legal analysis would be more lenient but still not clear.

In general it might be said that a doctor has to give all necessary treatment to a client/patient and this is understood by the nature of the professional relationship. Yet respirators are turned off when it becomes clear that the patient has lost all spontaneous capacity for life and is now machine-driven and machine-dependent. In these cases, the doctor is merely permitting death to show that it has already won. The human problem here should be as manageable for the law as it was for the Pope in his 1957 statement. And the law should make this clear.

Still, other omissions are not so easy and should be coped with. We alluded above to the position of moralists that a terminal cancer patient who is also insulin-dependent may licitly stop insulin and escape into death. What of that under law? Normally, insulin is such a commonplace in medicine that the administration of it to patients is expected and the failure to administer it would be murderous. So too, if a patient in the same terminal condition had pneumonia, instead of diabetes, could the physician abstain from giving antibiotics? Again, it is not clear that the law can cope with this in its present state. George Fletcher's conclusion on this is that it is up to doctors to fashion their own law in cases of prolongation of life.

By establishing customary standards, they may determine the expectations of their patients and thus regulate the understanding and the relationship between doctor and patient. And by regulating that relationship, they may control their legal obligation to render aid to doomed patients.[61]

All well and good, then. Doctors must establish the expectations and the law will honor the accepted expectations. Does this not, however, leave a sword of Damocles hanging over the doctor's neck? What if his patient does not accept the expectations of others? And what is the barometer of expectations? And who will check the justice of expectations? And what of the judge or jury who have not read George Fletcher's fine *Washington Law Review* article on the normative value of expectations, quoted above? What are *their* expectations? The law has a job to do here too.

Prospects for legislatures rising to this need are dismal. Consider the efforts of Florida's Dr. Sackett to get his "death with dignity bill" approved. He has failed repeatedly since 1968. In Wisconsin, too, efforts to pass quite modest bills allowing the right to die with dignity have failed. Doctors who feel that they could never be prosecuted for omissions might well be made nervous by this. Here are the words of a defeated bill: "Every person who is terminally and incurably ill and enduring severe pain and suffering shall have the right to die with dignity and to refuse and deny the use or application by any person of unnatural medical or surgical means or procedures calculated to prolong his life."[62] That may seem a reasonable bill, but not to Wisconsin legislators . . . or to legislators anywhere, apparently.

Legislators, in other words, are nowhere near where Pius XII was in 1957 when he said that there was no obligation to use extraordinary means. And Pope Pius XII was no radical in the area of ethics.

LEGAL DEATH

There was a brawl at Newcastle upon Tyne in June 1963, and quite a brawl it was. David Potter suffered extensive brain damage; here is the medical report on the case:

A 32-year-old man [David Potter] was admitted to Newcastle General Hospital with multiple skull fractures and extensive brain damage. Fourteen hours after admission, on June 16, he stopped breathing. Artificial respiration was then begun by machine so that one of his kidneys could later be taken for transplantation to another man. After 24 hours of artificial respiration a kidney was taken from the body on June 17. The respirator was then turned off and there was no spontaneous breathing or circulation.

NOTE. The reported comments by persons associated with this case are of interest: (1) The coroner stated that he thought the patient was alive when the kidney was removed, although there was no hope for him, but the coroner did not regard the doctors as having committed any offence. (2) A physician said that, in his opinion, when the patient ceased breathing on June 16 he had virtually died, but that from the legal point of view it would be correct to say that he died when the heart ceased beating and the circulation ceased to flow on June 17. In some reports, the physician is stated to have said that the patient was medically dead on June 16 and legally dead on June 17. (3) A neurologist said that, in his view, the man was dead before removal of the kidney. The brain damage was such that life was impossible, and the man was kept going by the machine to enable preparations to be made for the operation. (4) A pathologist stated that in his view the patient died from brain damage and removal of the kidney played no part in his death.[63]

The jury in this case returned a verdict of manslaughter against the particular brawler who did Mr. Potter in. In the Magistrates Court, however, the conviction was reduced to a charge of common assault. As Paul Ramsey puts the questions: "Why was Potter's assailant guilty only of assault and the surgeons not guilty of manslaughter, or, if the doctors did nothing wrong, why was the assailant not guilty of manslaughter? Recent proposals for updating the procedures for stating death are addressed exactly to these confused points."[64]

In another case in the United States, Clarence Nicks, a thirty-six-year-old man, suffered severe brain damage as a result of a beating.[65] Nicks' respiration stopped and brain waves were absent, but the heart was still functioning. One doctor pronounced him dead; another doctor disagreed. Nicks (or the body of the deceased Nicks) was placed on a respirator with an eye to heart transplantation. The heart was removed three hours later. The operation took place with some reservations since, if Nicks was not dead, the operating surgeons were killing him and "concealing evidence," i.e., his heart, in the chest of another person.

The definition of death issue hits the law in another way. Most jurisdictions have what is known as the "year-and-a-day" rule for punishable homicides. This means that death must ensue within a year and a day from the infliction of the mortal wound or it is concluded that death was due to other causes and the assailant escapes murder charges. With a respirator a victim could be kept "alive" for longer than a year and a day and murder charges would fail.

There is another area of the law which is out of joint with death in these times and which comes into analysis of mercy killing cases. This is the legal idea of "acceleration of death." This means that if there is only the slightest spark of life in a person and this is extinguished, this constitutes as much homicide as the killing of a healthy and vital person. The meaning of this provision is that in cases where someone has already felled a victim and a second party steps in and gives the *coup de grace*, the second party is guilty and may not use as defense that the victim was already beyond recall. (The first assailant, of course, is also liable for the death if his blow is deemed sufficiently mortal.)

This comes into mercy killing because of the argument that mercy killing is an acceleration of a death that is already in process. The retort offered is that this is no defense according to criminal law because of the acceleration provision. Again, in the noble cause of making distinctions where there are differences it should be acknowledged that the final blow in a murderous situation in which a man is brought from health to death is not the same as the acceleration of dying when dying is already in process. There is also the fundamental difference of malice in one case and not in another.

To take the terrible uncertainty out of cases like this, law must update its definition of death and thus enter the world of today in this important matter. There is some progress being made in this direction. On May 25, 1972, in a suit for wrongful death, a Richmond, Virginia, jury found that the transplant

team at the Medical College of Virginia had not caused the
death of Bruce Tucker by removing his heart in order to transplant it. The jury found that although the patient was breathing
by virtue of a mechanical respirator, he was, in fact, dead because of the absence of brain activity.[66]

Also, a 1970 Kansas statute permits death to be defined either
in the traditional way or because of the absence of spontaneous
brain function where further attempts at resuscitation would
not be useful. The outstanding part of this statute is that death
is to be pronounced before artificial means of supporting respiration and circulation are terminated and before any vital organ
is removed for transplantation.[67]

The General Assembly of Maryland made Maryland the
second state to move to the definition of death in terms of brain
death.[68] It is to be hoped that other states will follow the enlightened lead of Kansas and Maryland.

After heaping all these recriminations upon the law for its
laggardly state on the question of death and the right to death,
a final confession is in order. The reason why law is so timid and
remiss is that ethics has been similarly at fault. And the greater
sin is that of ethics. Ethics is the science which should be moving ahead, probing to see what humanizing forms man's developing freedom may assume. Ethics, more than any science, must
avoid entanglement in its own biases and jaded categories. Law
has more excuse for being conservative. Ethics, too, of course,
must conserve and fight loss. As anthropologist Margaret Mead
writes: "We know that again and again advances have been lost,
and we have no assurance that this will not happen in the
future."[69] The preservation of advances is an indispensable task
for ethics. But ethics is more than a preserver. It may not merely
sit on the status quo and pronounce *licet's* and *non licet's* like
a wizened old judge. Its supreme task is imagination. Ethics
must probe the ideal possibilities of the unfolding drama of
humanization. In doing this there is need for a balance between
carefulness and daring. But there is no room for timidity.

There is a new day adawning in ethics. We find ourselves in
a new moral atmosphere, and issues once thought to be closed,
are beginning to open. In the next chapter, we will take a look
at what some moralists are saying today.

FOOTNOTES—CHAPTER 2

1. Thomas A. Wassmer, "Between Life and Death: Ethical and Moral Issues Involved in Recent Medical Advances," *Villanova Law Review* 13 (1968): 776.
2. Case cited in Joseph Sanders, "Euthanasia: None Dare Call it Murder," *Journal of Criminal Law, Criminology, and Police Science* 60, no. 3 (1969): 351.
3. Ibid., p. 356.
4. Edward J. Gurney, "Is There a Right to Die?—A Study of the Law of Euthanasia," *Cumberland-Samford Law Review* 3, no. 2 (Summer 1972): 250. Gurney makes special note of this request and considers it significant in the final verdict.
5. The second case involves the chief surgical resident of the Nassau County Medical Center, Dr. Vincent A. Montemarano, who was indicted on June 27, 1973, on a charge of "willful murder." According to the indictment, he injected a fatal dose of potassium chloride intravenously while the patient was in a comatose state. See New York *Times*, June 28, 1973. At this writing the case has not come to trial.
6. They really might have mitigated their disappointment if they had pondered the causation issue on which the case turned. As I shall suggest below, there is a real physical difference between a death-causative action which affects a person on whom other death-causative factors are operating, and an action which is the exclusive and solitary cause of death. This physical fact does not define the moral and legal meaning of the act, but it is a reality to be weighed in a realistic assessment of the act.
7. Crim. No. 58-3636, Cook Co. Ct., Ill. (1958). For discussion of this case, cf. Gurney, op. cit., p. 250; for a transcript, see Glanville Williams, "Euthanasia and Abortion," *Colorado Law Review* 38 (1966): 178, 184–87.
8. New York *Times*, February 8, 1950.
9. New York *Times*, May 23, 1950.
10. On this case, cf. Helen Silving, "Euthanasia: A Study in Comparative Criminal Law," *University of Pennsylvania Law Review* 103 (1954): 354. For a listing and graphing of cases of "mercy killing" which shows the diversity of sentence and the strained reasonings of judges and juries in these cases, see Sanders, op. cit., pp. 355–57.
11. See Sanders, op. cit., p. 356, note 36, e.
12. Sanders v. State, 54 Tex. Crim. 101, 112 S.W. 68, 70 (1908).
13. Gurney, op. cit., p. 239.
14. Williams, op. cit., p. ix.
15. Gurney, op. cit., p. 238.
16. Arval Morris, "Voluntary Euthanasia," *Washington Law Review* 45, no. 2 (1970): 247.
17. *American Jurisprudence*, 2d. ed., Vol. 40 (Rochester, N.Y.: Lawyer's Cooperative Publishing Co.; San Francisco: Bancroft-Whitney Co., 1968), "Homicide" at 41.
18. Ibid., at 45.
19. Cited along with references to court decisions which use or borrow from this description in *American Jurisprudence*, at 51. I do not argue, of course, that Blackstone was attempting an exhaustive list of circumstances which evidence

"formed design." I do argue that his choice of circumstances coheres with the contention that malice involves ill will.

20. Malice in law need not imply spite, malevolence, hatred, or ill will to the person killed. It normally includes, however, a general malignant recklessness of the lives and safety of others. Thus *American Jurisprudence*, at 50, n. 6, citing Turner v. Commonwealth, 167 Ky. 365, 180 S.W. 768. In the case of mercy killing, the elements of recklessness and malignancy are arguably not present. Lawyers, with magisterial aplomb, point out to non-lawyers that in law, malice does not necessarily denote an evil state of mind. As a non-lawyer, I get the point but consider it absurd. Jonathan Matthew Purver goes so far as to argue that "malice aforethought" should be dropped from the definition of murder. That would indeed spare judges the onus of explaining non-malicious malice to juries, but it would also give tenure to the inadequate ethics inherent in current law. See Jonathan Matthew Purver, "The Language of Murder," *UCLA Law Review* 14 (1967): 1306–11.

21. See Gurney, op. cit., p. 240.

22. It is small wonder that legal reform is slow in this country, since Americans treat their law as fundamentalist sects treat their Bible. They may not obey it, but they absolutize it conceptually.

23. Iowa, Massachusetts, Texas, South Carolina, Kentucky, and Pennsylvania decisions are being quoted from here, see *American Jurisprudence*, at 49, n. 6.

24. Cf. *Black's Law Dictionary*, 4th ed. (1951).

25. One way that malice, at least implied malice, may be urged or made applicable to mercy killing is through the use of the wedge or domino theory. The malice could be said to consist of undertaking an action which will lead to a breakdown in respect for the sanctity of life. Thus, the argument could go, what is apparently benign in its immediacy is malicious in its long-term societal effects. The deficiencies of this wedge or domino theory will be considered in a subsequent chapter.

26. *American Jurisprudence*, ibid., at 53.

27. Vasquez v. State, 54 Fla. 127, 44 So. 739.

28. State v. Wilen, 144 Or. 251, 24 P.2d 1030; the summary is from *American Jurisprudence*, ibid., at 53, n. 15.

29. *American Jurisprudence*, ibid., at 53.

30. Ibid., at 54.

31. Ibid., at 54–76.

32. Jones v. United States, 175 F.2d 544, 552 (9th Cir. 1949).

33. The essential difference is not the fire, although it is quite relevant. Two people may be removing goods from the home during the same fire, one planning to keep some things, the other only wanting to save them for his neighbor. Again, it is motive that makes one a thief and one a friend.

34. See Silving, op. cit., passim; Gurney, op. cit., p. 240; Luis Kutner, "Due Process of Euthanasia: The Living Will, A Proposal," *Indiana Law Journal* 44, no. 3 (1968–69): 549.

35. "Euthanasia—The Individual's Right to Freedom of Choice," *Suffolk University Law Review* 5 (Fall 1970): 190–91.

36. American law does allow for the essential significance of motive in other crimes. In fact, motive enters life-taking cases in a real way in establishing the degree of murder or manslaughter and in cases of self-defense. It is operative in the usual usage of the term malice, but it is suppressed in the use of that term in mercy killing cases.

37. See *Time*, March 5, 1973.

38. The wedge argument could be pressed here. It will be treated subsequently in Chapter 6.

39. *Summa Theologica* I II q. 18, a. 3.

40. See Silving, op. cit., p. 350.

41. Penal Code of Uruguay, art. 37 (Law No. 9155), cited in ibid., p. 369, n. 74.

42. Ibid., p. 361 and n. 38.

43. German Penal Code #211, n. 2, cited in ibid., p. 363, n. 49.

44. Ibid., p. 367, citing the Swiss Penal Code, art. 64.

45. Swiss Penal Code, art. 115, cited in ibid., pp. 376–77.

46. The ambiguity concerning omission as a criminal act will be discussed below.

47. Sanders, op. cit., 351, n. 6.

48. Ibid.

49. Brim et al., op. cit., p. 306. The introduction to this volume observes matter-of-factly: "There is considerable evidence that doctors do terminate lives in certain situations" (p. xxiv).

50. *The Wall Street Journal,* January 31, 1972.

51. Louis Lasagna, *Life, Death, and the Doctor* (New York: Alfred A. Knopf, 1968), p. 236.

52. Ibid. Lasagna does not report which surveys provide these statistics.

53. Ibid., p. 235.

54. Earl Babbie, *Science and Morality in Medicine: A Survey of Medical Educators* (Berkeley, Los Angeles, London: University of California Press, 1970), p. 163.

55. In Brim et al., op. cit., p. 270.

56. "The Prolongation of Life, an Address of Pius XII to an International Congress of Anesthesiologists, November 24, 1957," *The Pope Speaks,* 4, no. 4 (1968), p. 397.

57. "The Right to Die," *Houston Law Review,* 7, no. 5 (1969–70), p. 659.

58. Cf. *The Good Samaritan and the Law,* ed. James M. Ratcliffe (Garden City: Anchor Books, Doubleday & Company, Inc., 1966). Note particularly "The Duty to Rescue: A Comparative Analysis," by Aleksander W. Rudzinski.

59. See George P. Fletcher, "Prolonging Life: Some Legal Considerations," *Washington Law Review* 42 (1967), reprinted in Downing, op. cit. For this kind of case, see p. 75. See also "J. Mooallen, "A Time To Die." *Case and Comment,* 78 no. 2, (March–April 1973) pp. 3–7.

60. Ibid., in Downing, p. 76.

61. Ibid., p. 84.

62. State of Wisconsin, Senate Substitute Amendment to 1971 Senate Bill 715, offered by Senator Soik on October 12, 1971.

63. Reported in "Moment of Death, Medico-legal," *British Journal of Medicine* 5353:394 (August 10, 1963). The summary given here is from M. Martin Halley, M.D., J.D., and William F. Harvey, J.D., L.L.M., "Medical vs. Legal Definitions of Death," *Journal of the American Medical Association* 204, no. 6 (May 6, 1968): 423.

64. Ramsey, op. cit., pp. 71–72.

65. New York *Times,* May 13, 1968.

66. Washington *Post,* May 26, 1972.

67. K.S.A., #77-202 (1970 Supp.), reported in Gurney, op. cit., p. 246, n. 63.

68. 54F (a) A person will be considered medically and legally dead if, based on ordinary standards of medical practice, there is the absence of spontaneous respiratory and cardiac function and, because of the disease or condition which caused, directly or indirectly, these functions to cease, or because of the passage of time since these functions ceased, attempts at resuscitation are considered hopeless; and, in this event, death will have occurred at the time these functions ceased; or

(b) A person will be considered medically and legally dead if, in the opinion of a physician, based on ordinary standards of medical practice and because of a known disease or condition, there is the absence of spontaneous brain function; and if based on ordinary standards of medical practice, during reasonable attempts to either maintain or restore spontaneous circulatory or respiratory function in the absence of spontaneous brain function, it appears that further attempts at resuscitation or supportive maintenance will not succeed, death will have occurred at the time when these conditions first coincide. Death is to be pronounced before artificial means of supporting respiratory and circulatory function are terminated and before any vital organ is removed for purposes of transplantation.

(c) These alternative definitions of death are to be utilized for all purposes in this State, including the trials of civil and criminal cases, any laws to the contrary notwithstanding.
Article 43 of the Annotated Code of Maryland (1971 Replacement Volume and 1971 Supplement), Section 54F, article approved and in effect as of July 1, 1972.

69. "The Cultural Shaping of the Ethical Situation," in *Who Shall Live?*, ed. Kenneth Vaux (Philadelphia: Fortress Press, 1970), p. 6.

CHAPTER 3

The New Mood of Morality

The moral theology of just a few years ago had many answers and few questions on the subject of our moral right to end life. In a military situation, we had copious moral authority to kill. The theoretically tidy principles of the so-called "just war theory" proved very stretchable in practice and the moral theologians over the centuries were able to find ethical warrant for all too many gory military adventures.

On life-taking issues such as abortion, mercy killing, and suicide, the situation in moral theology was one of utmost clarity. Certain truths were proclaimed to be self-evident, and on the basis of these truths doors were slammed shut in the face of many questions that were left to go abegging. Chief among these "self-evident" truths was the principle of the absolute inviolability of innocent human life. Direct killing of the innocent was absolutely impermissible. This meant that you could kill an unjust aggressor in war and self-defense. You could also execute a criminal who by his crime had lost his right to life, just as the aggressor had. Capital punishment was seen as an extension of killing in self-defense, but it is a loosely linked extension. The criminal is now a prisoner, not an aggressor, and a traditional reason for killing him was to show other malefactors the unenviable lot of the wicked . . . in other words, to make a point. Killing someone to make a point is, at best, dubious moral behavior, but more of that anon.

And so it was that the aggressive guilty could be terminated but the innocent could not. Notice how simple this rendered problems that are vexing us today. Observe this simplicity in the words of Gerald Kelly. After granting the right of killing the aggressor, he asserts that:

> neither the state nor private individuals can establish any authorization to kill the innocent. Hence, the principle that innocent human life is absolutely inviolable. By reason of this principle, we exclude all *direct* killing of the innocent, e.g., by destructive craniotomy of a living fetus, by "mercy killing," by all *direct* abortion, even for "therapeutic" reasons.[1]

The key word in that passage, and Kelly emphasizes it twice, is "direct." Kelly explains that word quite simply: ". . . the direct (i.e., the intentional) taking of innocent life is never permissible."[2] This concept of directness became a basic tool for much of the older theology, especially in Catholic circles. Not only theologians, but also popes and councils used this term to justify and explain their position on cases of life taking. So, for example, Pius XI asked; "What could ever be a sufficient reason for excusing in any way the direct murder of the innocent?"[3] And Pius XII condemned the "deliberate and direct disposing of an innocent human life"[4] and insisted that "neither the life of the mother nor that of the child can be subject to an act of direct suppression."[5]

This principle forbidding the direct killing of innocent human life, once it prevailed, was applied with consistency. Thus, if there should be a case where, because of the absence of skilled medical help (or due to neglect by the medics), it would seem necessary in a blocked birth process to kill the child to save the mother, the clear answer was *no*. Even if both should die as the result of non-action, no direct action could be taken against the innocent life of either mother or child.

To show how deadly serious some of the moralists were about the plying of this principle, one of them considered the case of a two-headed infant. In this hypothetical case, the physician discovers that the baby has two heads after the first head has been delivered. He wishes to amputate the second head to make delivery of the child possible. This moralist said that this would be gravely immoral because the two heads probably mean that there are two infants and so amputation would be direct killing of innocent life and therefore immoral . . . regardless of the consequences.[6]

Obviously, under this same principle, abortion, mercy killing of every sort, and suicide were always and everywhere wrong.

NEW QUESTIONS

Questions are terrible things, for they subvert and they subvert quite fairly. And subversive questions have undermined the old position. So, for example, philosopher-theologian John Milhaven, of Brown University, asked some hard questions in an article in 1966. He particularly accosts the principle of the absolute inviolability of innocent human life. Milhaven criticizes an article of a colleague who attacked abortion on the grounds of the principle forbidding direct killing. He notes that this colleague uses the principle of absolute inviolability but "he never indicates the reasons that prove there is an absolute inviolability, holding under all circumstances . . ."[7] Milhaven's telling questions are: "What proves that innocent human life is inviolable under all circumstances? How do we know this?"[8]

Charles Curran, a prominent theologian from The Catholic University of America, raised a similar question in a 1968 published interview: "We have never demanded that doctors use every means to keep human life going. But we have drawn the line at *positive* acts calculated to bring about the death of the patient. I think we can at least re-examine the morality of positive interference."[9] Curran was calling for a re-examination of a question most Catholics thought had been closed for all eternity.

Thomas Wassmer, a Jesuit moralist, moves in the same direction with his questions. He says that "it can plausibly be asked just where the difference lies in accelerating the dying process by acts of commission as well as by acts of omission."[10] He also goes after the old idea that it was permissible to give painkilling drugs even if it shortened life because it was the relief of pain that was intended, not the accelerated death. This meant that the doctor could give heavy doses of morphine or some other pain-relieving agent, could know that this would hasten death, but would will only the pain relieving, not the death. Says Wassmer: "It is hard to see how the effect of death is not involved in the very intentionality of the administrator."[11] Wassmer is obviously scoring a point here, because it is not fanciful to assume that there are many cases where both doctor and patient not only know about the death-hastening effect of the drug but wish for this ultimate release of pain which is death.

New Conclusions

One of the earliest harbingers of a new season in Catholic theology was an article by a bishop, Most Reverend Francis Simons, entitled "The Catholic Church and the New Morality."[12] The Catholic scene is worthy of special attention because, traditionally, Catholics have been the stronghold of conservatism in medical ethics. On life/death issues in medical ethics, they were comparable to what the Quakers and Mennonites have been relative to war and violence. Thus a change in the Catholic thinking is likely to be a significant indicator of developments in contemporary morality.

Bishop Simons develops a moral approach that puts great stress on the significance of a quasi-consensus of good people on certain moral questions. He goes head on into the question of killing the baby to save the mother. The bishop notes that some would say that this question has been made irrelevant by modern medicine, but he observes, from his vantage point in Indore, India, where he worked, that most of the world does not have modern medicine and so it is a real question. He notes the opinion of most of mankind, that "would allow the killing of the unborn child when this is honestly deemed the only means of preventing the death of both mother and child." He criticizes the old Catholic opinion that the child's right to life is fundamental no matter what the consequences, and he asks, "what 'fundamental right' is this by which an unborn child, without benefit to itself, can stand in the way of the preservation of the life of its own mother?"

The bishop also viewed favorably the licitness of suicide under dire circumstances such as when a person would be forced to divulge very damaging secrets under torture. Again, this was an area where no exceptions used to be made. Perhaps the revealing thing about Bishop Simons' article was that it did not create a big stir among Catholic moralists. Many Catholic moralists today would come to the same conclusions, each by his individual method. In general, most Catholic moralists were pleased to see some of the new positions of Catholic moral theology given prestigious expression by one of their mitered confreres. Since, however, Catholic theology is not monolithically liberal as it was once monolithically conservative, many theologians must have winced at the bishop's candid little essay.

Also in the Catholic sphere, Kieran Nolan, a Benedictine monk and professor of moral theology, addressed the question of acceleration of the death process in a little-noticed essay in 1968. In this essay, Nolan faced the question of what is popularly called mercy killing, but he does so in his own studied language. He asks: "Can the doctor increase the quantity of a particular drug or in any other way positively assist and accelerate the dying process?"[13] Father Nolan makes a distinction between rendering positive assistance to the suffer-dying, and "euthanasia," conceived of as the merciful relief of suffering when one is not dying.[14] He then offers this answer to the question about overdosing a patient to death. "Positive assistance to the dying process definitely seems to be encompassed in the reasonable understanding of the Christian and human right to die."[15] Fifteen years earlier, Nolan's conclusion that positive action to bring on death could be Christian and moral would have met a storm of resistance.

Bernard Häring, a Redemptorist priest and professor at the Accademia Alfonsiana in Rome, is one of the leading lights of moral theology. In a recent book, which reflects a course on medical ethics which he taught in Rome, Häring discusses a case presented by a gynecologist:

> I was once called upon to perform an operation on a woman in the fourth month of pregnancy, to remove a benign uterine tumour. On the womb, there were numerous very thin and fragile varicose veins which bled profusely, and attempts to suture them

only aggravated the bleeding. Therefore, in order to save the woman from bleeding to death, I opened the womb and removed the fetus. Thereupon the uterus contracted, the bleeding ceased, and the woman's life was saved.[16]

Häring approves of what the doctor did, even though, in older terminology, it was the direct taking of innocent life. Häring argues that what is wrong with abortion is that it attacks the right of the fetus to live. In this case, however, the doctor could determine that there was no chance for both the mother and the fetus to survive if he did not directly end the life of the fetus. In Häring's words: "He saves the life of the mother while he does not truly deprive the fetus of its right to live since it could not possibly survive in the event of the doctor's failure to save the mother's life."[17] He notes, too, that it is a service to life to preserve the mother's fertility.

Häring also takes a position on abortion which is not what many might expect to emanate from a Roman academy. He puts great stress on the determination of the point at which a fetus could really be called a "fully human being." He refers to this point as the time of "individualization."[18] Häring considers it probable that before the development of the cerebral cortex (sometime within the twenty-fifth to the fortieth day of pregnancy), "the embryo cannot yet (with certainty) be considered as a human person . . ."[19] Häring carefully stresses that he is not saying that the embryo lacks the basic human right to life before the cerebral cortex is developed. Nevertheless, he does reach this conclusion: "Up to the moment of complete individualization, the traditional judgment about the absolute immorality of the direct interruption of pregnancy might be modified in extreme cases of conflict of values and duties." He says, further, ". . . in difficult cases and particularly during the period where individualization has most probably not happened, we seem to be entitled to refer to the traditional doctrine of conflict of duties or conflict of values."[20] This doctrine would allow for exceptions to the moral principle against abortion and would thus allow for the possibility of a moral abortion. It is easy to see why, in the preface to his book, Häring says that

Catholic moral theology might "now [be] better termed 'ecumenical ethics.'"

JOSEPH FLETCHER

As Paul Ramsey says of Joseph Fletcher (before attacking him): "Tribute should be paid to Professor Joseph Fletcher for in season and out of season having kept open the question of allowing to die in the minds and consciences of the public beyond the limits of the medical profession."[21] Fletcher does this and more.

He has long since pleaded the case for both active and passive euthanasia. In his book *Morals and Medicine*, published in 1954, Fletcher devoted a chapter to his lonely battle for the freedom to end life when there is compelling reason to do so. He defines euthanasia as merciful release from incurable suffering. Fletcher takes the ten most common arguments that he has encountered against euthanasia and tries to decapitate them. He is a good debater. Briefly, here is the way the debate unfolds:

1. Objection: Voluntary euthanasia is suicide and therefore wrong. Fletcher: Life and length of days is not the *summum bonum* for Christians. To prolong life uselessly is no virtue. Just as you may risk and lose your life in a good cause, you may have good and noble reason to take it.

2. Objection: If euthanasia is involuntary, as when the patient is irreversibly comatose and did not ask for euthanasia, it is murder. Fletcher: Murder is made of malice. He urges the significance of motive and says that if motive does not matter, "then the thrifty parent who saves in order to educate his children is no higher in the scale of merit than the miser who saves for the sake of hoarding."

3. Objection: It is up to God to decide when life should end. Fletcher: Then stop all medicine, for that interferes with the time of death by postponing it.

4. Objection: The Bible says: "Thou shalt not kill." Fletcher: This means, Thou shalt not murder. And the Bible also says: "Blessed are the merciful."

5. Objection: Suffering is part of the divine plan. Fletcher: Then the Hippocratic oath is heresy, for it enjoins the physician to alleviate suffering.

6. Objection: Wait; a cure may be found. Fletcher: Some cases of advanced cancer get to the point where it is too late for the cure to help.

7. Objection: The patient might want to die and then change his mind. Fletcher: Make a careful law which requires a waiting period.

8. Objection: Adoption of euthanasia would weaken our moral fiber. Fletcher: It might take more moral courage to decide for death.

9. Objection: A physician may not kill. Fletcher: By relieving pain with heavy analgesics, he does, by the logic of morphine, bring on death. The Hippocratic oath commits the physician to relieving suffering. Sometimes death is the only relief. In his tenth and final thrust, Fletcher disputes the argument that all doctors disapprove of euthanasia and contends that doctors do in fact practice euthanasia clandestinely.

Fletcher does not do a systematic study of the ethics of euthanasia. What he does do, in all of his writing on the subject, is to charge the presuppositions and biases that block systematic discussion. Sometimes he wins only debater's points, but overall, his message on this subject is this: "It is harder morally to justify letting somebody die a slow and ugly death, dehumanized, than it is to justify helping him to escape from such misery."[22] To those who would give this proposition the back of their hand, Fletcher insists that they had better have something better than their hoary old saws to support the closed state of their minds. Fletcher is a successful provocateur who has a way of annoying minds open. He is good at this. Right or wrong he always provokes, and causes people to tighten their defenses or take a new measure of their positions.

PAUL RAMSEY AND TWO POSSIBLE QUALIFICATIONS

Paul Ramsey, the Harrington Spear Paine Professor of Religion at Princeton University, is probably the most influential writer in contemporary ethics. Few subjects have escaped the vigor and nuance of his attention, so that, whether you agree with him or not, you must deal with him when you do ethics. For this reason, Ramsey's treatment of death by choice is highly significant in the current ethical milieu.

Ramsey builds a strong case for the categorical moral imperative always to care for the dying and never to hasten the dying beyond the reach of our love and care. Arguing largely from Christian categories, Ramsey says that it would be a contradiction of Christian charity to cease from caring "before [being] released from the claims and needs of a still living fellow man."[23]

Nevertheless, Ramsey concedes that there may be two qualifications of our duty to care for the dying. Here are the exceptions that Ramsey would allow:

> We may say, Never abandon care of the dying except when they are irretrievably inaccessible to human care. Never hasten the dying process except when it is *entirely indifferent to the patient* whether his dying is accomplished by an intravenous bubble of air or by the withdrawal of useless ordinary natural remedies such as nourishment.[24]

Ramsey argues that a moralist cannot really say whether there are such cases which fall under this justification of direct killing. This would be for physicians to say. If there are, direct killing is moral and not an unacceptable exception to the principle of always caring for the dying. This first exception depends on whether a patient's physiological condition actually renders him beyond our love and care. If his comatose condition is such that he feels no hunger, then he will not experience the withholding of nourishment. If it is determined that the patient is in this state, then, Ramsey feels, it is a matter of complete indifference "whether humankind's final act toward him directly or indirectly allows death to come."[25] This is not an effort to escape the demands of charity prematurely, but to acknowledge that charity makes no more commands to company with this person who is now beyond all our caring.

Ramsey's position here does not make of him a raving euthanasiast by any stretch of the imagination. Indeed, he has placed an almost impossible condition in the hands of the physician, namely, to determine the kind of psychological blackout that Ramsey postulates. Can such a state be verified? Or has ethicist Ramsey managed to have his exception cake and eat it too? As moralist Richard McCormick says, commenting on Ramsey's position: "On what grounds would physicians make this judgment? They would have to guess, would they not? They are in no better position than anyone else to tell us whether the patient is experiencing anything or is beyond care."[26]

Also, the German theologian Helmut Thielicke, while not addressing Ramsey's position, cuts into Ramsey's exception, based as that exception is on the issue of consciousness and awareness. Giving full rein to his imagination, Thielicke writes: "It is conceivable that a person who is dying may stand in a passageway where human communication has long since been left behind, but which nonetheless contains a self-consciousness different from any other of which we know."[27] Since we could, with Thielicke, speculate rather endlessly on possible mental states of the dying, Ramsey may have introduced a condition that could only be verified by a number of persons who rose from the dead to give us some data on the descending phases of terminal self-awareness.

Still, I would argue that Ramsey's first exception is not entirely beyond application. If, as the result of an accident, there was clear evidence that the cerebral cortex had been drastically damaged and only the brainstem continued to be functional, it would seem clear that personal life has been extinguished. Then, to use Ramsey's words quoted above, it would seem that it would not matter to this patient "whether his dying is accomplished by an intravenous bubble of air or by the withdrawal of useless ordinary natural remedies such as nourishment." There may be other cases, too, where massive evidence of cerebral death could become sufficient to warrant the judgment that the patient is, in Ramsey's strict terms, beyond human caring.[28]

Though Ramsey may not seem to have moved far here, he has actually moved further than American law would permit a physician to move. There is no room for bubbles of air in American law, however laboriously circumscribed the conditions for their administration may be. Given the prestige of Paul Ramsey in the field of ethics and his conservative credentials, this first exception of his is well worth the note we are making of it.

His second exception is even more noteworthy. It is this: with regard to dying persons, never "take positive action to usher them out of our presence or to hasten their departure from the human community *unless* there is a kind of prolonged dying in which it is medically impossible to keep severe pain at bay."[29] Again, Ramsey says that a moralist cannot say whether there are any members in this class. Persons dying from bone cancer may be members, he says, but he notes that in hospital situations it is probably possible to suppress all kinds of pain. If, however, there is such a case, then it is comparable to the case of a man seriously wounded during a military mission in a jungle who cannot go on with the group and cannot be carried, and would therefore have to be left behind to be devoured by insects. In such a case, Ramsey says, it might be permissible to kill the man or leave him a gun with a warning that whatever happens he should save the final bullet for himself.[30] Likewise it could be permissible to bring about the death of a terminal patient suffering uncontrollable pain. In his words: "One can hardly hold men to be morally blameworthy if in these instances dying is directly accomplished or hastened."[31]

Let us be clear, then, about what is being said here. If a dying person has undefeatable and unsupportable pain, he is, like the patient in the first exception, beyond reach of the ways in which we could keep company with him. In such a case it may be morally permissible to take direct action to end his life.

Again, the question could be asked, has Ramsey really conceded anything or has he given us an exceptional class without members? No, it would seem he has conceded a lot and this class of exceptions has potentially many members. First of all, Ramsey says that the proper meaning of "euthanasia" is "direct killing."[32] Ramsey has therefore approved of certain carefully specified kinds of euthanasia, by his definition of that term.[33] He even has faced up, albeit briefly, to the principal argument brought against making any exceptions to the principle forbidding direct killing, viz., that this will lead to abuses. He concludes that if the strict limits of the exceptions are observed as he circumscribes them, further and reckless extension need not be feared.[34]

We said that this second exception of Ramsey's could potentially include many members. This is so because it is based on the notion of "undefeatable agony," uncontrollable pain. Pain, however, is a subjective state.[35] Different people have varying thresholds of pain: tolerance varies. And, most importantly, the worst pain may not be the pain of an aching tumor but rather the mental pain such as Mrs. Postma deemed most intolerable for her mother.

Furthermore, physical pain can only be controlled in its most terrible forms in a hospital setting, and, then, not in every hospital setting. This is an area of medical science which is making great strides and which promises even more in the future. Pain management now involves not just the use of drugs but also such things as neurosurgical procedures which can be quite effective. All this is fine, but it presents two large problems: not everyone wants to be or can be in the hospital setting where pain can be so controlled.

Older moralists used to say, quite humanely, that there was no moral obligation to leave one's home and go away to a more healthful climate to be cured. This was seen as something that could be too painful or too inconvenient to be considered obligatory. In the spirit of this insight, a person might not want to go to the hospital for pain relief, especially if it meant being sustained in a semi-stupor until death ensued. This prospect might be more painful to some persons than many kinds of physical pain. Also, in some countries, it would be necessary to go a very long distance to get to a hospital equipped for this kind of pain relief and in many parts of the world, it would be economically infeasible to seek and find such care.

Therefore, this second category of Ramsey's is a class with members . . . members who do not have access to good hospital care and members who do but who might vigorously prefer to face death at home rather than in a humanly sterile medical location. For both of these types of persons, there could come a time when, in their dying process, their unmanageable pain puts them squarely into Ramsey's second exceptional class.

Ramsey's two qualifications to his cardinal rule of always caring for the dying may have certain weaknesses. I believe they do, since I will argue that some persons who are quite accessible to human caring might, in spite of their accessibility, find good reasons to prefer death to continued living. They might find themselves in a situation where the care they most want from us is assistance in hastening death when death is perceived as a friend. Care for the dying might involve positive acts to hasten death even before the extreme conditions stipulated by Ramsey.

But his two exceptions are important because they represent something other than the absolutism which previously prevailed in many scholarly circles regarding direct action to terminate life. Also, while legality is not morality (and we have already rejoiced over that fact when viewing the state of the law) it is still something to ponder that both of Ramsey's stringent exceptions would, if acted upon, probably be classified as first-degree murder in American law. Here, again, morality is moving beyond law and away from law in a divorce proceeding that is unnatural and inimical to the common weal.

EVENTS IN THEORY

We have already looked at some of the new questions regarding mercy killing and at some of the new conclusions being reached and defended. Two examples of changes at the fundamental level of theory are also worth a moment of our effort and time. The two influential moralists whom we will look at here do not reach conclusions that mercy killing is morally defensible. In fact one of them, Richard McCormick, explicitly argues against it. But both of them provide a theoretical approach to moral questions of life and death that evacuates the grounding of the older position on the absolute inviolability of innocent life. That older position might somehow be reinstated, but it would have to be reinstated on new pilings. One need not be a trained ethicist to see the implications of this shift in theory.

PETER KNAUER

Peter Knauer is a German theologian with a special interest in ethical theory. As was mentioned at the beginning of this chapter, the terms "direct" and "indirect" were staple ethical fare for centuries. Peter Knauer has a new and radical reinterpretation of the notion of directness. Knauer does not attack the old formula that innocent life may never be taken directly, but he redefines "directly." He puts it this way: "I say that an evil effect is not 'directly intended' only if there is a 'commensurate ground' for its permission or causation."[36]

If this statement confuses the reader, it is because the reader is thinking clearly. Knauer is changing the meaning of direct so much that it has no relationship to its previous meaning. What he means is that the taking of innocent life is wrong if there is no commensurate reason for taking it. The old position, however, was that there could be *no* commensurate reason for intentional taking of innocent life. While holding on to the old terminology, Knauer has abandoned the old position. In clearer language, he puts it this way: "Moral evil, I contend, consists in the last analysis in the permission or causing of a physical evil which is not justified by a commensurate reason."[37] Or, clearer yet: "Whether there is a violation of a commandment (that is, whether an act is murder, lying, theft) can be ascertained only if it is established that the reason for the act in its existential entirety is not commensurate."[38] Thus, if someone cuts off your leg, that is surely a physical evil. We do not know if it is a moral evil unless we know if there is a proportionate reason for this serious act. If the leg were affected with advanced cancer or gangrene, that would be a commensurate reason for the surgery and the act is morally good. If the surgeon just wanted amputation practice, the reason would not be commensurate and *therefore* the act would be immoral.

Let us apply this theory then to life-taking cases in a way that Knauer does not do with this specificity, but in a way that his theory allows. It is wrong to take innocent life (that of a fetus or that of a dying person suffering from incorrigible pain who begs for death) unless there is a commensurate reason. If there is commensurate reason, then it would not be immoral. At the theoretical level then, Knauer's ethical theory allows for euthanasia, suicide, or abortion under his dominant rubric of "commensurate reason." He slips out from under the old rule against intentionally taking innocent life and comes up with the position that commensurate reason is what counts.

Let it be said, however, that there are indications that Knauer is not willing to go as far as his theory goes. By putting tremendous stress on the long-term effects of an action, he can avoid conclusions and hide behind the inevitably imponderable quality of very long-term effects. In other words, unless you know all the long-term effects, how do you know if there is commensurate reason for your action? Thus does Knauer avoid hard answers to concrete cases.

An example of this occurs at the end of the article from which we have been quoting. The editor asks Knauer how his doctrine of commensurate reason would apply to the case of a woman who is asked to commit adultery in order that her children may be rescued from a concentration camp. Does she not have commensurate reason for the adulterous act, and would this act not therefore be morally good? In response, Knauer flies to the abstract and wrings his hands about whether life or freedom would have any value if one is forced to give up all human rights and be exposed to every extortion. That is certainly a valid and worthy question, but it is not an answer. He does not apply his commensurate reason theory nor does he answer the question. Fine! Knauer is not the first academic to be stronger on theory than on application. But his theory is important, because working in a conservative Catholic context, Knauer comes up with the conclusion that whether life is taken directly or indirectly is not so much the point as whether or not there is proportionate reason for taking it. This theory would open up the approach to all the problems we have been discussing. With this theory, not everyone would come up with the same answer, since not all would agree on what was commensurate, but no question would be closed. And that is a change.

RICHARD McCORMICK

As an ethicist, Richard McCormick is a master surgeon who cuts finely when he analyzes. As a result, his work is highly esteemed by moralists of every stripe. Because of the weight his thought carries, he is an important final witness for this chapter.

Richard McCormick, like Knauer, goes after the old standby "direct/indirect" which guided a lot of thinking in areas such as self-defense, abortion, euthanasia, and suicide. McCormick says that while the notions of directness and indirectness of psychological intent do have importance in ethics, they are not utterly decisive in determining what is right or wrong. "What was and is decisive is the proportionate reason for acting."[39] Thus, for example, it used to be said that the direct killing of innocent persons in war was evil *in se*. In the old view, that meant that such killing was morally evil regardless of the circumstances and the consequences. McCormick argues, however, that it is "precisely because of foreseen consequences that such a principle is a practical absolute."[40] The undesirable consequences would be such as to far outweigh whatever short-term gain might be gotten from direct assaults on innocent persons. In other words, there would be no proportion between the ills consequent upon the action and the gains gotten. The bads would outweigh the goods. Such action would, McCormick argues, brutalize sensitivities in such a way that in the long run, more lives would be lost. This is what makes a principle such as non-combatant immunity a kind of practical absolute or "virtually exceptionless."[41]

What McCormick is doing here is giving us some of the key ideas for handling cases such as we are treating. When McCormick applies his thinking to cases of euthanasia, he comes out with the conclusion that euthanasia is always wrong in the same sense that the slaughter of innocents in war is always wrong.[42] From the foreseeable consequences of making exceptions in mercy killing cases, he tends to the conclusion that mercy killing should always be seen as wrong. No proportionate good could come from allowing exceptions here.

However, McCormick's conclusion is one thing, the implications of his theory, another. In summary, here is what McCormick comes up with: actions which cause a physical evil (such as loss of life or limb) are moral only if there is a truly proportionate reason which justifies the actions. Taking life is wrong, *unless there is proportionate reason to do so* and this will be determined by a long hard look at the immediate effects *and* "the social implications and reverberating after-effects in so far as they can be foreseen."[43]

In Knauer, commensurate reason was the master rubric; in McCormick, who borrows selectively from Knauer, the idea of commensurate or proportionate reason is fleshed out with more stress on consequences. What is important is that McCormick's method breaks the absolutist bind in which questions such as mercy killing cannot even be considered. Though McCormick uses his system to question euthanasia, his system can be used to support it. For when it comes to judging whether or not there is proportionate reason for ending a terminally ill patient's life, we are facing a question which is by its nature open, not closed. It becomes a matter of assessing the proportionate reasons and here judgments vary. One man's proportion may be another man's poison. As McCormick says: "The judgment of proportionality in conflict situations is not only a very decisive judgment; it is also a most difficult one."[44] Recognizing this, he wisely calls the lecture from which we have been drawing *Ambiguity in Moral Choice*.

These matters are ambiguous, not crystal clear. Because of that, these issues are open to discussion, not to anathema. This is redolent of the new moral climate, and in this moral climate it becomes clear that many issues, including issues such as mercy killing, were artificially closed to reconsideration. The artificial wraps are starting to come off. Abuse could follow from this. Abuse can follow from anything good including the creation of persons as free beings. At any rate, as Justice Brandeis was wont to say: "Sunlight is the best disinfectant." And sunshine is getting into some of the nooks and crannies which were hitherto recessed in shadow.

FOOTNOTES–CHAPTER 3

1. Kelly, op. cit., p. 63.
2. Ibid., p. 65.
3. *Acta Apostolicae Sedis* (AAS) 22 (1930), p. 563.
4. AAS 43 (1951), pp. 838–39.
5. AAS 43 (1951), p. 857.
6. Healy, op. cit., pp. 252–53. Healy concludes his discussion of this case with this advice: "During such a dangerous parturition the physician should remember to administer baptism to both heads if both can be reached."
7. John Milhaven, "Towards an Epistemology of Ethics," *Theological Studies* 27, no. 2 (June 1966): 233, n. 7.
8. Ibid.
9. *The Sign*, March 1968, p. 26. The article cited as a transcribed dialogue between Dr. Robert White, Director of the Brain Research Laboratories at Cleveland Metropolitan General Hospital, and Father Curran.
10. Wassmer, op. cit., pp. 766–77.
11. Ibid., pp. 766–77.
12. *Cross Currents* 14, no. 4 (1966): 429–46.
13. "The Problem of Care for the Dying," in *Absolutes in Moral Theology?*, ed. Charles Curran (Washington and Cleveland: Corpus Books, 1968), p. 259. The volume contains eight essays by Catholic moralists on a variety of moral issues and it was intended by the editor and the contributors to show the new face of Catholic moral thought which now coexists with an older face in the phenomenon of a pluralistic Catholicism.
14. Ibid., p. 260. This definition of euthanasia is not common since most use the term euthanasia to mean positive action to bring on the death of a person *in extremis*. In fact, in common parlance, what Nolan recommends would be considered euthanasia.
15. Ibid.
16. Bernard Häring, *Medical Ethics* (Notre Dame, Ind.: Fides Publishers, 1973), p. 108.
17. Ibid., p. 109.
18. Ibid., p. 101.
19. Ibid., p. 84.
20. Ibid., p. 101.
21. Ramsey, op. cit., p. 148.
22. "Ethics and Euthanasia," *American Journal of Nursing* 73, no. 4 (April 1973): 671.
23. Ramsey, op. cit., p. 160.
24. Ibid., p. 161.
25. Ibid.
26. "Notes on Moral Theology," *Theological Studies* 34, no. 1 (March 1973): 68.
27. "The Doctor as Judge of Who Shall Live and Who Shall Die," in Vaux, op. cit., p. 163.

28. See p. 16 in Chapter 1.

29. Ramsey, op. cit., p. 162.

30. Ibid., p. 160, n. 59, and p. 163. On this case, Ramsey refers to his essay "The Case of the Curious Exception" in Norm and Context in Christian Ethics, ed. by Gene H. Outka and Paul Ramsey (New York: Charles Scribner's Sons, 1968).

31. The Patient as Person, p. 163. This would be another case where the distinction between omission and commission may be abrogated, according to Ramsey.

32. Ibid., p. 149.

33. Ramsey's exceptions are painstakingly sectioned out and therefore he would understandably wish to avoid listing them under the term "euthanasia," overladen as that term is with varying and even contradictory meanings. His exceptions, however, are not narrow, as we have been seeing.

34. Ramsey, op. cit., p. 164. To understand Ramsey's confidence in the durability and validity of principles, see his Deed and Rules in Christian Ethics (New York: Charles Scribner's Sons, 1967), and his essay "The Case of the Curious Exception," noted above. Ramsey does not see the exceptions or "unlessments" as tearing apart the integrity of the principle.

35. Ramsey acknowledges this, in The Patient as Person, p. 163, n. 60.

36. "The Hermeneutic Function of the Principle of Double Effect," Natural Law Forum 12 (1967): 137.

37. Ibid., p. 133.

38. Ibid., p. 150.

39. Richard McCormick, Ambiguity in Moral Choice: The 1973 Pere Marquette Theology Lecture (Milwaukee: Marquette University Theology Publication, 1973), p. 84.

40. Ibid., p. 86.

41. Ibid., pp. 86–87. McCormick borrows the term "virtually exceptionless" from Donald Evans.

42. See "Notes on Moral Theology," Theological Studies 34, no. 1 (March 1973): 70–74. In these notes, McCormick questions the major conclusions of my article "The Freedom to Die," Commonweal 46 (1972): 423–27. His objection is, in essence, that the consequences of not treating the ban on euthanasia as an absolute are foreseeably so bad that exceptions should not be made.

43. Ambiguity in Moral Choice, p. 95.

44. Ibid., p. 95.

PART TWO

The Ethics of Death by Choice

Up to this point, I have been proceeding under the mantle of an almost unfair immunity, the immunity of the commentator. I have toured some of the areas of medical progress that pose perplexing questions without bearing the physician's grave burden of responsibility. Non-lawyer though I be, I have deplored the inadequacies of American law vis-à-vis the human right *to die humanly*. Even when I treated some of the significant openings in my own field of ethics, I chose to recount and comment on the theories, questions, and conclusions of my colleagues. All of this was in an effort to show the new climate in which death is being considered and to urge that new thoughts on death are not only thinkable but to be thought.

In this section, I propose to show how I as a moralist treat the subject of death by choice. Every moralist is as good as his method and so it is necessary to know something of a moralist's method if you would know the worth of his conclusions. The method presented here is geared to the solution of all of the kinds of cases that we have been touching upon, whether these involve choosing death for yourself or death for another, whether you step in and take positive action to end a life or whether you omit supportive measures and let "nature take its course." Obviously there is an immense difference between deciding on your own death and deciding on the death of another. Different and distinct objections can be lodged against each of these actions, and after the presentation of my method, these objections will be confronted separately and in the necessary detail. What I hope to show in this chapter is that, by the very nature of ethics, all of these cases are open to discussion. Or, more directly, there may be cases where action (or inaction) to end one's own or someone else's life may be moral and good human behavior. It is my contention that to deny that possibility *a priori* is to betray a taboo mentality which proscribes certain actions without sensitivity to their meaning-giving circumstances. But now, on to the method.

CHAPTER 4

Ethics: How to do It

Ethics is the science which seeks to bring sensitivity and method to the human task of discovering moral value. With that said it should be clearer what an ethicist (moralist, ethician) is. Two questions leap out of that definition: 1) What does an ethicist do that everyone else does not do, since everyone is involved in knowing moral values? 2) What does moral mean?

Answers: Nietzsche is right when he says that man is a valuing animal. Programmed though he may be, he is not as programmed as a squirrel, but is rather "condemned to freedom," to some freedom at least. Human consciousness brings with it the noble onus of having to sort and pick amid competing and often conflicting values to determine which options are moral and which are not. Therefore, it is true to say that every man is an ethicist in pursuit of moral value. The special task of the professional ethicist is to attempt to bring sensitivity, reflection, and method to the way in which his fellow humans have learned to do, or stumbled into doing, ethics. The ethicist stops to think how moral judgments are and should be arrived at; most people do not so stop and so think. They should have something to learn from the ethicist who does.

The second question was: What does moral mean? Moral (as opposed to immoral) means that which is normatively human—in other words, that which humans ought to be. An example: most humans decide that sexual fulfillment ought not to be found in rape. A rapist is not what humans ought to be, which is to say that rape is immoral. When we call something immoral, we mean that it is incompatible with humanity. Conversely, that which is truly fulfilling of our humanity is moral.[1]

Some primitive peoples have a very suggestive punishment for incest. The incestuous couple are forced to eat with the hogs for a period of time. However indelicate the example, the symbolic dramatization of immorality is powerful. They have acted in a way that is piggish, counter-human, not human. That is what the judgment of *morality* is all about. (We prescind from whether this guilt rite does any injustice to the mores of the pigs.)

In asking whether a person has the right to end his own life, or the life of another, we are asking whether this is compatible with humanness as we understand it. I will argue that positive action to bring on death in certain circumstances is truly human and moral.

How, then, does one go about deciding whether one's judgment of humanness and moralness is right or wrong, especially in disputed matters where a lot of other humans disagree? Or, in other words, how do you do ethics?

The first step in ethics is to set up the moral object. Moral object is a term of art. It means an act with all of its attendant and meaning-giving circumstances. An action considered by itself aside from its circumstances has no moral dimension. Thus suppose one gentleman is putting a bullet into another gentleman's head. This raw fact, however impressive, does not give us a moral object that can be validly judged. Until we add the *circumstances*, we do not know whether this action is moral or immoral. Is it a killing emanating from robbery, self-defense, or caprice? When we know that, we will have the circumstances that allow moral judgment. We will have the moral object.

The moral object can be known through a series of reality-revealing questions. Each of these questions is important and it is ethical heresy to neglect any one of them. The bane of ethics is incompleteness, and incompleteness is the product of unasked questions. The goal of the doctrine of the moral object is to get as much of a grasp of the reality as possible because *morality is based on reality*. If you do not ask all the reality-revealing questions, your judgment will be based on only part of the reality and it will be right only by accident. Therefore, no moral judgment can be reached until all questions have been answered as fully as possible.

THE REALITY-REVEALING QUESTIONS

The trouble with the questions to be set out here is that most of them are obvious, but, unfortunately, it is the obvious in ethics that is most often ignored. Hopefully the examples given throughout will illustrate this. The first question, then, is *what?* The question "what?" is really the beginning of ethics. And it is a beginning that most people resist. The implication, lest it be missed, is that people usually do not know *what* they are talking about. It is the way of men to skim off an impression of reality and treat it as though it were the reality itself. Therefore, "what?" is a formidable question. It must be asked because the answer involves concrete facts and data which are loaded with moral meaning.

Let us test this first simple question on something like abortion. Some people argue that a woman has a clear-cut right to an abortion at any time for any purpose since she has a right over her body and the fetus is, in effect, an appendage of her body. I would suggest that anyone who would so argue does not know *what* he or she is talking about. Such an argument might be closer to reality if the woman alone were to be considered. Pregnancy, however, is not a condition of aloneness. Someone or something else is part of the *what* that we are talking about. And this someone or something is not just an appendage. Good ethics would ask *what* it is. Knowing what it is will not give the answer to the morality of abortion, but it will be a marvelous beginning. Look at some of the facts about fetuses and you might sense the unreality of considering the fetus as mere appendage or mere tissue or mere anything.

What you have is a genetically unique individual. Around four or five weeks after conception, when a mother might just be beginning to think she is pregnant, the foundations of all the organ systems of the fetus have been laid. A cardiovascular system has already begun pumping. Primitive brain vessels are developing. By the eighth week, it is possible to get an EEG reading. During the ninth and tenth weeks, the little creature is capable of reflex activities such as squinting and swallowing. All of this has happened before the mother feels fetal movements, "quickening," as it is called. Mere appendage or mere tissue this is not.

If you would judge the morality of abortion, know *what* you are aborting. There may indeed be some tragic but morally compelling reason why this "miraculous" ensemble of cells which is concertedly expanding toward infant and personal life might have to be squelched and rejected. But no one who does not know *what* he is expelling, could judge that.[2] The judges of the Supreme Court of the United States might have ruled differently on abortion had they seen and touched a few fetuses whose life processes were interrupted in the first months. The Court effectually discounts the value of the fetus during the first six months of its uterine existence by denying it the protection of law. Though abortion may at tragic times be moral, it is not because the fetus at any point is of dubious value. Justices who knew *what* they were talking about would have taken account of this in their ruling.

Another example: persons who speak glibly about the moral use of napalm in counterinsurgency warfare may indeed be right. Its use may in certain circumstances be moral. But that judgment should be based on a clear knowledge of what napalm is. As in the case of the fetus, the empirical facts are a highly meaningful part of the reality to be judged moral or immoral. Napalm is a gel formation of gasoline. It enhances the destructive properties of burning gasoline by concentrating the flame which can burn to a temperature of more than 2000° C. White phosphorus is used in the ignition systems of napalm bombs and land mines. This and other elements produce a dense, white smoke which retards fire fighting or rescue operation. Napalm bombs contain up to 165 gallons of napalm, which may spread over a wide area. Napalm casualties usually suffer third-degree burns because of the prolonged burning time and the high temperature. Such burns usually result in death or deformity. Napalm burns are often complicated by carbon monoxide poisoning. Children suffer a disproportionately high mortality rate because of the special problems of the burned child.

So that is *what* napalm is. There may be some tragic but morally compelling reason why napalm should be used in warfare, but whoever judges that must know the empirical facts of the case. Empirical facts in a human context have moral meaning. Not knowing the facts skews moral judgment.

In a case of death by choice in a medical context where intolerable suffering is the motivating factor, some may say that suffering does not give proportionate reason for terminating life. Those who argue this way may in many cases be right, but they had better begin their ethics by knowing *what* the patient is suffering and *what* that suffering means to the sufferer. In the cause of empirical sensitivity, we might look at the facts of one instance of suffering.

> One day a middle-aged woman became suddenly blind in one eye. The terror of this unheralded experience was rapidly offset by recovery of vision in subsequent weeks. Attacks of giddiness and shaking of the legs and head followed, again to improve but again to reappear. This was the onset of multiple sclerosis, a disorder where disseminated foci of damage occur throughout the brain and spinal cord. Slowly but inexorably the patient was forced to bed and was ultimately unable to leave it because of paralysis of the lower limbs. Soon, control of the bladder and anal muscles led to incontinence of urine and feces. Bed sores developed and were so large and deep that the underlying bones of the pelvis were eroded as well.[3]

Some people in this condition may wish to continue in spite of the pain and indignities. Others may wish that antibiotics be stopped or even that more positive action be taken to bring on death. Could a lethal injection of potassium be morally justified in such a case? *What* the mental and physical sufferings of the patient are must be factored into the moral judgment here because they are an important and integral part of *what* is being judged.

One of the things that is frequently said is that mercy killing in the case of a consenting subject is exactly like suicide. This is erroneous. There are real differences at the level of *what*.

Suicide, self-killing outside of a medical context, is the interruption of a health process. The suicidal act is the sole and exclusive cause of death. Death by choice in cases where there is a terminal illness is the interruption or acceleration of a dying process. In this case, there are other causes operating to produce the effect of death. These causes are adequate to effect death in their own time. The terminal patient who opts for death is not precisely a suicide for this reason. He may wish that he were well and hale, but given the disastrous medical facts, he prefers death now. The adequate causes of death are not operative in the suicide. By applying all the questions listed in this section on the moral object, further differences would be disclosed. Somewhat defensively, I must urge that this is not quibbling. It is an effort to say that if you start out to evaluate two acts and do not see the differences in those two acts, you are off to a bad start. Better to know *what* you are talking about.

The second reality-revealing question is *why?* This refers to the motivating reason or intention of the agent.[4] One person may be giving money to another person. The mere *what* is not very significant in this case. The morality could emerge from the *why*. If the money is being given to embarrass the recipient later by revealing the debt, the act takes on one moral meaning; if the money were being given out of compassion, the morality would be different. What we are speaking of here is the moral significance of motive.

In the example given above by Joseph Fletcher, saving money to educate a child and saving money for mean and miserly purposes changes the moral quality of the money saving. Becoming a lawyer to help the poor and becoming a lawyer to help the Mafia are two morally different realities and they are different because of the different motive, because of the different *why*.

Performing a craniotomy to save the mother is not the same as doing a craniotomy to eliminate a competing heir. A different *why* makes a different reality. If an abortion is motivated by a change of vacation plans since being pregnant will be inconvenient at the beach, it would have one moral meaning. If the abortion was performed due to a sudden critical development in the mother's health, the case is not the same. If a doctor injects a fatal dose into a patient's vein because the patient has repeatedly begged for release from agony, it is not the same as if the doctor is doing it because he finds the patient a cantankerous old buzzard who is a nuisance to treat.

What all of these examples illustrate is that *motive gives essential and constitutive meaning to human action.* We have not passed judgment on any of the above cases, for to do so would be to break the rule that no moral judgment should be made until all the reality-revealing questions have been asked. We are only saying that to exclude motive is to exclude reality to a substantial degree.

Good motive alone, of course, is not enough to justify an action morally. Poisoning a city's water supply would not be justified by the motive of easing population pressures. Likewise the noble motive of checking air pollution would scarcely justify a systematic plan to assassinate oil magnates.

An example of the inadequacy of good motive alone is easily found at the collective level of life where a one-rubric ethic of motive is regularly plied. Thus the avowed motive for the bombings of Hiroshima and Nagasaki, which terminated or maimed an enormous number of lives, was "to save American lives." Many sensitive persons have judged this good motive grossly insufficient to justify the holocausts in those two population centers. Similarly many of the things that nations do "to make the world safe for democracy" or "to promote the revolution of the proletariat" can hardly be sanctified by good intention alone. The American colonel who stood in the ashes of Ben Tre and proclaimed: "We had to destroy this village in order to save it," had good intentions. The survivors of Ben Tre could attest to the insufficiency of good motive alone.

The motive factor does not of itself give the moral answer to cases of abortion, suicide, or mercy killing, but it is intrinsic to that answer. All terminations of life are not the same morally since they do not all have the same motive. It is *morally* and *really* absurd to equate the mercy killer with the robber killer and the rapist killer. There are real differences at many levels in these types of cases and certainly at the level of motive. Legal or moral judgment that does not recognize this is unreal.

The next reality-revealing, and thus morality-revealing question is *how?* What we are saying here is that the manner or style of an action contributes to the constitution of its morality in an integral way. Driving a car can be good, but *how* you drive can make it a moral crime. Sexual intercourse can be a morally fine action but if it is brought about by force or deceit, it will be morally defective at the circumstantial level of *how*. It could be defective for other reasons, too, which would be unearthed by other reality-revealing questions, but the point here is that *how* something is done is morally significant.

What you might be doing may be good; *why* you are doing it may be excellent; but the action may fail morally by *how* you do it. For example, if someone goes into the poverty-stricken inner core of his city to help the poor, he may pass the *what* and the *why* questions with flying colors and fail the *how* by acting with an air of superiority that offends. In this way, a good action could become insulting and therefore bad.

In the area of mercy killing, *how* is again of great importance. Here is one place where omission and commission make a big difference. At times, if death is decided upon, omission may be the only way to bring it about, because positive action may be psychologically unbearable or legally prohibited for the persons involved. On this basis it might be decided to suspend intravenous feeding rather than give an injection. Or if it is decided to take positive action, again there are various ways in which the life may be terminated. You might, for example, repair to the seventeenth-century custom in Brittany where an incurable sufferer could appeal for the Holy Stone. The family gathered, the religious rites were performed, and the oldest living relative raised the large stone over the sufferer's head and let it fall.[5] That is one way of doing it. And it is a good way to show that *how* makes a difference. One might, however, prefer an excessive dose of pain-killing drug. The way an abortion is performed could make it immoral. The way in which a person is overdosed or fatally injected affects the morality of the act, as would the means used, e.g., cyanide or morphine.

Again, this is not to say that if you do it nicely, it is good. It is simply to say that how you do it matters morally. The *how*

question is closely related to the matter of *means*. The wrong
means to the right end equals a wrong action. *How* matters.
It is not a matter of indifference whether you use a sledgeham-
mer or a pill to respond to someone's request to put him out
of his misery. If it is determined that on every account the act
is moral, the means chosen could make it immoral.[6]

Who? is also a critical question. Every who, i.e., every person
is unique. He has his own unrepeatable story that is embodied
in his personality and outlook, his own degree of sensitivity, his
own conscience and his own superego, and, if the thesis holds
that we are all neurotics, his own neurosis. To do ethics abstractly and ignore the who that you are dealing with is a
tragedy. Perhaps this is what is behind Sartre's poignant observation that the greatest evil of which man is capable is to treat
as abstract that which is concrete. In making ethical judgments
we can easily consider everything except the person involved.
We can abstractly pass over the wisdom of the old adage that
one man's meat may be another man's poison.

Note what is being said here: the subject—the *who*—constitutes part of the objective reality to be evaluated. Note what is
not being said here: this does not mean that what Lola wants is
good for Lola. It does not mean that an arbitrary subjectivism
where everyone does his own normless thing is being suggested.
It merely means that if you do not know the *who* with all his
hopes, needs, and personal possibilities, you do not know what
you are judging.

An abortion may seem morally indicated in the case of a rape
victim who has a history of mental illness and who is clearly
traumatized by the sexual assault. If, however, the girl is so
constituted by training and disposition that she could not ap-
prove of an abortion, she could not morally decide for one.
A fortiori, it could not be decided for her. Likewise, it is, I
believe, immoral to draft into military service a thoroughly non-
violent man. The full reality of the *who*, as he is, for better or
for worse, must be factored into the final moral judgment. If
mercy killing is seen as moral, it is possible that a medical doctor is not the right *who* to do it. The word "medicine" comes
from the Latin *mederi*, meaning to heal. Maybe doctors should

only heal and not be involved in terminating life. If this hypothesis is true (and we shall discuss it later), then it might be immoral for a doctor to terminate life for any reason precisely because of *who* he is. Some other profession might have to be created to deal with the imposition of death.

Does this mean that what is objectively moral for one person may be objectively immoral for another? The answer is yes.[7] An example from anthropology can illustrate this. It is reported that in the past, Eskimos would let their grandparents go off to freeze to death at a certain point because this was their way of keeping population within the limits of food supply.[8] The grandparents did this willingly. The story is told, however, of some missionaries who went to the Eskimos, discovered this practice, and condemned it roundly in terms of divine authority. The Eskimos were mightily impressed with the missionaries' veto of their long-standing custom. With their point made, the missionaries departed, promising to return in a few years to see if the faith was being kept alive. They returned and found that the group had died out, presumably enervated and finally killed off by the relative population pressure and lack of food.

The story, if true, shows the moral and real significance of several of our reality-revealing questions. Of the questions we have considered so far, the missionaries obviously did not know the *what* or the *who*. On the contrary, in the absence of viable alternatives, these Eskimo *whos* knew *what* they were about in practicing socially motivated geriatric suicide. The missionaries did not understand either the culture of these people or their ecological situation. As a result they did bad ethics and they killed, as bad ethics can often do. (They also failed to ask other reality-revealing questions we will list, concerning alternatives and effects.)

In the absence of alternatives, the Eskimo practice of benevolent suicide would appear to have been quite moral. The action of the missionaries was objectively immoral, although their intentions were the best, because they ignored the reality of the case for which they so confidently prescribed and because they did not explore alternatives.

Some persons (i.e., some *whos*) might be able to suffer in

some peace what others would find utterly unendurable. One person who has multiple sclerosis with paralysis of the legs and no control of urine or feces, might be able, by the singular force of his personality, to bear this suffering with equanimity and resourcefulness. Another person, because of special sensitivities and personal standards of dignity, might find the same condition utterly unbearable. The *who* question, therefore, brings us into the relativity of suffering. Since, as we have observed, pain is a subjective state with many variables and facets, some pain might make death a friend for one person and leave it still an enemy for another.

Some of the other interrogatives essential for good ethics are *where?* and *when?* Very often these questions will not evoke morally relevant information. If someone shoots you on a Monday or a Tuesday, at home or away, it probably will not affect the moral substance of the act. But it might. Loading a gun is a constitutionally proper and typically American act, and it might also be quite moral. Loading one in a crowded bus might not be. The *where* would suddenly be quite significant. Having an abortion in a back room abortion mill could render immoral what might have been a morally defensible act due to the overwhelming weight of conflicting values. The *where* could be decisive.

When could be most important in evaluating an abortion. An abortion around the fourth week of pregnancy is not the same as an abortion around the sixth month of pregnancy. The time factor affects what you are dealing with; it influences the chain of effects, and the alternatives open to you. So the *when* question in these cases brings a good deal of reality into focus. This is not to establish then that any abortion is moral, but to say that the age of the fetus is relevant. The more advanced the fetus, the more compelling the reasons needed to justify aborting that fetus, if one holds, as I do, that abortion might, at times, be justifiable. Only one who has no awareness of the empirical moorings of human ethics could say that the age (the *when*) of the fetus does not matter.

The final two questions used to set up the moral object and thus make moral judgment possible are: *What are the foresee-*

able effects? and *What are the existent viable alternatives?* First to the effects. Effects or consequences are so important in ethics that there is a particular ethical leaning known as consequentialism, which argues in substance that actions are good or bad depending on their consequences. The consequentialist strain, if we may call it that, is good as far as it goes but it does not go far enough. There is more to life than effects and consequences; there is also more to ethics, since ethics is the science of human life. Thus merely looking at effects is to succumb to the lure of a simplistic one-rubric ethics.

There is no doubt that effects are a major factor in establishing moral meaning, in knowing whether acts are good or bad. If atomic testing in the atmosphere is immoral, and it seems to be, it is so because of effects. If reproduction or adoption of children by single persons is morally right, the moral judgment would emerge largely from an analysis of effects. If the recent Supreme Court ruling on abortion is wrong, it will be so because of any damaging effects on American society. Thomas Aquinas justified the existence of prostitution in society because of the probable bad effects of its abolition. A war is judged as justifiable or unjustifiable largely on the basis of its effects.

And issues of abortion, suicide, and mercy killing will also be justified or condemned to a great degree by their effects. Indeed, this is the most frequent argument brought against any breakdown of the absolute against mercy killing. Opponents of mercy killing usually cite the breakdown of respect for life in Nazi Germany and try to trace that to accommodations on the subject of euthanasia. The text usually adduced is from an article in the *New England Journal of Medicine* which studied the breakdown in German mores regarding the taking of life. The article says:

> The beginnings at first were merely a subtle shift in emphasis in the basic attitude of the physicians. This attitude in its early stages concerned itself merely with the severely and chronically sick. Gradually the sphere of those to be included in this category was enlarged to encompass the socially unproductive, the ideologically unwanted, the racially unwanted and finally all non-Germans. But it is important to realize that the infinitely small wedged-in

lever from which this entire trend of mind received its impetus was the attitude toward the non-rehabilitatable sick.[9]

It would certainly be true that if the position I defend would bring about results such as those described in the text, then such a position is indefensible. If the choice is between an absolute negative on mercy killing and Nazi "eugenics," then we must stand with the absolute negative on mercy killing. (As I shall suggest in considering this serious objection, the situation is not so simple as to be reducible to two such stark alternatives.)

With regard to the question on alternatives, it might be said that this last question is the most neglected of the questions. All of these questions are in pursuit of reality. And just as foreseeable effects pertain to the reality that must be judged, so too do alternatives. A realistic moral judgment looks at all the alternatives, or possible forms of reality, open to the agent. To do less is to divorce yourself from part of the real. It might be said by way of baleful comment on humankind, that in any situation involving a hundred alternatives, we see and act on about ten of them. It is the role of man's creative imagination to sense and seize upon alternatives and thus to expand the possibilities of life. Imagination is the transcending, expansive faculty of man, his highest faculty, I judge. Unfortunately, it is, in almost all of us, withered, like an arm that was tied to one's body at birth and hence is undeveloped because unexercised.

Let us see how neglected alternatives can be determinative of morality in death-dealing situations. One might decide that an old man should have the right to die if he is so miserable that he begs for release from his mortal malady. It is true that he might have that right, but it is also possible that we are neglecting an *alternative*. Perhaps the desire for death is due not so much to the illness as it is to the dehumanized atmosphere others have created for the old man. Perhaps he has never been taught the humanizing and liberating truth that usefulness and meaningfulness do not coincide. Perhaps he has been made to feel useless and thus worthless.

One alternative to his voluntary death might be to create an atmosphere in which he might want to live, an atmosphere in which he may learn that utility is not the measure of man. The "useless" person can be capable of joy and love, of ecstasy and of humor. In fact the "useless" person can also, paradoxically, be useful. He can show pragmatic modern man that there are richer forms of living, that to say *homo faber* (man the maker) is not to say enough about man.

If all this were a viable alternative in the hypothetical case we are considering here, it would make the termination of that man's life immoral in the extreme. We should always strain to say yes to life and to say no to death when death is premature and not meaningful. We should therefore strain to find alternatives to the imposition of death. We may not find them, and then death, voluntary or otherwise, may be the blessed and natural consummation of life. Life is so replete with possibilities and surprise that good ethics should not leave a possibility unturned. Before death is decided upon, every alternative should be probed and every effort made to say yes to life before saying yes to death. Death should be considered an enemy until it shows itself as a friend.

With the completion of these questions . . . what, why, how, who, where, when, what are the effects and the alternatives? . . . we have done what we can to set up the moral object. Now moral judgment can be made and we turn our discussion to some of the ways ethics uses to evaluate the moral object. The moral object constitutes what might be called, in lawyer's language, a fact sheet, a complete laying out of all the essential circumstances of the case. The first tool for the evaluation of this object that we will look at is moral principle. What are principles and how do they help you distinguish right from wrong?

PRINCIPLES

Moral principles are the repositories of human ethical experience. More technically, they are propositions that express a value judgment about what befits or does not befit the behavior of human beings. Examples of principles are: do not kill; keep promises; tell the truth; pay your debts; do unto others as you

would have them do unto you; act in such a way as to promote
human harmony and community, etc. Principles obviously can
be positive or negative in their formulation and they can be
very generic (Do good and avoid evil) or rather specific (Thou
shalt not commit adultery). The question is, what are they
worth?

If there are principles for every moral situation, it would certainly simplify the work of ethics. All that one would have to
do in situation x is find the appropriate principle and follow its
guidance. Unfortunately for our love of ease and simplicity,
ethics is not done by principle alone. Principles, however, do
contain a distillation of moral insight and a proper understanding of them is required for moral acuteness.

The manifestly relevant principle for cases of death by choice
is, in its classical formulation, "Thou shalt not kill." And there
are satellite principles that come with this: never do anything
to hasten the death of a patient; you must use ordinary means
to preserve life. If these principles are true, and sufficient for all
the complex situations of life, then any action performed to
speed up death is immoral. If, however, morality dictates not
only principles but also exceptions to those principles, then the
question of death by choice is open to further treatment.

GOOD EXCEPTIONS TO GOOD PRINCIPLES

It is part of the common wisdom to say that a man who has
no principles is a knave and not to be trusted. But what of a man
who is replete with principles which he wields unbendingly?
Could he not be the kind of good man who features as the saint
in the satirical definition of a martyr: a martyr is someone
who has to live with a saint. To be without principles is to be
evacuated of much moral wisdom; but not to know the limits
of principles can be equally dehumanizing and cruel.

The precise task of ethics is to find the meaning of human,
moral behavior. Principles are relevant generalizations about
the normally valuable. They contain a lot of meaning. But human meaning is not entirely generalizable, because it derives
from persons who are not entirely generalizable. Principles are

fine . . . as far as they go. But they do not and cannot cover every case. Ethics is more than an enterprise of principle.

Let us take the principle "Thou shalt not kill." Where did we get this principle and what are its limits? This principle, like every principle, was born of an experience of value. Suppose we go back imaginatively to the first persons of our species. Suppose we tell *a story*.

Our story begins way back when evolution had just pushed men over the brink into what would later be called specifically human consciousness. These first newly evolved persons would look at themselves and at one another, and value experience would begin. They would readily sense that all life, whether it be in leaf, flower, bird, or beast, is marvelous, a kind of miracle of energy and organization. In looking at human life they would see its special powers transcending anything else. Here are creatures who can perceive not only what is but what can be and can bring it about. They can find and create beauty. They can speak and sing and laugh and be merciful. They can and sometimes do transcend everything, even their own selves, in the phenomenon of benevolent love which can extend to supreme sacrifice. This kind of life, they might conclude, is outstandingly valuable. They might even reach for superlatives and call it sacred.

From this experience an ethical conclusion would follow naturally, to the effect that this kind of life should be treated as inviolable. Awe and love are the proper response to such life. Violation of such life is wrong.

At this point, our first humans have become ethicists. From their primal experience of human life as uniquely awe-inspiring and valuable, they drew forth a principle: Thou shalt not kill. They might, at this point, feel that their ethics was done. After all, they had had a primal value experience and they had formed a principle to guard the experienced value. That should do it. Human affairs would then be manageable by principle, at least as regards killing. Killing is something you do not do. So be it.

Sooner or later, however, as it always does in ethics, the context that spawned the principle begins to talk back to the principle and the deficiency of principle begins to show. Let us suppose that this happened to our first primitive group when one of their members, an older man weakened and slowed by the years, was coming home from the hunt with a load of venison. Another member of the group spies him while he is still a distance from the camp. And this other member has a little "value experience" of his own. He reasons: there are two ways to get venison. I could go off on the hunt, which is exhausting and often dangerous, or I could knock off this old fellow, which is clearly more efficient, and produces just as much venison.

But, alas, the best-laid plans of mice and primitive men often go astray. The old man, hobbled and all as he was by old age, carried a big stick and with this stick he bludgeoned his iniquitous marauder and killed him. And being an honest man he came home and reported his tragic deed.

"Murder" cry the others when they hear of it. "This contradicts our primal value experience of human life as sacred and it breaks the principle to which that experience gave birth." So now what!

Well, the tribal sages would convene and what later ethicists would call the exception-making or "unlessment" process would commence. Some of the sages would point out that if they had been in this situation and had realized what the assailant was about, they would have fought him off by every means even if it regretfully meant killing the assailant.

"Would that not make us as bad as the assailant?" others asked. These were the ones who believed that their established principle was an absolute. But the wiser sages would argue that it is one thing morally to kill for gain and another thing to kill in self-defense. The motive makes it a different reality meriting a different moral judgment, provided, of course, that there were no viable alternatives to killing and that the foreseeable effects were acceptable. With all these conditions met, killing in self-defense could be licit.

And so it was that ethics made the fateful step to the third level, the troublesome level of unlessment, where you say that this principle holds, unless . . . "But do not fret," the happy exceptionists told the absolutists. "This third level has only one entry. Your principle is almost intact." The absolutists grumbled about the breakdown of morals and the permissiveness of their new society, but the unlettered people generally thought and felt that the self-defense clause was a great one and it became a matter of moral consensus.

All was well until one day the context talked back again. During a birth process, the baby was being presented in such a fashion that the midwife could not get it out. She was an experienced midwife and she explained to the people around what this meant. "During the absolutists days," she said, "I saw cases like this and both mother and baby died. But now that we have made one exception, couldn't we make another since this is such a good one. If we make the exception, we will have one death; if we do not, we will have two." After her speech, the midwife, being a practical sort who knew there was no time to wait for the academic types to unravel this, went in and performed a primitive act of feticide or infanticide and saved the mother.

This, of course, was not the end of the matter. The old absolutists shrieked: "We told you so! We told you when you made that first exception that you had entered on a slippery slope and that you would slide further into exceptions." "That first exception was like a wedge," one of them said; "now the wedge is being driven further and who knows where it shall end." "Why, it is like dominoes," exclaimed another staunch citizen. "The mistake was in tipping over the first one. On the long haul, the old absolute would do less harm than we are going to see done now." Cries of "the camel's nose under the tent" and "the crack in the dike" filled the assembly.

But then the mother who had been saved by the killing of her child came in and stood before them. The assembly hushed and became still as she bore quiet but eloquent witness to her great sadness that her child had to be killed lest she and it die together. "This was tragic," she said with deep feeling, "but I do not believe it was immoral. Morality like life would appear to be the art of the possible. We must seek to achieve as much value as we can but when values conflict as they did in this case, even death-dealing actions . . . though still utterly tragic . . . may be the best we can do in the service of the good."

Well, that little speech changed the mood of the assembly. Some of the male chauvinist elders huffed and puffed and saw the speech as suspect in its origins. They were supported by the lawyers, who pointed out that the woman was an "interested" witness and therefore biased. But, by and large, most people were glad that the woman was still alive to be with them and with her children. And they liked her distinction between the tragic and the immoral and they agreed that this case was tragic but not immoral. Another entry was put into the line of exceptions.

Eventually other exceptions followed. For example, some of the rogues in the community got to be so hardened in crime that the assembly regretfully instituted capital punishment as a way of coping with the spread of serious crime. Later, some mothers with an eye on the infanticide case, had their fetuses removed from their wombs because they were so ill that they did not think they could in any way survive the pregnancy. And further on, some mothers had their fetuses removed just because they found pregnancy such a bore, and so abortion for some became their manner of birth control. Some added other things to the exception list: duels in cases of honor, infanticide, euthanasia in its active and passive forms, killing off the mentally defective, killing people from supposedly defective races, and eventually almost any kind of killing. As time and reason made them more wise, however, it became clear to most that a lot of the exceptions were bad exceptions. And they realized too that no two exceptions were completely alike, and that therefore, in cases apparently identical, you might grant one exception and deny the other.

The self-defense doctrine, however, persistently expanded for cases in which other communities of humans attacked *en masse* and this came to be known as war and it became one of the most popular exceptions. Not even the old absolutists objected to this, though they still protested all the other exceptions. In fact, what developed as the exceptions multiplied is that different people got sensitive about different kinds of killing but very few were sensitive all the way across the line. Some people could swallow wars and slaughters like oysters in season, but would react with horror to the very prospect of an abortion or euthanasia. Others were out to liberalize all the abortion customs but saw war as an unredeemable moral leprosy. And a lot of people were just confused.

People started to put stickers on their carts to show their views on life/death issues. (The wheel had now been invented, though it is a matter of no small note that men thought of killing long before they thought of the wheel.) Some carts would have inscriptions on one side saying: Life is sacred; stop the war! And, on the other side: Liberalize abortion laws! Other carts urged the people to support "our boys" who were away somewhere killing in the national interest, and, alternately, they would condemn all abortion. The people had good reason to be confused. And so they lived not so happily ever after.

At this point we can leave our fictionalized account of the beginnings of the human ethical drama with the quandaries thereof, and see what it teaches. First, it teaches that there are three levels of reality to be distinguished in discussions of moral principle. Graphically they appear as shown below.

The problem presented here is how to know whether the principle is a good principle and how to know whether the exception is a good exception. In general it can be said that the principle is a good principle if it is truly rooted in the primal value experience and expresses that experience in a concrete way. Graphically, if you can draw a line from level 2 to level 1, then level 2 is legitimate, and a true moral principle.

1. Primal value experience   Life is sacred.

2. Principle   Thou shalt not kill.
          unless

3. self-defense	war	capital punishment	feticide to save mother	abortion of convenience	abortion after rape	suicide	passive euthanasia	active euthanasia	genocide, etc.

What about the *unless* line? Of the unlesses or exceptions it can also be said that they can only be justified if they proceed from the primal experience of the value of human life and *if they express in exception form what the principle expresses in rule form.* An exception to the principle "Thou shalt not kill," if it is a good and moral exception, must be an expression of the appreciation of the sacredness of life. If killing in self-defense when there are no alternate modes of protection is a good exception—and all but absolute pacifists say it may be—it is because life is so sacred that this kind of action protects and enhances the very sacredness of life. Even though it involves killing and thus ending an individual's life, it promotes the over-all conditions of life. In our still barbaric state, the right of self-defense gives life the possibility to continue without being overwhelmed by evil.

Graphically, therefore, if you can draw a line from an exception listed on line 3 to the primal experience of line 1, it is a good exception. A bad exception exists when the line cannot be drawn. Such an exception is not rooted in the primal experience. On war and on capital punishment, people differ on whether such a line could be drawn, as they do on most of the other issues that could be listed on line 3. If euthanasia is justified, it is because it seems that sacred human life is such that voluntary moral dominion over its demise is befitting to it. In summary, therefore, the principle and the exception, if they are good, are good for the same reason—they express the concrete demands of the sacredness of human life in a specific situation.

Patently, this does not mean that the principle against killing is not a good principle just because it is open to exceptions. Rather, it is good as far as it goes, but it does not go all the way since individualized situations cannot be comprehended by generalized principles. It is perhaps best to say that practical moral principles have limited applicability. A very generic principle like "Do good and avoid evil" has unlimited applicability because it is "uncontaminated" by particularizing circumstantial content and because it is, in essence, an unapplied explanation of the terms good and bad. Good is that which should be done; bad is what should not be done.

As Thomas Aquinas says, in speaking of what I call practical moral principles: ". . . although there is some necessity in the common principles, the more we descend into particularities, the more frequently we encounter defects."[10] This means that the principle is good but not without what Aquinas calls *"defectus,"* deficiency, limit. There are cases where greater values than those contained in the principle supervene and prevail. Thus in the case of killing in self-defense, the value of self-preservation in the face of evil may prevail over the value of not killing.

Ethics is a conversation among competing values and the ethical choice seeks the most valuable option obtainable, although in so doing other values will be lost and left unrealized. My argument for positive action to induce death is based on the fact that in some cases a thorough study of the moral object shows that induced death may be more valuable than protracted living. In those cases, the good principle of maintaining life yields to the higher value that is found in inducing death.

This could also be explained by saying that when a principle proves deficient, it is because another principle proves applicable. Thus if an armed man intent on murder asks me where his intended victim is hiding and I deny him that truth by telling him an untruth, the truth-telling principle has yielded to the principle which contains more value here, i.e., the life-saving principle. Therefore, the truth-telling principle is good as far as it goes, until it meets a situation where another principle better expresses the value needs of that particular case. Ethical inquiry, therefore, is an exchange between the moral meaning found in the empirical context, and the moral meaning found in the several principles contending for application in this concrete case. Thus the principle of prolonging life might, in view of the full reality of the case, have to yield to the principle of achieving a good death. In value language, the value of death might become greater than the value of continued living. In that case the pursuit of death becomes a more morally valuable act.

In conclusion regarding principles, it must be noted that principles are not all equally open to exceptions. Some have greater elasticity than others. The general norm in this regard is that the more generic a principle is, the less likely is it that the empirical context (where ethical meaning is also found) will talk

back in the form of exceptions. Thus, "To each his own" is
generic enough to be rather free of exceptions.[11] The same is
true for "Do good and avoid evil." Likewise, if a principle has
so many circumstances larded into it that it comes to describe
something outlandishly evil, it is likely that it will not have any
exceptions. Thus the principle "Do not rape a girl who is suffering from mental illness" imports an action that is so ghastly in
its meaning and consequences that the principle would appear
to be absolute since no competing values could seem to outweigh the harm such an action portends. Some people argue,
and I disagree, that the principle against ever doing anything
positive to hasten the death of a terminally ill patient is in this
category. To make this case, it would be necessary to show that
the foreseeable consequence of any forms of mercy killing are so
disastrous that they outweigh all possible contending values. It
is my position that this case cannot be made.

Thus far, then, with principles. Whatever their limits, they
are indispensable for the business of ethics.

OTHER MEANS FOR EVALUATING THE MORAL OBJECT

If there is one topic which reveals what an ethicist is and
how he thinks, it is his discussion of principles. For that reason,
I lingered a bit on that topic.[12] There are, however, other tools
and faculties which are essential to good ethics and I will touch
on those that most affect conclusions on the right to die by
choice. Each of these, in its own way, converges on the moral
object and aids in the delicate task of weighing the values contained in that object.[13]

Alongside close attention to in-principled moral wisdom, we
can place *reason* and *analysis*, an ethical process that is tedious
and therefore neglected. Reason and analysis here means dis-
cursive, perspiring thought and research. Ethics must do its
homework or be poor ethics. The reason for this attaches to
what we said about the moral object. Morality is a dimension
of reality and if you have not done your homework, you are
probably settling for figments of the real. Thus reason must
glean from the data and the debris of human experience in all

of its empirical and conceptual complexity. If morality were merely a matter of deducing principles from a contemplation of our nature abstractly viewed and then deducing answers from those principles, ethics would be more simple and more sure. On the contrary, empirical facts have moral import and must be probed and picked apart analytically. If you are dealing with an irreversibly comatose patient, the empirical/medical fact of that person's condition must be part of your moral judgment. If a pregnant woman has cancer of the uterus, that empirical fact is morally significant. The hydrocephalous condition of an infant is relevant to the judgment on how to treat that child when it comes to ordinary and extraordinary means for preserving its health. If the prognosis is good, bad, or uncertain, that counts heavily in determining the moral meaning of the various options.[14] Good prescription (i.e., prescribing well what ought to be done or not done) derives in major part from good description, and reason and analysis, by discovering and comparing, reveal the telling facts.

Gemüt is another faculty for moral discovery. In general it is a good principle to beware of pedants bearing foreign words and telling you there is no word like it in the larders of one's own native tongue. But Gemüt is a word worth borrowing from German moralists. It is usually translated as sentiment or feeling. It is a rich word, however, and we will use it as denoting an affective perception of moral truth. More simply, in the phrasing of Pascal, the heart has reasons of which the mind knows nothing. Gemüt refers to what the heart knows.

It is, I judge, a palpable fact of life that very often the heart is wiser than the head when it comes to judging what is morally good. Of course, the heart can also be mean, self-serving and dead wrong. But ethics has all too often neglected the special contribution that our feelings and affections can make if we will pay them heed. Let me go to my favorite ethicist, Thomas Aquinas, for a word on this. Thomas did not neglect the role of affectivity and feeling in moral appreciation. He said there are two ways of coming to a correct moral judgment, by a perfect use of reason and study, or by having a kind of connatural instinctive feeling for the truth. By way of illustration, he says that one could know the moral truths about chastity by learning what formal ethics has to say about it, or by the distinct route of a connatural feeling which grows out of a love for the value which chastity imports.[15]

Henri Bergson in different language points to the same cognitive power of affective experience. "There is a genius of the will as there is a genius of the mind . . ." he writes.[16] This should not really be surprising if one reflects on the fact that knowledge is conscious awareness; it is an opening of the consciousness to reality. Awareness, however, is not just a phenomenon of the intellect; through emotion and feeling and affection we become aware and open to new aspects of reality. After all, the one subject thinks and feels and both thinking and feeling sensitize and open his consciousness to reality.[17]

In discussing cases of mercy killing, there is usually an effort to disparage feeling, as though it were necessarily distorted by the stress and agony of the situation. And yet this is a topic where the feelings are most active, especially when it is one's self or one's loved one who is coming to the point where death would be a friend. It is too much to say that all feeling here would be set awry by the crisis context and thus be untrustworthy. If we would be wise in this difficult matter we should be attentive to all genius including the genius of the will.

It should be noted here too that *Gemüt* is a product of nature more than of education, though it is, of course, affected and conditioned by education. Thus the *Gemüt* of the unlettered might be as reliable as the *Gemüt* of the learned. Very often in the history of the race, the *illuminati* of the land would have done well to attend to the wise *Gemüt* of the lowly.

In cases of death by choice, the *Gemüt* of many people, especially those who have watched a loved one go through an extended final agony, is favorable toward the idea of hastening death. For the most part, people think that this type of thing is forbidden by God and the societal norms of morality because they have been so taught to think, but it is not hard to elicit from them a *feeling* that there are cases where these norms are too absolute. The experience of many people in this regard would appear to be close to that of persons in a primitive society who begin to sense that a reigning taboo is not entirely realistic but who hesitate to challenge it because this taboo enjoys the prestige of the supernatural.

I am not attempting to show that the *Gemüt* of people regarding individual cases could be easily assessed or polled and that this would prove that death by choice is moral. In fact, many people who, with reference to a case very near to them, will say they feel that it would have been a blessing if death had been hastened, would respond negatively to a public poll on euthanasia. What I am saying is more modest than proof. I am saying that it would do a moralist good to leave his library and walk among the people who have suffered through a prolonged dying process with someone, or who are now suffering through it themselves. They have touched the problem in the immediacy of painful experience and their reactions—which are more affective than thought-out—are a direct response to the values and disvalues of this kind of a situation. A study reported in the *Canadian Medical Association Journal*, reports on surveys done on the subject of euthanasia. Questioned were dying patients, other patients, psychiatric patients, and non-patients. In each group a majority favored euthanasia, but it was most favored by the dying patients.[18] Again, this does not determine the moral issue here nor turn ethics over to George Gallup's pollsters. What it does indicate, and what the reactions and nonreactions of juries and the public to mercy killing cases indicate, is that death by choice often produces a positive reaction at the level of *Gemüt* and that the immediate *experience* of dying often opens up minds on this subject.

For now, however, let this be the final word on *Gemüt*. Moral inquiry will go astray if it proceeds from either headless heart or heartless head. *Gemüt* is the *votum* of the heart. *Gemüt* may need to be corrected or overruled by reason, but it should always be heard.

Creative imagination is, I submit, the supreme faculty of moral man. Philosophers have been challenged for centuries to distill the quintessential human quality that marks out human life as unique. Some have said that man could be defined as the *animal rationale,* the animal capable of reason. Others have thought, quite ingeniously, that man's distinctive essence is better captured in the title *animal risibile,* the animal capable of amusement. I think that more basic than either of these would be the title *animal creativum,* the animal capable of creativity.

The root of man's creativity is in his consciousness not only of the actual but of the possible. Other animals can know what is and react to it; man can know what might be, and create it. Creativity is the high point of the human spirit.

As mentioned above in our treatment of viable alternatives, man's creative imagination is an all too rarely exercised power. This is unfortunate for human life, and therefore for ethics. If man does not respond creatively to his context of conflicting values and disvalues, his response will be less than fully human and therefore less than moral.

On matters relating to death by choice, man's native creativity is challenged in two principal ways: first of all, is the exercise of freedom to induce death a fitting development in man's growth toward fuller moral freedom, or is it a backward step? Creativity can go in full reverse, in accord with the fatal principle that nothing is so good that it cannot be abused. There is such a thing as fiendish creativity. And so moral man must wonder whether he is daring here new initiatives that are the fruit of a vaulting ambition overreaching itself.

This is an old problem. It dates back to man's first perceived opportunities to do what was previously not done because of taboo or lack of technology. Many ancient myths touch upon this moral drama of imaginative man.

Prometheus, the philanthropic god who stole fire for men, was judged by Zeus to have gone too far. Bellerophon in the Iliad came to a sorry end for trying to ride to the Olympus of the gods and for thinking "thoughts too great for man." And Icarus, exulting in the technology of man-made wings, flew too close to the sun and perished. These myths, like the myths of Babel and Adam's sin, are relevant to the moral dilemmas of inventive man, particularly in the face of man's control of death. What thoughts are "too great for man"? Where are the sacred borders between the *can do* and the *may do*? Where does presumption enter into the knowledge of good and evil?

May mortal man, graced with imagination, will his death and bring it about, or must he await it in passive obedience to organic developments which must be considered normative? May he seek out with sensitive imagination, the moral possibilities of other kinds of death and realize them in freedom? Imagination is the power that helps us break out of unnatural binds into which our truncated thinking leads us. It would seem that man, the only animal who knows he is going to die, has unique advantages in the face of death. He can foresee it and forestall it when it is clearly an "untimely frost," or he could go forth to meet it when it is a friend he needs. Such an assessment of imagination would seem to have much to recommend it to a reasonable conception of human moral freedom.

The second major challenge proffered to imagination by the phenomenon of elective death, relates to the exploration of all the alternatives to death. As already stated, death should be presumed an enemy until it presents itself as a friend. Life has too much marvelous resiliency to be negated without a strainingly imaginative quest for its possibilities. Ethics must operate with an explicit and active bias for life, and an imaginative, vital ethics must be slow to opt for death. Opt it may, but only when imagination has borne no alternatives.

Group experience is another necessary ethical instructor. Even in matters that seem entirely personal and private, the sensitive moral thinker must glean from the experience of other men and groups of men. Group experience has many *loci*; it is found in tradition, principles, customs, literature, and in analytical studies of the practices of other peoples. Good ethics, in other words, has good antennae. It listens.

Good ethics knows that morality is not a self-evident property of human situations. Morality is not like a color, so that as I see that an object is yellow, I also see that abortion is immoral. In our immaturity, it did seem that way, and getting disabused of this simplism is one of the pains of growth. Morality, rather, is a relational matter. It has less in common with a physicist looking into his microscope and more in common with a detective looking at a host of clues and seeing how they band together. When he sees how the slipper and the key and the phone number all *relate*, he has his insight.[19] And when the ethicist sees how all the factors and values relate in the most humanly valuable way, he has moral insight. Because of the enormous number of complexities, imponderables, and unpredictables involved in this, one must go to the various archives of human experience and see how the same or similar problems were met. It is so easy to embrace merely apparent value and miss true value. Group experience is a check on this.

For example, on the subject of abortion, the United States has by reason of the Supreme Court's decision in *Roe* v. *Wade* and *Doe* v. *Bolton*, set the stage for a permissive societal stance on abortion. What have other societies learned from the experience of permissiveness?

Japan has the most permissive system in the world. Their record is, therefore, instructive as to the morally important consequences of a permissive system. The relative numbers of abortions and live births is the principal indicator of what permissive law can precipitate.

In 1949, there were 246,104 reported abortions and 2,696,638 live births. By 1953 the figure was 1,068,066 reported abortions and 1,868,040 live births; and, by 1955, there were 1,170,143 reported abortions and 1,730,692 live births. There are many reasons why abortions are not reported in Japan, including tax and insurance benefits, and thus the real figure is considerably higher than the reported figure.[20] Thus in Japan we see a system in which abortions almost came to equal live births, at least in the year 1955. Reflecting back to our graph on exceptions to principles, the question arises as to whether respect for human fetal life could in any sense be thought to have endured in the face of these stark statistics.

Japan, of course, also illustrates that such a trend does not necessarily persist. By 1965, live births were nearly double the number of reported abortions. While granting that Japan is not the United States, still we must look at Japan's experience with abortions as we drop most of the legal barriers to the termination of fetal life. An enlightened Supreme Court might have done more consulting of group experience and less textual nit-picking in the decision.

Anthropologists also tell us of groups whose experiences may be meaningful for us. Margaret Mead, for example, comes out strongly for a retention of the Hippocratic oath rigorously interpreted.[21] She says that "having lived in societies in which killer and curer is the same person," she is very opposed to involving the doctor in the termination of life. Though the legal and cultural realities of our society are vastly different from those studied by Dr. Mead, nevertheless, we must incorporate the experiences she relates into our calculations even if we draw different conclusions.

The Nazi experience with euthanasia is something we will consider very carefully in assessing the arguments against death by choice. It may or may not be relevant, or it may be relevant in some respects only, and this must be seen if we would be fully open to the implication of what we are doing in making a choice for death.

ON KNOWING WHAT NOBODY ELSE KNOWS

In the persistent effort of humankind to practice reductionism in ethics, there is a popular tendency to reduce ethics to conscience. Much language about the absolute freedom of conscience is tinged with this reductionism. It would seem that nothing is needed except to be faithful to one's conscience and to respect people who are being faithful to theirs. Beyond that, all discussion of ethics is in the category of pedantic trappings.

The problem with this is that conscience can be wrong. A formidable amount of harm is done by people who are acting in perfect obedience to their consciences. If someone were in conscience to decide that infant sacrifices were necessary to placate the reigning divinities, there would be little talk about freedom of conscience in the public and legal response to this plan. The role of subjective discernment, however vital and irreplaceable, is not a substitute for a systematic ethics which tries to decide what makes some consciences right and some wrong.

With that said, however, the question of the signal role of the judging subject, i.e., of the person in the situation, awaits us. The judgment of the concerned party (parties) is of singular significance in moral inquiry. There is something that the subject knows that no one else knows. The person involved in a moral decision has a role that is unique and untransferable. There is a contact with reality that the subject has which cannot be supplied by any ethical methodology or any moral principle. This has got to be disconcerting to any professional ethicist who wants to wrap it all up at the more manageable level of theory and principle. And maybe that is why this central fact of ethical life is more than a little neglected in formal ethics.

There are three basic reasons to stress the inalienable role of the discerning subject; first, only the experiencing subject has an immediate awareness of the concrete and unique realities of his case. Now, of course, we have to contend with the point of the old adage, *nemo iudex in suo casu,* no one is a judge in his own case. This means that you cannot expect the highest degree of objectivity from the man who is sliding into second base as to whether he should be deemed safe. In judging our needs, the wish is often the father of the self-serving thought. On the other hand, the man who experiences his foot on the bag *before* he experiences the ball on his shoulder has an experience that the umpire looking through the swirl of dust does not have, even though he may have to take the memory of this experience back to the dugout with him after being called "out." (He has every right to remind the umpire of the inalienable credentials of the discerning subject.) The ethicist judging through the swirl of competing principles and theories can also be wrong and may miss the true value of the situation, which only the person suffering the circumstances directly may appreciate.

As we have stressed in treating the moral object, moral meaning derives from the empirical realities of the case, and only immediate experience touches that. When Mrs. Martinez, the seventy-two-year-old Cuban refugee, begged the doctor to stop treating her and let her die, she was in a unique position to evaluate the procedure which involved cutting her skin open and forcing blood into her veins. Fortunately the judge allowed her to do what she should have been allowed to do without a

legal judgment, i.e., to refuse the treatment and to die. No one
in that case had the "authority" that Mrs. Martinez had, not
even the judge of the Dade County Circuit Court. It is more
than unfortunate that society recognizes his authority in this
instance rather than hers. It is unfortunate because another
judge might have ruled differently, so that her right to die is
really up for judicial grabs.

Principle-ists (and by that I mean those who have an unwarranted confidence in the universalizability of principles) indulge
in a game of simplism. The gain of the game is clear. If we stress
the similarities and constancies of human affairs, ethics can become a kind of magisterium which absolves individuals of their
unique role in evaluation—rather, it arrogates that role to itself.
This also lends a greater sense of order in ethics, though surely
a lesser sense of reality.

Moral judgment is a judgment of how persons relate to other
persons and to things; but it is concrete persons and things who
are related. It is in their concreteness that they are ultimately
morally meaningful, however many constancies may be detected
in the web of relationships. Let us bring this to bear on the
subject at hand. Of each person and of each approach to death
it can be said that there has never been another one like it.
There is here a uniqueness and unrepeatableness that is underestimated by the principle-ists. The principle-ist can be so impressed with what is normally good that he forgets what is good
here and now. It has been said that generalization is the root of
all error. That overstates the case but the overstatement sins by
excess where the principle-ists sin by deficiency.

A second reason for the irreplaceability of the subject's role
is that the truth in moral matters is often found by way of affectivity and intuitive feeling and by creative imagination. The
discerning power of these faculties cannot be encapsulated in
principle form. They comprise a task that only the subject can
accomplish. Of these two faculties we have already spoken.

Thirdly, within the exclusive preserve of the subject there is
what I choose to call the sense of profanation.[22] Most peoples
consider it wrong to shoot captives by way of reprisal. Thus in
the Second World War there was much publicity about German

troops who reportedly would round up a number of civilians and shoot them in reprisal for a sniper shooting of a German soldier. Why is there such a general consensus that this is wrong? Some ethicists would say that the negative judgment springs from a calculus of the short- and long-term effects of such activity. This consequentialist calculus, it is said, would show that although there may seem to be short-term gains from such intimidating tactics, overall the act intensifies hatred and eventually evokes an even greater loss of life. That is true as far as it goes, but I believe there is something more to be said here. At this point the sense of profanation enters.

A story might illustrate this. It comes out of World War II and involves a German soldier in Holland who was on a firing squad which was assigned the task of shooting innocent hostages. Suddenly he stepped out of rank and refused to shoot them. His officer charged him with treason and lined him up with the hostages, whereupon he was promptly shot along with them by his erstwhile companions.[23] Knowing the territory as he did, this soldier could not have failed to foresee the results of his act. Yet he refused to kill the hostages and took the ultimate penalty of death in preference to doing so. In so doing he acted out Socrates' dictum that it is better to suffer injustice than to commit it. Why? How did this soldier come to this sudden and heroically self-sacrificing conclusion?

Does it seem realistic to say that he, even implicitly, conducted a calculus of the long-term results of this kind of activity? Or did he not look at the hostages huddled together, limp with terror, and realize that he was being ordered to commit a moral crime? Was it so much a reasoning process as it was a shrinking from moral horror that moved him? Was it a "conclusion" that he reached or a profound experience of evil that overwhelmed him and made him prefer death? Cardinal Newman once said that men will die for a dogma who will not stir for a conclusion. Dogma in that sense denotes an experience of the sacred. Did not the German soldier experience the sacredness of the innocent life lined up before him, and the horror of its violation? If an ethicist could have provided him later with a full consequentialist analysis of the correctness of his decision, would he not, most likely, have felt that this intellectual explanation, however accurate, was not, even in a seminal fashion, what pulled him from the ranks of the killers into the ranks of the condemned? It seems better to attribute this to a native deontological[24] sense of what ought not to be done. This reaction would seem to be more instinctive than rational, an eruption from the precordial depths of personal consciousness, where feeling and thought are even more intimately commingled and whence a cry of pain is likely to burst out in the face of profaning evil.

Another example might serve to press this point. In 1972, during the war in Vietnam, there was a famous picture of a little Vietnamese girl named Kim running from a napalm attack with her clothes and flesh afire. This became one of the classical horror photographs of that war. For many people it took napalm and Vietnam out of the abstract, and it touched the consciences of many Americans who had been viewing the war through the rose-colored glasses of patriotic cliché. The response was one of moral shock. What was happening to that little girl was wrong. It ought not be. There was, I would hazard, a strong sense that no matter what rationale could be put forth to try to justify this burning of children, the impression of wrongness would not go away. It was wrong to dump napalm on Kim. It was a profanation of something sacred, namely, Kim's life and bodily integrity. The prime issue was not long-term or short-term consequences but a rudimentary awareness of wrongdoing at the sight of this child on fire.

The reaction of moral shock is not a reaction born of syllogism or intellectual effort. It is analogous to the sense of the sacred, for it is its opposite. It is a sense of profanation of the sacred. It is an experience that is by its nature prior to ethical deliberation, which might or might not follow from it.

Of course, this deontological sense, or sense of the profanation of the sacred, is not infallible. It could be contradicted by subsequent reasoning. Perhaps little Kim and others like her were part of the tragic but unavoidable "collateral damage" of a just war that did more good than harm. Maybe this war could be shown to have so changed the quality of life in Vietnam that future Kims will have a better existence. And maybe the damage done to Kim and millions of other Vietnamese children and adults will be more than balanced by the improvements brought about by the war. Maybe. But it is not easy to overrule this fundamental value experience. The experience becomes a spring of skepticism that rises stubbornly in the face of all efforts at justification.

It must be noted too that this sense can be muted by the savage environs in which our moral faculties take shape. Capital punishment was once a public and even festive event. There was very little sense of profanation in evidence. The sense of profanation, however, has grown, and now capital punishment is done privately if at all. The immorality of capital punishment can be argued in several ways—by stressing that it does not really deter as it is supposed to—that it is ultimately vindictive and primitive, etc. But I believe that if persons were forced to company with a person before and at his execution, the sense of profanation could be stimulated. This would be an instructive experience different from but supportive of reasoned criticism of the institution of punitive killing.

There might be room, too, for the sense of profanation in our sterile and marvelously efficient hospital settings. Look at a dying person, bedecked with tubings and gadgets, with doctors and nurses working over her like witches at their brew, and wonder what became of the good idea of a peaceful death, *bene* · *mori*. Is there not also something profaning about the unreasoned effort to keep a body artificially respirated long after hope for a return to consciousness is gone? Is it befitting human life to keep a body breathing and circulating through mechanical wizardry with life reduced to the vegetative level?

Is there not something profane about acting as though death · were not a fact of life? We treat death as though it had no · meaning or justification in the nature of things, whereas it is every bit as natural as birth. The medical profession reflects the cultural malaise with death by relentlessly attempting to ward it off with pyrotechnics of every sort. The words of Carl Jung have to be jarring to our mind-set on the question of death: "We grant goal and purpose to the ascent of life, why not to the descent? The birth of a human being is pregnant with meaning, why not death?"[25] The denial of death in our setting is something of a profanation because it distorts and shuns the mortality that is our lot.

The discerning subject, we may conclude, has his work cut out for him. To make good moral decisions, we must be faithful to our total experience of life and a good part of that experience is highly personal. It expands within the multiple ways in which we react evaluatively to our moral context. A neglect of our basic perceptions will leave us open to an abstract and cold ethics that will eventually become cruel. At the same time, no individual subject can cut himself off from the matrix of the historical human family with its accumulated wisdom and its principles and methods. The marriage of subjective discernment and shared theory was made in heaven.

FOOTNOTES–CHAPTER 4

1. The term moral can be the opposite of immoral or of amoral. As the opposite of amoral, it means that a subject is open to value judgment of an ethical sort. So, for example, to say that war is a moral matter means that war can be evaluated morally, not that this war is a good war. Moral as the opposite of immoral means good as opposed to bad. Thus this is or is not a moral war.

The term human also can have two meanings; descriptive or normative. Thus, descriptively, it can be said that it is human to lie. That is, humans do it. Normatively, one could say, it is not human to lie, meaning humans ought not to do this. Normative language is ought language.

2. The morality of abortion will be treated more fully in Chapter 8.

3. Downing, op. cit., p. 148.

4. The words "motive," "intention," "why" are large and potentially ambiguous words. Historically, ethicians have made a host of distinctions within this category. The favored Latin word was *finis* and distinctions were made between the *finis operantis*, the *finis operis*, the *finis qui*, the *finis cui*, etc. This was not useless quibbling; sensitivity to the nuances in critical categories is the glory of careful theory, however much it may tax the theorist. For an example of sensitivity to the meaning of *finis*, see Vitus de Broglie, S.J., *De Fine Ultimo Humanae Vitae* (Paris: Beauchesne et ses Fils, 1948). De Broglie opens with the acknowledgment: "*Finis, universim sumptus, non facile definitur.*" For our purposes, when speaking of the *why* I am speaking of the *finis operantis*, the good desired by the actor, the

motive. The question *what* can also admit of wide interpretation encompassing all of the other questions. I use it to evoke awareness of the basic facts of the case, usually the physical facts, but recognizing that the question could evoke a good deal more than that. Overlap can occur with other questions used in this presentation, but I believe that the congeries of questions as presented is calculated to enhance completeness.

5. Cited in Joseph Fletcher, *Morals and Medicine* (Boston: Beacon Press, pa., 1960), p. 180.

6. Relevant here is the old adage from Scholastic philosophy: *Bonum ex integra causa malum ex quocumque defectu.* This means that the goodness of an act could perish due to a defect discovered in any of the aspects being discussed through the probing medium of these questions. Thus the what, the why, the when, the who, etc., could be morally praiseworthy, but the action fails at the one level of how, etc.

7. The word "objectively" is inserted here to show that we are not talking about subjective guilt. Subjectively, we might say that Hitler was morally innocent if he truly and utterly came to believe that the establishment of the Reich was necessary and good. Subjective guilt refers to the case of a person acting in bad faith. So, again, a criminal might be free of subjective guilt if he truly believes that the mob's way of life is a normal and acceptable way of life. By objective standards (and objective standards are the goal of ethics) we would judge both Hitler and the mobster to be wrong.

8. Margaret Mead alludes to this saying, however, that it was the "grandmothers" who were so allowed to depart. See "The Cultural Shaping of the Ethical Situation" in Vaux, op. cit., p. 5.

9. Leo Alexander, "Medical Science Under Dictatorship," *New England Journal of Medicine* 241 (1949).

10. ". . . *etsi in communibus sit aliqua necessitas, quanto magis ad propria descenditur, tanto magis invenitur defectus*" (*Summa Theologica* I II q. 94, a. 4). Thomas says (ibid. and a. 5) that principles are applicable most of the time (*"in pluribus"*); in particular cases (*"in aliquo particulari et in paucioribus"*) they may not apply. Thus he says that it is a good principle to give things back to their owner when these things are held in trust. But if the owner manifests the ethically significant circumstance of doing serious harm with the object held, then the principle can be seen as non-applicable and the object should be retained. In this case values more important than the principle take precedence. Thomas by no means saw principles as the all-embracing derivatives of a nature statically conceived. Thus he says "The Nature of man is mutable" (II II q. 57, a. 2, ad 1). Unlike the divine nature, our nature is variable (Supp. 42, 1, ad 3, 65, 2, ad 1; *De Malo*, 2, 4, ad 13). On the position of St. Thomas regarding exceptions to moral principles, see John C. Milhaven, "Moral Absolutes and Thomas Aquinas," in Curran, *Absolutes in Moral Theology?*, pp. 154–85.

11. Eminent domain might be considered an exception to this principle since when the common good prevails, each one may lose his right to what he has legitimately considered his own. Also emergency hunger may justify taking what is someone else's if it is needed to stay alive.

12. There is, I believe, another area that is highly revelatory of the heart of one's ethical method . . . sin. A full discussion of the theory of what sin does or does not mean—which would not be in place within the purposes and confines of this volume—shows forth almost every presupposition in one's theory.

13. The term value is highly generic and not every value is a specifically moral value. There may be esthetic or economic or military values which, considered in themselves, do not admit of moral valuation. They do admit of moral evaluation when put into their full circumstantial human situation since morality is a

dimension of all human activity. Here we are using the term value in a broad sense of that which is good for man. Thus it includes health, relief from pain, peace of mind, peace of conscience, good medicine, community, friendship, etc. In a moral analysis it usually becomes clear that any choice locks out some values and embraces others. To make the most valuable selection in a way that, overall, befits man as man, is the work of ethics.

14. The terms reason and analysis, of course, admit of a rich development in ethics. For a discussion of the profound significance of reason as a moral category in Thomistic thought, see Joseph Pieper, *The Four Cardinal Virtues* (New York: Harcourt, Brace & World, 1965), pp. 155–58 et passim.

15. "*Sicut de his quae ad castitatem pertinent per rationis inquisitionem recte iudicat ille qui didicit scientiam moralem: sed per quandam connaturalitatem ad ipsa recte iudicat de eis ille qui habet habitum castitatis*" (II II q. 45, a. 2). Connaturality for Thomas comes about *per caritatem*, through love.

16. *The Two Sources of Morality and Religion* (Garden City: Anchor Books, Doubleday & Company, Inc., 1956), p. 58.

17. Theologian John Macquarrie puts it this way: "Being, then, gets disclosed in existing. But existing is not just beholding or contemplating or perceiving, for it is also concern and involvement and participation. Feeling is always a constituent factor in existing . . . We are, however, disclosed to ourselves, and being is discussed, in affection and volition as well as in cognition, or perhaps better expressed, all affective and conative experience has its own understanding." *Principles of Christian Theology* (New York: Charles Scribner's Sons, 1966), pp. 87–88.

18. D. Cappon, "Attitudes of and Toward the Dying," *Canadian Medical Association Journal* 87 (September 1962): 693–700.

19. For this comparison I borrowed from Bernard J. F. Lonergan, *Insight* (New York: Philosophical Library, Longmans, 1957), p. ix.

20. See Daniel Callahan's monumental study of this question: *Abortion: Law, Choice and Morality* (London: Macmillan & Co., Collier-Macmillan, 1970), pp. 251–77.

21. Mead, op. cit., p. 13.

22. This sense may fit within a treatment of what I call *Gemüt*, but it deserves special mention here in this discussion of the unique credentials of the discerning subject. This sense also can be a collective experience.

23. This story is recounted by J. Glenn Gray in *The Warriors: Reflections on Men in Battle* (New York, Evanston, and London: Harper Torchbook, Harper & Row, Publishers, 1959), pp. 185–86. This book is a neglected classic.

24. This ethical term derives from the Greek word meaning *ought*.

25. "The Soul and Death," in *The Meaning of Death*, ed. Herman Feifel (New York, London, Sydney, Toronto: McGraw-Hill Book Co., 1959), p. 7.

CHAPTER 5

Four Questions

Before completing our tour of some of the methodical ethical considerations which guide our judgment of death by choice, we must needs look at four of the classical questions used in these cases. These are: 1) what is the morality of doing nothing at all? (the moral difference between omission and commission); 2) what difference does it make if death comes directly or indirectly? 3) what is the morality of doing enough or more than enough? (the question of ordinary and extraordinary means); 4) what could be proportionate to the taking of a life? (the principle of proportionality in death by choice cases).

THE MORALITY OF DOING NOTHING AT ALL

There was a case in Germany some years ago where a husband and his wife had a quarrel. In his rage, the husband hanged himself before the wife's very eyes. She did not cut him down, but was, as the court understated it, "satisfied with the course of events—events which had occurred without any action on her part."[1] After complicated proceedings at law, the woman was convicted on the grounds of failing in her duty to help prevent a suicide. She was guilty before the law because of an omission.

Law as we have seen has had to struggle with the idea of guilt by omission. What has ethics done with this notion? Can you be morally guilty for what you do *not* do? The question is quite practical for the consideration of death by choice and is behind the distinctions that tend to be made in the usage of the term euthanasia. Thus discussion of negative, passive, or indirect euthanasia usually refers to letting the patient die by not providing the extraordinary means that would prolong the dying process but not cure the patient. It refers to omission.

Although under American law the doctor practicing omission to allow death to ensue is by no means legally protected, there is evidence that doctors feel sure about the morality of this procedure. Dr. R. H. Williams of the University of Washington polled the members of the Association of Professors of Medicine and found that 87 per cent of those responding said they favored negative euthanasia; 80 per cent said they themselves had practiced it.[2] In a related study, 90 per cent of fourth-year medical students interviewed favored negative euthanasia. In the same study, however, only 15 per cent of the doctors quizzed favored positive euthanasia, as opposed to the 87 per cent favoring negative euthanasia.[3] Although polls on the subject of euthanasia vary rather drastically (a 1947 poll of four thousand New York physicians showed 80 per cent favoring "mercy killing"),[4] this poll is probably accurate in showing the tendency to find it easier to justify omission rather than commission even when the result is the same—death.

On the other hand, there are some, like Joseph Fletcher, who do not see much moral difference between omission and commission in the matter of mercy killing. Fletcher sees the omission/commission dichotomy as "a very cloudy distinction." He asks: "What, morally, is the difference between doing nothing to keep the patient alive and giving a fatal dose of a pain-killing or other lethal drug? The intention is the same, either way. A decision *not* to keep a patient alive is as morally deliberate as a decision to *end* a life."[5]

Thus it would seem that the common wisdom makes a distinction between omission and commission, and some moralists disagree. The common wisdom would appear to have the better of the argument here. Omission and commission are different realities and since morality is based on reality, a *real* difference could be expected to make a *moral* difference. How then, do they differ?

Fletcher says they are the same because the intention is the same and because both are deliberate. There is more, however, to the reality of human acts than motive and deliberateness. I believe there are four ways in which omission and commission differ in a death by choice situation:

1. They may differ in their effects. Psychologically, the effects of giving a fatal dose of a pain-killer may be more disturbing to the bereaved than not treating pneumonia and letting the pneumonia bring on death. Death under any circumstances tends to stimulate guilt feelings. People wonder whether they should have done more for the departed, whether they had made proper amends for all their differences, whether a little more treatment at an earlier period would have prevented the final crisis, etc. Such feelings are common even in cases where the care for the dying has been heroic and edifying. If, on top of this, they knew that they had given the final and definitive impetus that brought on death, their guilt problems and regrets might be compounded . . . even if the dying patient had begged them to hasten his death.

On the other hand, it is just as possible that the memory of a prolonged and terrible final agony might make the survivors feel regretful that they did not take some action to shorten the final torture, especially if they hear of others who did this for their loved ones. As this kind of action becomes more discussed, this kind of reaction becomes more possible. Omission is not necessarily more benign in its psychological effects.

It would also seem that omission and commission vary in their effects on the medical profession. Since doctors in most cultures are trained in a tradition that is absolute toward maintaining life, since the influential oath of Hippocrates warns them not to give "deadly medicine to anyone if asked, nor suggest any such counsel," it will be easier to stop supportive or resuscitative measures than to give a deadly injection. The cessation of various medical procedures may bring on death almost as quickly as some positive means, but the doctor could feel that he had not terminated life in his care, but had only let death have the victory which it had already won. This is not to say that direct termination could not be moral. It is merely to say that a doctor would understand if you said that omission is not the same reality as commission in these cases.

Lawyers also would agree on this. The fact that there does not appear to have been any case of prosecution of a doctor in the United States for omitting care that would have prolonged life, is the first indicator. It would, of course, be difficult legally to prosecute for omission. Juries, as we have seen, tend to be lenient in mercy killing cases and to seize upon any defect in the evidence as a reason for acquittal. There would seem to be even more reasons for acquitting in cases of not acting.

Omission and commission also differ in their effects on society. This would be most persuasive to those who subscribe to the wedge theory, which would anticipate all manner of evil effects coming forth if we allow any exceptions on mercy killing. But even if one justifies some kinds of mercy killing, he would have to concede that there are different foreseeable effects for omission and commission. Death by commission gives more control to the one who dispenses death and this could be abused for tax or inheritance purposes. So here again, for better or for worse, omission and commission are distinguishable by their effects. As a result, it might be easier to justify one than the other. For this reason the distinction is practical.

2. Omission and commission may differ in their deliberateness. Omission may result from a kind of paralysis and immobilization as a result of being caught in the crunch of conflicting needs and desires.[6]

Omission, or not doing anything, can be the result of not being able to decide what to do. It is a current truism that not to decide is to decide. It must also be said that not to decide may be not to decide. Non-deciding may be the result of not being able to overcome the non-volitional drag of inertia and confusion. Whether this kind of omission is morally good or bad is not the point here. The point is that it represents a different kind of reality from commission, where judgment is made and acted upon.

Of course, some omissions are fully deliberate and decisive acts of mind and will. There are cases where not deciding is deciding in a complete and even agonizing way. The decision not to operate on a gravely defective child can be a thoroughly willful act. But it is not the same psychological act that moves you to give that child a fatal shot. Either one may be moral or immoral but they are not the same, and sometimes the difference may make one easier to justify than the other.[7]

The difference between not operating and injecting a fatal dose is also altered by the knowledge that the injection has a complete finality about it. It closes off this life and bars unforeseeable alternatives. This too must affect the deliberateness of the committing will and necessitates more serious reasons to justify commission.

3. In omission, agency is diffuse. It is easier to say who did it than to say who did not do it. A question arises as to who was in the best position to do that which was not done. If what was omitted should have been done, who was most responsible, since it is literally true that *everyone* did not do it? If an angry father asks his five children who did not take the newspaper in out of the rain, he faces the problem of diffuse responsibility. If the misdeed that irks him is a broken lamp, finding the one agent who broke it is a simpler process.

In omission, the case always comes down to who should have done it, if it should have been done. In moral analysis of particular cases, this can make a major difference. If life-saving medicine was not administered, who should have given it? And so again, the distinction between omission and commission is really not all that "cloudy." It is a real distinction that can make a real moral difference.

4. Finally, omission and commission differ because they take on their own variety of forms. There are many kinds of omission, as there are many kinds of commission. Consider the moral differences in these omissions: not steering your rolling car away from a child in its path; not stopping to tackle an armed robber; not giving insulin to an otherwise healthy diabetic; not giving insulin to a terminal cancer patient in pain; not attending to and caring for a dying patient after all medicine has been stopped. These are all omissions, but none of them is the same *really* or *morally*. Commissions, too, can take an infinite variety of forms. I could terminate life with a shotgun or needle. So not only does omission differ from commission, but one omission differs from another, and so too for commission. Good ethics makes distinctions where there are differences and there are differences here. The difference, however, is not that one is right

and the other wrong. Both may be right or wrong depending on
how they feature in the value equation.

On Being Direct or Indirect

Closely related to the omission/commission discussion are
the categories direct and indirect. We have seen that moralists
for years defended the principle that there may be no *direct*
termination of innocent life. A whole system of the ethics of
controlling death hung on this concept. The insight behind this
distinction here is basically a valid one. It is that the moral
quality of an act will be affected by the attitude of the will toward the evil effect. To *will* an evil effect (death) is not the
same as *permitting* the evil effect. Thus, for example, to excise
the uterus of a pregnant woman because it is cancerous is not
the same as abortion. In the case of the cancerous uterus, what
is directly intended is the saving of the woman by the removal
of the malignancy. In abortion, the death of the child is directly
intended. The baby dies just as surely in both cases, but the
psychological reality of the act is different. This could lead to
differences at the level of effects on the agent, on society, etc.
To this point, this distinction was correct. It was staking out a
difference as good distinctions should.

However, this fine distinction was made to bear a freight that
it would not carry. It was used to say that outside of a self-
defense situation, direct killing is always wrong. This had two
bad effects: 1) it led to too much artificiality by inaugurating
a facility to countenance *indirect* killing of the innocent in a
way that gave an undue tidiness to military slaughter; 2) it con-
tributed to an unnuanced absolutism which negated *a priori*
all direct termination of innocent life for good reasons other
than self-defense. This is a problem since it is neither revealed
nor self-evident that self-defense is the only justifying cause
for terminating innocent life.

First, then, to the way this distinction was used in the just
war theory. One could kill thousands and thousands of innocent
people *indirectly*, and therefore morally, in bombing or shelling
a legitimate military target if there was proportionate cause for

waging the war and all the conditions of just war were deemed present. In this case it was said that the destruction of the target was *directly* intended; the death of the innocent bystanders was only *indirectly* intended. The deaths of these people were permitted, not willed. Given the right conditions for warring, killing them was moral.

Practice took its toll on this theory. Directness and indirectness became all-important in determining morality. What was down-played was whether or not there was a proportionate reason for the bombing at all.[8] Proportionality should have been stressed. It was stressed in the just war theory, but, in practice, it seems that the principle of proportionality was dropped before the bombs. Indirectness tended to become a self-sufficient moral defense.[9] The deaths of the people of Hiroshima and Nagasaki *may* have been indirectly willed, but those bombings were rather patently immoral. They were immoral because there were neglected military and diplomatic alternatives to these acts of total war. They were immoral because there was no proportionate gain. They may also have been immoral because it strains credibility to say that these population centers were bombed without our *directly* willing the death of the population. It seems that the direct purpose of those bombings was to break the will of the Japanese government or to impress potential post-war enemies by the doomsday annihilation of two cities. Therefore, directness can affect morality, but it is not the only criterion.

The artificiality of overloading this distinction can be further seen in the treatment of an old-time favorite case, the plight of the sexually threatened maiden. May she jump to certain death to preserve her virginity? Some of the old authors said yes, and some said no. One author put it this way: she did not have to jump, but she could do so morally even though death was certain to follow. He uses the idea of indirectness to avoid the charge of suicide which he could not allow since it is direct killing of innocent life. Here is how he does it:

> Thus, she may leap from a great height to certain death, for her act has two effects, the first of which is to escape from violation,

the second, her death, which is not directly wished but only permitted. The distinction between the jump and the fall is obvious. In the case, the maid wishes the jump and puts up with the fall.[10]

In the case of this maiden as in the case of the bombardier, the issue is not the *indirect willing* of the suicidal death and the killing of civilians. The issue is whether, in view of all the effects, alternatives, and other circumstances, there was proportionate reason to compensate for this termination of life.

The second ill effect of a false reliance on this distinction is that it precludes a discussion of whether or not there is proportionate reason to end innocent life directly in situations that have nothing to do with self-defense or the preservation of chastity. As Richard McCormick puts it, "[In] those instances that have been traditionally viewed as immoral because the intentionality was direct, the psychological directness itself is not decisive. The immorality must be argued from lack of proportionate reason."[11]

In conclusion, therefore, whether an effect such as death is directly willed or not is a factor that should be calculated for what its moral worth may be from case to case. But both direct and indirect termination of life (whether that life is innocent or the life of an unjust aggressor) can be moral or immoral according to the circumstances that give them moral meaning. Directly or indirectly killing the innocent is evil if there is, in the concrete circumstances, no proportionate reason for doing so.

WHAT'S ENOUGH?

Dr. David A. Karnofski, of the Sloan-Kettering Institute for Cancer Research, has advocated in strong terms the use of what he calls "aggressive or extraordinary means of treatment." With not a little sardonicism he observes:

> Withholding of aggressive or extraordinary treatment can be urged and supported by state planners, efficiency experts, social workers, philosophers, theologians, economists and humanitarians.

For here is one means of ensuring an efficient, productive, orderly and pain-free society by sweeping out each day the inevitable debris of life.[12]

Karnofski gives an example of what he means by aggressive care. He tells of a patient with cancer of the large bowel. A colostomy was performed to relieve the intestinal obstruction. A recurrence of cancer in another nearby area was treated by X-ray. Then the abdominal cavity began to fill with fluid and radioactive phosphorus was used to check this. Next, the liver began to fail and a variety of supportive measures were employed. With all of this, the patient lived for ten months; without these measures, death would have occurred within weeks or even days. Karnofski puts it this way: "When should the physician stop treating the patient?" Answer: "I think that he must carry on until the issue is taken out of his hands."

Should the spirit of Karnofski be the spirit of medicine? Should all means, ordinary and extraordinary, be morally mandatory? Perhaps, but here again there is a traditional wisdom that would seem to be a bit more wise. This wisdom is filed under the rubric of ordinary/extraordinary means. In this view, ordinary means must normally be taken; extraordinary means are usually morally optional. Even a non-professional ethicist can sense that these terms are a bit slippery. Slippery they may be, but not useless. Here is how these means have been described:

> Ordinary means are all medicines, treatments, and operations, which offer a reasonable hope of benefit and which can be obtained and used without excessive expense, pain, or other inconvenience. Extraordinary means are all medicines, treatments, and operations, which cannot be obtained or used without excessive expense, pain, or other inconvenience, or which, if used, would not offer a reasonable hope of benefit.[13]

This definition could, I think, be improved by changing the expression "hope of benefit" to "hope of a return to reasonable health." To use the case of pneumonia occurring in a patient in the later stages of bone cancer, the use of antibiotics could be said to have some "hope of benefit." There is not, however, hope of a return to health. Therefore, under this rubric, the antibiotics would be extraordinary, and not morally necessary; to omit them would be moral. To omit insulin under similar conditions would likewise be moral for the same reason. There are cases, too, where intravenous feeding could also be extraordinary, as when it preserves the life of someone judged to be irreversibly comatose. The use of an iron lung would clearly be an extraordinary means, as would the use of the kidney machine. It should, of course, be noted that to say that a means is extraordinary and therefore not morally obligatory, does not say it is wrong to use it. In complex human situations, there are often several arguably moral courses to follow. Often enough, there is not one right answer, but several alternatives, each morally defensible. Thus it could be morally defensible to go off dialysis to make the kidney machine available for someone else or for some other reason, and, at the same time, it could be morally defensible to stay on dialysis. Morality is not like bookkeeping, where there is only one right answer and where all other answers are wrong.

So the old ordinary/extraordinary means idea was a useful tool. It is not, however, a panacea for ethical quandaries. For example, if you apply it to the case of the parents who refuse life-saving surgery for their mongoloid infant, it does not solve the case. Can you say that the surgery will not return the mongoloid child to "health" because it will still be mongoloid? Is being a mongoloid incompatible with health? Is this the same as refusing what would otherwise be ordinary means for the terminal cancer patient? Obviously, it is not the same, since you are deciding for someone else, since that someone is not dying from a terminal illness, since it is chronologically at the beginning of life and not at the end of it. The decision to refuse a necessary operation on a mongoloid could only be justified by a judgment that death is of higher value than life for such a child, not by a narrow consideration of whether the operation is an extraordinary means. Therefore a simple use of this rule will not yield clear advice on such a case. Allowing the mongoloid child to die may be morally justifiable but that decision could not be reached merely by a consideration of ordinary and extraordinary means.

Furthermore, the definitions offered above and slightly amended, are very general in their language. They admit of a lot of relative variables. "Excessive expense" is relative to the wealth of the patient. Pain, too, is a subjective state and when it becomes excessive and unbearable varies from person to person. Pain also is not just of the physical kind; the mental suffering might be worse than the physical in certain kinds of debilitating illnesses. And, of course, the expression "other inconvenience" could include a host of things. Going to a faraway hospital in an alien setting could be for some persons "excessive inconvenience." For some sensitive persons, it may be "excessive inconvenience" to have their life prolonged when they see what it is doing to their loved ones.

It should be obvious that the terms as defined are broad and go well beyond merely medical considerations. The definitions are moral and seek to embrace all that constitutes morality by viewing the whole human situation of the patient. The decision on the use or non-use of ordinary or extraordinary means is a moral, not a medical decision. Indeed, doctors often use these terms in a different way.

Paul Ramsey cites three differences in the way doctors and moralists use these terms. First, the doctor is likely to use the distinction to mean customary as opposed to unusual procedures, without as much reference to the particular medical history of this patient. Second, the decision to stop extraordinary treatment is made by the moralist as easily as the decision not to start it. For the doctor, it is more difficult to stop it, once begun. Thirdly, moralists view the whole domestic economy of the patient and even his religious situation. The doctor, understandably, would take a more narrow view.[14]

Obviously, the judgment as to whether means are ordinary or extraordinary, and the decision to use or not use them is not the business of the doctor, unless there is no one else to make the decision. His particular competence merely qualifies him to supply the medical information that is one component of this moral decision. To the exaggerated and sacralized conception of the doctor's role in life/death issues, we shall return.

PROPORTIONATE TO WHAT?

The moralist Richard McCormick reflects much ethical wisdom when he says that "the basic category for conflict situations is the lesser evil, or avoidable-unavoidable evil, or proportionate reason."[15] There are situations where you are apparently damned if you do and damned if you do not. To determine what is moral in these situations, you have to envision the non-moral or physical evils (loss of life, loss of limb), and see if there is a proportionate good that would balance and compensate for those evils. In these cases, the physical or non-moral evil would remain unfortunate, even tragic, but it would not be immorally caused.

Thus, if the American Revolutionary War was justified, it was because certain qualitative changes in American life would result from it and would compensate for, or be at least proportionate to the loss of life and goods that the war entailed. The right of the American people to live in freedom and independence was seen as more important than the lives of Americans and others who would be lost in the war.

A few years ago in the United States, when the riots of the dispossessed were frequent, there was much discussion about shooting looters during the riots. Some prestigious Americans even urged the policy of shooting looters. Many people—one would like to say most people—found the idea morally abhorrent. The principle of proportionality would help explain this moral revulsion. There was no proportion between the lives of these looters and the television sets and other goods that they were stealing. There was good cause to stop the looting, but there was no proportionate reason to kill in so doing, given the presence of other alternatives.

To remove a woman's uterus because it is shot through with cancer, and, as a result, to sterilize that woman in spite of her desire to have children can be morally justified because saving her life is more than proportionate to the loss of fertility.

To give one of your kidneys to a member of your family whose kidneys have both failed does involve a physical or non-moral evil, viz., the loss of one's own kidney, a loss that could some day be fatal to you if the remaining kidney fails. Using the principle of proportionality, a moralist can argue that it is a moral action since your risk is compensated for by the "gift of life" (as the National Kidney Foundation calls it) that your kidney gives to another.

A defense of death by choice, whether you are deciding for yourself or for another, will depend to an important degree on the idea of proportionality. If we decide that a patient reduced to vegetative status should be terminated, it would be because of a determination that the physical and non-moral evil of that person's *complete* death is more than compensated for by proportionate values. Among these would be: ending the macabre spectacle of maintaining a body in biological life after the personality is extinguished, ending the hopeless expense for treatment that cannot cure, relief of a grieving family, reallocation of medical resources, etc.

What happens in such cases, of course, is that a calculus takes place to balance the competing claims of contending values. In a conflict situation, where some goods will be lost no matter what you do, such calculus is not unworthy; it is inevitable. It need not be utilitarian in its inspiration, in such a way as to submerge the good of the individual in the amorphous needs of the group. But ethics must calculate and balance values, especially in conflict situations.

Consider the case of a conscious terminal patient who is in unsupportable pain which cannot, in his circumstances, be relieved. What is the morality of his opting for termination? Vis-à-vis proportionality, this person must weigh the value of continued living in his condition and balance that against the values deriving from an earlier death. Unless someone holds to the position that continued living in any condition is always preferable to all other values—a position impossible to prove since no one can know all other values as they relate to a concrete case—unless someone holds that impossible position, he must enter into proportional calculus. He must see whether the termination of his life, which is a value even in his desperate state, is more valuable than following passively the slow trajectory of his ongoing collapse.

Judgments of proportionality cannot be computerized. They are rarely self-evident. They are not susceptible to neat and tidy rules. And when these judgments are made, they do not dissipate a sense of apprehension and fear that they may not be correct. Persons looking at the same case will differ in their judgments of proportionate reason. How then do you decide what is truly proportionate? This question is as large as the question: How do you tell right from wrong? The whole purpose of ethics is to attempt to find the answer to those questions. This is the purpose of all of the elements of ethical method that I have treated here: careful and complete analysis of the moral object, a discriminating use of principles, *Gemüt*, group experience, imagination, subjective discernment, category analysis, etc. All of these are geared to the achievement of a sensitive judgment in a case of conflicting values. Again, two persons using these methodic elements that I have suggested can come to opposite judgments. Also, using this approach, one person might come to the conclusion that there are several morally defensible choices open to him and that the selection of one course or another is something of a leap. It is the goal of ethics to make that leap as guided as possible and to make it less arbitrary. The moralist cannot dissipate the ambiguity of morality, for he cannot reshape the real world, where moral meaning is found in the midst of mystery and not a little confusion. But he hopes at least to turn dark to dusk and to sharpen as best he can the perceptual powers of "the valuing animal."

In these chapters, I have explored the nature of ethics as it faces up to the problem of our moral dominion over death. Throughout I have been attempting to show that at the level of theory, the morality of terminating life, innocent or not, is an open question although it is widely treated as a closed one. It is also an awesome question and an intricate one, but it is not an avoidable one. In issues of war, self-defense, or capital punishment, few people scruple at terminating life. Indeed there is a mammoth carelessness about so terminating life, to the point where history has been accurately described as "a butcher's bench." Outside of the arena of self-defense, there is considerably more stringency with regard to ending life. It is this stringency that I see as open to question since it would seem that there are values proportionate to the value of defense that could warrant the taking of life in other situations.

Those who deny this fit into two categories: either they are functioning at the level of taboo and thus do not face the issue reflectively, or they face it very reflectively and they conclude that in view of all the circumstances and theoretical factors, death by choice in these cases is wrong. They bring strong argumentation against any exceptions. It is these strong objections that I will consider in the next two chapters. In confronting these objections, my own position will be further revealed and, I trust, substantiated.

FOOTNOTES—CHAPTER 5

1. Silving, op. cit., p. 373, n. 94.
2. Reported in David Hendin, *Death as a Fact of Life* (New York: W. W. Norton & Company, 1973), p. 91.
3. Ibid.
4. See Selwyn James, "Euthanasia—Right or Wrong?" *Survey Graphic* 37 (May 1948): 241, cited by Healy, op. cit., p. 266.
5. "The Patient's Right to Die," in Downing, op. cit., p. 68.
6. Studies on what is known as the Good Samaritan crisis (the failure of persons to come to the rescue of others, even when this could be done without danger) show that the non-responders have a distinctive kind of psychological reaction. For one thing, they are surely not apathetic. They show great nervousness, blood pressure rise, sweaty hands, etc. And yet they do not act. They seem blocked by their strongly felt but conflicting emotions. See John Darley and Bibb Latane, "When Will People Help in a Crisis?" *Psychology Today* 2, no. 7 (December 1968): 54.
7. The will is ultimately geared to the concrete and commission touches the concrete and activates the will in a way that omission does not do, since, however deliberate it may be, it is still a sort of abstention.
8. On this, see McCormick's excellent analysis of direct and indirect willing in *Ambiguity in Moral Choice*.
9. For an analysis of what this can mean in practice, see John C. Ford, S.J., "The Morality of Obliteration Bombing," *Theological Studies* 5 (1944): 261–

309. Ford underscores the problem of a bombardier dropping the bombs but withholding the intention.

10. Henry Davis, *Moral and Pastoral Theology*, 6th ed. (London and New York: Sheed & Ward, 1949), Vol. 2, p. 144. On the use of the direct/indirect categories, Joseph V. Sullivan says: "Direct killing means an action or omission which has no other immediate end than the death of a person. The death is intended as an end in itself or as a means to an end. If a man is killed out of revenge, then the death is inflicted as an end desirable in itself and hence is direct killing. If a man is killed in order that a secret be maintained or that an end be put to his sufferings, then the death is inflicted as a means to an end, but this is also direct killing. In either of these cases the death inflicted is the only immediate effect. Direct killing must be understood in contradistinction to indirect killing, which may be defined as an action or omission having some other immediate effect in addition to the death of a person. Such a death, even when foreseen to follow an act, need not be intended in itself, but can be merely permitted." *The Morality of Mercy Killing* (Westminster, Md.: The Newman Press, 1950), pp. 38–39.

11. McCormick, op. cit., p. 84.

12. "Cancer and Conscience," *Time*, November 3, 1961.

13. Gerald Kelly, S.J., "The Duty to Preserve Life," *Theological Studies* 12 (December 1951): 550.

14. *The Patient as Person*, pp. 120–24.

15. McCormick, op. cit., p. 77.

CHAPTER 6

Deciding for Yourself: The Objections

It is fair to say that if you do not know the objections to your position, you do not know your position. This was a firm conviction in the great medieval universities, where the position of the adversaries was given unique prominence. The *Summa* of Thomas Aquinas, for example, leads off each article with the objections to his position, and quite regularly he makes the principal points of his case not in exposition but rather in response to the objections. There is a wisdom in this medieval tactic (I refuse to accept the term *medieval* as pejorative) that we could well reappraise and reappropriate. In modern terms, it recognized the dialectical nature of our approach to truth, or, more simply, it recognized that the delicate reality of truth is grasped by our minds only in the tension of point and counterpoint, position and counterposition. "We know in part," said Paul the Apostle with masterful epistemological insight. And only by staying in contact with the parts that others are on to can we move our knowledge from more imperfect to less imperfect. That said, let us look at the main objections to the idea of choosing to end your own life by positive means. The objections to ending someone else's life, who is not capable of consenting, will be met in the next chapter. Obviously, some of the objections treated here will relate to that more difficult problem of deciding for someone else.

The Domino Theory

Writing in the *Indiana Law Journal*, Luis Kutner observes matter-of-factly that efforts to legalize "voluntary euthanasia" have been persistently rejected because they "appear to be an

entering wedge which opens the door to possible mass euthanasia and genocide."[1] What Kutner says is a commonplace in
the literature that treats of death by choice. He is evoking, of
course, the ghost of Nazi Germany, where some 275,000 people
are thought to have perished in "euthanasia centers." There is
no precedent that is more regularly brought forward than this
one, and well it should be, for what happened in Germany did
not happen in an ancient tribe centuries ago, but in a modern
state with which we have not a few bonds of cultural kinship.

Analogies, of course, are our way of knowing. We meet something new and immediately a number of similar or analogous
realities come to mind. We come to know the unknown by
relating it to the related known. That is all well and good. But
analogies are also tricky, and the mind can indulge in false
analogues. By this I mean that we can compare a present situation to a past one and be so impressed by the possible similarities that we miss the differences.

It is argued that German euthanasia in the Nazi period began
at a more moderate level. It was to involve only the severely
and hopelessly sick. Originally, it was not to be allowed for
Jews since it was seen as a privilege for "true" Germans. But
once begun it grew and spread preposterously, until hundreds
of thousands of socially unproductive, defective, and, eventually,
racially "tainted" persons were liquidated. "Useless eaters," Hitler called them. And it all started, as Leo Alexander writes, "from
small beginnings."[2] The conclusion drawn from this is that if
we allow any exceptions, any "small beginnings," we too shall
fall into the excesses of the Nazis. For this reason positive acts
to end the lives of consenting persons, or life-ending actions
taken by those persons themselves, are to be seen as absolutely
unconscionable.

Let me begin to confront this Nazi analogy by the technique
which past logicians called *retorqueo argumentum* . . . turning
the example back on the one who uses it. This technique does
not disprove the argument offered, but it does conduct explora-
tory surgery on its presuppositions.

Therefore, let it be similarly argued that the Nazi war machine began from "small beginnings." It began when the first

humans began to kill one another to settle differences. Through the process of military evolution, this grew to the preposterous point of *Blitzkrieg* and the Nazi military atrocities of World War II. Therefore, relying on the Nazi experience and relying on many other ghastly historical examples of the abuse of military kill-power (which can make this case stronger than that against euthanasia) we can conclude that all forms of killing, even in self-defense, should be morally banned. We should, in a word, become absolute pacifists, and not allow the "small beginnings," which have throughout history generated bloodbath after bloodbath. If the Nazi analogy forbids euthanasia, then it should also, and indeed *a fortiori*, given the history of military carnage, forbid war.

We could make a similar *retorqueo* argument regarding sterilization. The Nazi practice of eugenic sterilization might be argued as the basis for an absolutist stance against all sterilization. Add to the Nazi experience here the excesses revealed in the United States, where children were sterilized apparently without consent.[3] Given these facts of abuse, should not the possibility of abuse be precluded by an absolute moral ban on sterilization?

Similarly, and finally, could not a case be constructed against the morality of developing and retaining nuclear weapons by citing the Hiroshima and Nagasaki atrocities? Such attacks could happen again. Development and deployment are not even "small beginnings." Therefore, if the thrust of the Nazi analogy used against death by choice is valid, all these should be considered, again *a fortiori*, as beyond the moral pale.

The answer that would be given to my *retorqueo* arguments here would be that I am overworking analogies and not noting the differences between past and present situations. I would make the same response to the analogy regarding death by choice.

There are many differences between our setting and that of Nazi Germany, however many alarming similarities can be found. I shall note four of them. First, the euthanasia program of the Nazis was an explicit repudiation of the individualistic philosophy that animates this country. Mercy killing for the benefit of the patient was not the point in Germany, and was rejected. People were killed because their life was deemed to be of no value to German society. The uselessness of the patient to the community was decisive. Though this idea was resisted heroically by many Germans, and though the mass destruction of mental patients even had to be revoked by the Nazis due to public outcry, still the German context was all too susceptible to this collectivist form of ethic. The motif of individual rights simply was not as ingrained in the society of Nazi Germany as it is today in our society. Indeed, in our society, it tends to be exaggerated. This makes for a major difference to which the Nazi analogists should advert.[4]

A second weakness in the Nazi analogy is that our society is not nearly so homogeneous as German society. American society, we are discovering as we emerge from illusions of oneness, is made up of "unmeltable ethnics" and conflicting cultures. This does not mean that the whole country cannot get jelled into oneness when civil religion gets activated by some national crisis, though even that is getting more difficult to do. But it does suggest that on matters of individual morality, our pluralism is incorrigible. This would seem to augur well for the possibilities of critical debate on any issue such as death by choice. Again, it is a difference worth noting before we concede that the Nazi "parade of horrors" will be our portion if we admit the possibility of some exceptions in the area of voluntary imposition of death.

A third reason to limit the Nazi analogy is the Nazi experience itself. We now have that grotesque episode emblazoned on our cultural memory. The stark experiences of Nazism have become important symbols in our collective consciousness. This does not mean that knowledge is virtue, but it does suggest that deeply ingrained knowledge of human wickedness can help to deter. The wickedness has a harder time now slipping in unbeknownst. Our *when* is different from their *when*, and that is a difference. Their experience gives us a vantage point that makes our situation to that degree advantageously dissimilar.

Fourthly and finally, the opening of the question of voluntary dying is now arising in an atmosphere where death is being re-evaluated as a potential good, not in an atmosphere where the utilitarian value of certain lives is the issue. How a question arises is important for the conclusions that may follow. The question currently is not whether life is worth living, but whether death, in its own good time, is worth dying.

This cultural re-evaluation of death is another major and influential difference.

In conclusion then, on the Nazi analogy, it is illuminating. It gives us an example of the iniquity of men that in our earlier naïveté we might have thought implausible. It must never be allowed to leak out of our memories, for of such chastening memories is moral progress made. We must face the painful fact that the Nazis were, like us, members of the species that calls itself *sapiens*, but is nevertheless capable of staggering malice. One can grant all of this and still be able to say that the decision to end life voluntarily in certain cases may be moral if there is proportionate reason to do so.

The domino or wedge theory, however, may be presented in more subtle dress. It is inferred that if we allow exceptions even in the case of a mature adult who wishes his death in the face of unbearable alternatives, the logic of the dominoes will still obtain and send us cascading all the way to compulsory imposition of death. As G. K. Chesterton put it:

> Some are proposing what is called euthanasia; at present only a proposal for killing those who are a nuisance to themselves; but soon to be applied to those who are a nuisance to other people.[5]

At the very least, it is argued, there will be as a result of this a general erosion of the respect for the sanctity of life. Those who object in this fashion do not see exceptions as the harbingers of a new Hitlerian *Reich* but as dangerous slackenings in our already precarious grasp of the sacredness of life.

I respond to this version of the domino theory by distinguishing between the theory and the socio-psychological effects of exception making in the matter of death. Theoretically, the objection fails; psychologically it has something going for it. At the level of theory, the objection is saying that if X is allowed, then Y and Z follow. If you grant X, you cannot draw a line before Y and Z. The assertion is theoretically gratuitous. It has been said that ethics like art is precisely a matter of knowing where to draw lines. Without the drawing of lines, there is no ethics or no art. More directly to the point, the cardinal fact here is that X *is* not Y, nor *is* it Z. And since they are different realities, they may merit a different moral judgment. Ethics is not just a matter of logical deduction from principle. It is also a matter of evaluating different empirical realities in their morally meaningful concreteness. For this reason a moral principle (like "Thou shalt not kill") is not like a balloon, which, if pierced at the point of X, deflates also at the points of Y and Z.[6]

Psychologically, however, it should be granted that an impetus toward excess can be created when we make exceptions. There is a danger here that must not be minimized. The history of warfare proves it and after any war, there tends to be an increase in violent crime when the warriors return home. It seems hard for some to turn the killing off. The history of abortion in many countries indicates a similar psychological thrust toward excess. We can dissipate a principle in exceptions.

This reaction is especially likely when a taboo begins to crumble. Taboos forbid certain actions absolutely. Taboo is not open to reasonable exception. It simply forbids—by edict, as it were. When reason and light begin to pierce the province of a taboo, the situation is both promising and dangerous. It is promising because ethics by taboo is not ethics. Taboo does not give reasons; ethics must. Movement out of taboo then, intimates progress. It is dangerous, however, because a study of taboo shows that taboos, even those that seem silly at first blush, are rarely mindless or valueless. They often represent a primitive way to fence off a value by banning intrusion with no ifs, ands, buts, or unlessments. Taboo, therefore, represents one far swing of the pendulum. Reaction to taboo can swing you to the other extreme. The experience of liberation from taboo is exhilarating and a heady wine. It can lead to a binge of exceptions before the value experiences once encapsulated in unyielding taboo can become ensconced in a mature and discerning ethics.

This possibility of abuse might suggest two remedies: keep the taboo (on the grounds that where there are *no* exceptions there can be no *abusive* exceptions) or make the necessary distinctions where there are differences and strive to contain the possible abuses. There is an old Latin axiom that pertains to this problem: *abusus non tollit usum*, the fact that something can be abused does not mean that it should not be used. Rather, the use should be promoted if it is good, and the abuse curtailed by every means available.

To say that there is no possible way of curtailing abuse if we grant the morality of some voluntary, self-imposed (or assisted) acts of death by choice, and then to conclude that because of that impossibility, no such act can be moral, is an immense and· unwarranted leap. Such an argument would not be accepted· in other contexts. Suppose one were to argue that all investigatory or experimental medicine, even when performed on consenting subjects, is immoral on the grounds of the extreme danger of abuse. If one were to impose the logic of the domino, a similar case could be made. One could say that, theoretically, the domino or wedge theory does not hold, but given the nature of man, abuse will follow upon use, involuntary experimentation upon voluntary. To support such a case one could turn to Dr. Henry K. Beecher, who reports on the kinds of experiments that go on. He is not selecting rare and extraordinary cases, but assures us that "examples can be found wherever experimentation in man occurs to any significant extent."[7]

To cite a few of his randomly selected examples: thirty-one subjects, twenty-nine of them black, were used in a study of cyclopropane. Toxic levels of carbon dioxide were achieved and maintained for considerable lengths of time, creating a condition that often leads to fatal fibrillation of the heart.

Whether or not the subjects gave consent, this type of experimentation is a sort of medical roulette. Without the consent of the subjects, the experiment would be gross in its immorality. With the consent, the case becomes open to discussion, but one wonders whether thirty-one subjects could be found to accept experiments at these stakes if they were really informed as to the nature of the stakes.

In another case, twenty-two human subjects were injected with live cancer cells. They were "merely told they would be receiving 'some cells.' "[8] One of the investigators admitted that he would not have submitted to such a risky experiment himself.

In another case, a small piece of a patient's cancerous tumor was transplanted into her mother. The mother volunteered for the experiment. The purpose of those who reported the experiment was "the hope of gaining a little better understanding of cancer immunity and in the hope that the production of tumor antibodies might be helpful in the treatment of the cancer patient."[9] The daughter died the following day. The mother died 450 days later from the cancer that had spread from the original transplant.

A final example concerns the treatment of patients suffering from acute streptococcic pharyngitis. For experimental reasons, penicillin was withheld from 525 men despite the investigator's avowed knowledge that "penicillin and other antibiotics will prevent the subsequent development of rheumatic fever." Dr. Beecher reports the result: "Thus, twenty five men were crippled, perhaps for life." He adds the significant data that the subjects were not informed, did not consent, and were not aware that any kind of experiment was being performed.

Note well, Dr. Beecher is not detailing experiments conducted in Nazi Germany, but "practices found in industry, in the universities, and university hospitals and private hospitals, in the government, the army, the air force, the navy, the Public Health Service, the National Institutes of Health, and the Veterans Administration." He cites a salient and portentous motive for research experimentation by observing that, in recent years, few if any doctors achieved professorships until they proved themselves productive in investigatory research. From the patient's viewpoint, that introduces a conflict of interest. In spite of these gory examples, which Beecher says "are by no means rare" and which indicate not what might happen but what has happened, I would not see the domino theory as proving that all human experimentation is immoral. Neither do I find my colleagues in ethics rushing to that conclusion. A harsh judgment must be levied against abuses of investigatory medicine, and defenses against them must be mounted, but experimental medicine, under proper conditions, justified by proportionate reasons, may be morally good. The abuse does not make all use wrong.

The matter of experimentation is, I judge, especially useful because it shows the fallacy in the use of the domino or wedge theory used against death by choice. Whereas actual and very impressive abuses in experimentation (including death, mutilation, and deception) do not lead to the conclusion that all experimentation is immoral, the *potential* abuses of death by choice are offered to support the judgment that all death by choice is immoral. If it can be shown that the dangers inherent in death by choice are worse and unavoidable, the case against death by choice will stand. Short of that, this argument fails.[10]

Those who use the domino theory to ground their assertion that each and every act of voluntary death by choice is immoral are trying to prove an immense thesis in terms of foreseeable effects alone. This is a species of what I have been calling one-rubric ethics. It is a simplistic and partial approach to the question. It furthermore does not prove that moral doomsday follows inevitably from the admission that some mercy killings appear justifiable. It simply presumes that we have no way of preventing abuses of this moral freedom.

Also, those who argue this way leave themselves open to the charge of the British philosopher Anthony Flew. Flew argues for voluntary euthanasia only. He does not argue the case for ending the lives of those who are not in a position to consent because they are permanently unconscious. Flew is impatient with those who respond to this argument by saying that they cannot countenance the involuntary euthanasia which presumably would follow from the voluntary kind. His retort:

> Anyone, therefore, who dismisses what is in fact being contended on the gratuitously irrelevant grounds that he could not tolerate compulsory euthanasia, may very reasonably be construed as thereby tacitly admitting inability to meet and to overcome the case actually presented.[11]

The domino or wedge theory warns us against the possible diminishment of respect for life that may flow from the acknowledgment of another exception to the principle that forbids killing. To this extent it is to be taken seriously. It focuses our attention on foreseeable effects, and good ethics requires this because effects *partially* constitute the moral object. The domino theory does not, however, prove that every single act of voluntary death by choice is immoral. To attempt to achieve so much so simplistically is to fall under the indictment of the ancient adage: *qui nimis probat, nihil probat.* He who proves too much, proves nothing.

ABSOLUTISM AS THE LESSER EVIL

One of the arguments brought against allowing death by choice as an exception to the principle against killing, is that the common good would be best protected by an unbending absolute. This has been compared to the situation when the law forbids outside fires during a drought. Though an individual fire might do no harm, the law is unbending because of the danger of people making a wrong private judgment and starting a holocaust. Such a law would not be based on the ability of the legislators to "prove" that each and every individual fire would be "evil" but on the presumption that the common danger can only be contained by an absolute negative. This argument implies that an individual fire might not only be harmless but even good for those who light it, but this good must be sacrificed to the common good.

There would seem to be three weaknesses in this argument. First, it is a covert form of the domino theory and thus is liable to all the criticisms offered above. The imagery switches from domino and wedge to fire, but the thought is the same. The first exception will lead the parade of horrors and therefore each and every exception ought to be considered immoral, however dissimilar they are.

Secondly, this argument confuses law and ethics. Law has to work at the level of general presumptions. Law seeks to set up general norms for society. It cannot hope to know what would be moral for each person in every concrete circumstance. Ethics, on the contrary, has a more difficult task. It cannot remain at the level of the presumptively good but must seek out the actual here-and-now good. Thus, if there were a law in the case given, it would be illegal to light an outdoor fire during the drought, but it is not clear that it would be immoral, because there may be a proportionate reason for taking this risk in a given case. A carefully circumscribed fire might be needed for an emergency situation. In that case, it would be moral but presumptively illegal.

Of course, even the law recognizes the possibility of an excusing factor, and the virtue of epikeia, of which we have spoken, is the virtue which helps one discern the true exceptions where the letter of the law may be set aside. So if we were to apply this anti-fire drought law to the question of death by choice the possibility of exceptions would still be open. Therefore, the legal problem should not be equated with the moral problem but, even if it is, the possibility of exceptions remains.

Thirdly, this objection is utilitarian in the objectionable sense of the word. There is a natural tension between the needs of the individual and the needs of the group. Utilitarianism eases the tension by an excessive concession to the group. Of course, private good may have to be sacrificed to the common good. Taxes and eminent domain illustrate this fact of life. But the tension should remain. The objection we are treating here implies that all instances of mercy killing should be treated as wrong even if they cannot be proved in each case to be wrong so that the good of the group will be preserved. To make this objection stick you would have to prove that the good of the group is totally dependent on an absolute negative and cannot be provided for in any other way, and that this kind of simplistic utilitarian ethics is at all valid. I submit that neither of these points could be established.[12]

PLAYING GOD

In one form or other the objection is often heard that to take steps to end life is playing God, for it is God's prerogative to determine the end of life, not man's. To terminate a life is to violate the property rights of God.[13] As the objection is often phrased, it sounds like a program of pure pacifism. Interrogation, however, usually reveals that the objector does not object to killing in war. There, apparently, we have a permit from God to go at it, using appropriate ethical calculations.

The objection is, at root, a kind of religious, biologistic determinism. Now that, admittedly, is a mouthful. In more kindly language, what the objection implies is that God's will is identified with the processes of man's physical and biological nature. When God wants you to die, your organs will fail or disease will overcome you. Organic collapse is the medium through which God's will is manifested. Positive action to accelerate death, however, would amount to wresting the matter out of God's hands and taking it into your own. It is a sin of arrogant presumption.

If this objection were taken literally, it would paralyze technological man. And this, of course, would mean that it would paralyze medicine. For if it is wrong to accelerate death, by what right do we delay it by ingenious cures and techniques? Is not medicine tampering with God's property rights by putting off the moment of death and thus frustrating God in his effort to reclaim his property?

Men who believe that God's will is manifested through the physical facts and events of life would have to sit back and await the good pleasure of Nature. All efforts to step in and take over by reshaping the earth in accord with our own designs would be blasphemous. We are here at the level of discourse expressible in the statement: if God wanted you to fly, he would have given you wings.

The mentality of this objection is utterly at odds with genuine Christian theology. According to the Christian view, man is created in the image of the creator God. He is thus himself commissioned to creativity, a co-creator with God destined to exercise fruitful and ingenious stewardship over the earth. He is not a pawn of the earth's forces, but a participator in God's providence, invited by his nature and his God to provide for himself and for others.[14] This, of course, is not to say that Christian theology is committed to death by choice. It is, however, to say that the presuppositions of the "playing God" objection are not Christian even though Christians are among those who offer it.

Philosophically, there is in the "playing God" objection a problem with the idea of authority. Many people have difficulty believing that they have moral authority over their dying. One of the principal reasons why this question is opening up for reconsideration today is that the idea of authority is being rethought. This is due in no small part to technological man's new awareness of his abilities. Professor Diana Crane alludes to this when she says that there has been

> . . . a change in social attitudes toward human intervention at both the beginning and the end of life. Birth and Death are now viewed as events which need not be blindly accepted by human beings . . . Suicide and euthanasia are being tolerated to a greater extent, or at least viewed differently. Consequently, we are in the midst of developing new ethics.[15]

The natural course of events is less and less seen as normative. Unlike his ancestors, technological man is inclined to rise up, not lie down before fate. Obviously, he can overdo this, as our ecocatastrophe bears witness. But it is an apparently irreversible fact of our lives that we envision ourselves less as *homo actus* (man acted upon) and more as *homo agens* (man achieving).

The notion of moral authority is unavoidably affected by this major shift in self-consciousness. If we go back into the centuries, we find that the effort to explain unaccustomed exercises of moral freedom relied heavily on divine intervention. Thus Samson's pulling the house down on himself was seen as justifiable suicide. The justification, however, came from the fact that Samson was divinely inspired. Otherwise there would be no way of knowing that this was a good act. Likewise St. Apollonia saved her virtue by throwing herself into a fire. Her action, too, was deemed good because she was judged to be divinely inspired.[16]

Thomas Aquinas even managed to justify acts of adultery and fornication by this notion of divine authority. He did this by saying that these acts of intercourse with someone who is not one's wife, were not really fornication or adultery when they were divinely mandated. Thomas puts it this way: "Consequently intercourse with any woman, by the command of God, is neither adultery nor fornication."[17] (Clearly, a divine command in these matters is not easily come by, so Thomas was not being all that permissive.)

Thomas uses this same approach to justify the direct taking of innocent life. He considered the case of God's command to Abraham to kill his own son and concluded that whoever kills either the innocent or the unjust by divine command does not sin.[18] Thus direct ending of innocent life is moral and good if God commands you to do it. Thomas is not saying that something is good just because God commands it. It is his position that God can only command that which is good.[19] Thus, in these cases, Thomas is conceding that the direct taking of innocent life such as Abraham was ordered to do was a good moral action. The command of God *revealed* that it was good; it did not *make* it good. Thomas was a realist, not a nominalist. This meant that he believed that things are not good because commanded; they could only be commanded if they are good. For Thomas and his colleagues, given their cultural setting, suicide or direct ending of life could only be known to be good if God gave an explicit order. Authority was from on high. Thus, in effect, there could be no knowable exceptions to the self-killing principle without a mandate.

This thought is not very palatable to a twentieth-century mind for this reason: we have come to see that it is not through burning bushes but through thinking minds that God reveals the holy places of human freedom. The divine mandate is to think and feel and listen and do all of the things that make a moral being fully alive in all of his sensitivities. Moral man does not stand idly all day looking into the heavens awaiting a miracle of knowledge; the miracle is his own mind. And modern religious man is no less religious for so locating the miracle and for availing himself of it. Moral authority is seen now as coming, not from a mountaintop, but from within the struggling moral community, where men attempt to know the limits of their God-given moral freedom.

Notice, however, that we are not entirely parting company with the ancients on the issue of whether direct termination of life could be moral, but only on how we know that it can be moral. Moral authority is now seen as discoverable. Applied to the question of death by choice, we need not await a miraculous divine revelation of the sort that Abraham is said to have had, to assume this freedom. Rather we must probe and see whether there are proportionate and good reasons to recognize this moral dominion over our dying. To do this is not to play God but, if you will, to play man. It is to do what is proper to man as man, a being with power to deliberate and to act on his deliberations when that action appears to achieve what is good.

Christians and other religious persons who would oppose mercy killing must not pretend there is a divine edict against it. Father Bernard Häring, who opposes euthanasia, puts it this way:

> In earlier times, the general argument, "You may not choose when to fall into the arms of God who alone is Lord over life and death" seemed sufficient. Today however, it is not as simple as that because Christian Scientists and the Witnesses of Jehovah invoke this argument equally in proscribing blood transfusions.[20]

Häring might also have added that the same argument was used by Catholics and others against the control of birth as is now used against the control of death. When Häring goes on to argue against euthanasia, he does what he has to do. He tries to find reasons against it. The reasons that he offers (e.g., "the wedge reaction") I do not find compelling, but his manner of argumentation is correct. He is seeking reasons to support a position that is not self-evident one way or the other.

CONSENT OR DESPAIR?

In this chapter we are considering the objections against death by choice when the patient makes the decision for himself. These cases are easier to judge morally than cases where the decision is made for someone else now unconscious. How can we judge that a person has made a free decision for death?

Is the patient just undergoing a temporary period of depression? Or could it be something worse than depression—his relatives? Could those who care for him be tiring of the burden and communicating to him subtly that he avail himself of his moral freedom for death by choice? Could there be, as in the mystery stories, an eager band of relatives chafing at the bit in anticipation of a rich legacy? Though this is more of a danger when we speak of deciding for someone who has lapsed into coma, the desire for death could be prompted by the selfish needs of others.

It is, of course, a fact that a person suffering does have his moments of despair when he feels that his resources of patience are spent and he can endure no more. Then he says with Job: "Strangling I would welcome rather, and death itself, than these my sufferings!"[21] However, Job did have better days. "After his trials, Job lived on until he was a hundred and forty years old, and saw his children and his children's children up to the fourth generation."[22] Job's story of despair, then, had a happy ending. A terminal patient cannot perhaps expect as much, although there are remarkable cases of remission of the worst of illnesses. Still, the possibility for a premature wish for death is a real problem.

Dr. G. E. Schreiner of Georgetown University Hospital reports on a kidney patient who asked to be taken off dialysis. The result of this, of course, would be his death. Dr. Schreiner gave the patient a very thorough dialysis treatment to put him in excellent chemical shape and then asked him if he still wanted to discontinue. "Don't listen to me," he replied. "That's my uremia talking, not me. I want to stay in the program." Another patient, however, said the same thing and was given the same special treatment. He persisted in his desire to stop treatment and so he withdrew and died.[23] (Interestingly, Dr. Schreiner says, "we allowed him to withdraw," as though the decision were the doctors' and not the patient's, even though the patient was in full and reflective possession of his senses.)

In other illnesses, it is not possible to give a treatment that will provide such favorable physical conditions for a decision. The problem of temporary depression is more difficult in these cases. Some proposed euthanasia bills have tried to meet this problem. The Voluntary Euthanasia bill offered in 1969 in England proposed a thirty-day waiting period after a person made a declaration for death by euthanasia. The declaration could be revoked at any time in that period. In some cases, this could leave a person in unrelievable pain for a longer period than he might wish, but it does represent an effort to guarantee real consent.

The ways in which relatives and/or medical personnel could suction the desire to live out of a patient are not easily warded off by legislation. At the level of morality, however, the sin of such persons is heinous. We spoke of the danger of making a sick person feel useless and *therefore* worthless as though our ability to be of use was the base of our human dignity. Likewise, uncomfortable as we tend to be with suffering and the approach of death, it is possible to insinuate some of our inability to cope with the fact of dying. This, too, could create a premature desire for the release of death.

Most important in this regard is an awareness that it may be the patient's uremia or something else that is requesting death. If the patient is open to it, good counseling can help him evaluate his situation. Sometimes, the closer you are to the patient, the less help you would be in this kind of a decision; other kinds of closeness can give a friend or relative better qualifications than a professional counselor. Overall, the problem of consent is not insuperable, but it is also not to be minimized.

Suppose a Cure is Found

In 1921, George R. Minot was found to have diabetes at the age of thirty-six. For the next two years he fought a losing battle to control his disease by diet, the only means then available. In 1923, insulin became available and Dr. Minot's life was saved. After this, Minot went to work on a series of experiments that culminated in his 1927 report that large quantities of liver could bring about the regeneration of red cells in the bone marrow. This was an effective treatment of pernicious anemia and won for Minot the Nobel prize in 1934.

This story called dramatic attention to the possibility of a new cure being found to bring sudden and unexpected help for a disease that had been fatal. Many people use this as an argument against death by choice, the idea being that a cure might be just around the corner. Medical science has surprised us before.

The problem of what medicine might do is compounded by what medicine might not be able to do. I refer to the not very fine art of prognosis. Dr. Lasagna calls this art "an elusive one" and notes that "many an embarrassed doctor has failed to outlive the patient whose immediate doom he prophesied."[24] There are also numerous cases of regression of a disease, including cancer, for no apparent reason. Dr. Lasagna writes: "Even where questionable cases are ruled out because of inadequate information, there are still a sizeable number of patients considered by cancer experts to show spontaneous disappearance of what appears to be typical malignant disease."[25]

Therefore, prognosis is fallible, diseases go into unaccountable remission, the power of life is unpredictable. How could we ever impose death—an irreversible condition—since, where there is life, there is hope?

In response, I would say that for all its fallibility, prognosis can enjoy a high degree of certainty. The percentage of correct diagnosis is exceptionally high in cancer cases, and these are the patients most likely to opt for death by choice. Other terminal conditions, especially in their later stages, are open to very precise prognosis. These are cases where there is life but no hope.

With regard to the possibility of a cure, there are advanced cases where death would remain a certainty even if a cure were to be found today, due to the extent of deterioration. Also, as Anthony Flew says:

> . . . the advance of medicine has not reached a stage where all diseases are curable. And no one seriously thinks that it has. At most this continuing advance has suggested that we need never despair of finding cures *some day*.[26]

This objection sins by abstraction. It tenders a vague hope for medical miracles as an argument against death by choice.

In particular cases this vague hope can be dismissed by the concrete facts.

THEY SHOOT HORSES, DON'T THEY?

Euthanasia is a bad word. It is bad for two reasons: first, it means too many different things to too many people. Secondly, it is bad because it connotes an attitude on suffering that is false.

As to its indefiniteness, Paul Ramsey says that in current usage it means direct killing and that efforts to use the term in some other way do not succeed.[27] Yet, for example, lawyer Arval Morris uses it in another way when he says that Pius XII did not uniformly condemn euthanasia.[28] As direct killing Pius certainly did condemn it. The Euthanasia Educational Fund uses the term in two senses and therefore must employ the modifiers active and passive. A New York *Times* editorial speaks of the frequent practice of euthanasia in this country and abroad, and then explains that normally this takes the form of a cessation of extraordinary measures.[29] Moralist Gerald Kelly has to point out that he is not using the term euthanasia to denote the mere giving of drugs to a dying patient to ease his pain, as some theologians do.[30] Some use the qualifier "pure" euthanasia to describe the use of pain-killers which do not shorten life.[31] Also, in some cases the term has been used to describe dangerous medical experiments performed on human beings.[32] As a result of this confusion, many people sense the need to move away from that term and develop terms that do justice to the various and different ways of meeting death. And so we meet the terms orthothanasia, agathanasia, benemortasia, dysthanasia, anti-dysthanasia, and mercy killing.

Most often, however, the term euthanasia has reference to direct killing with an accent on relief of suffering. Thus a dictionary definition calls it "an act or method of causing death painlessly, so as to end suffering; advocated by some as a way to deal with the victims of incurable disease."[33] The Voluntary Euthanasia bill of 1969 in England defined euthanasia as "the painless inducement of death." It is to this accent on painlessness that a false philosophy of suffering easily attaches. One of the bad arguments that persistently surfaces in the literature defending euthanasia is in reference to what we do for animals. As the argument goes, we see it as cruel and inhumane to leave an animal in hopeless pain and so we "put him to sleep." Could we do less for one of our own?

Because of this kind of argument, one of the arguments that is brought against any liberalization of the moral right to death by choice is that those who press such a right are infected by a crassly materialistic philosophy of suffering. Since a mistaken philosophy of suffering is reductively a mistaken philosophy of man, this objection is serious. In responding to it, I find myself responding to those who support death by choice with bad arguments (They shoot horses . . .) and to those who rely on those bad arguments to object to death by choice.

The philosophical error involved here is one that should be refutable by observation. Horses and men are different in some rather impressive ways. A horse can be relieved of his suffering but he does not have the human power to transcend that suffering by giving it meaning.

Man is a meaning seeker. Where he finds meaning he is fulfilled and, by a remarkable alchemy, he can find meaning in the most unlikely experiences. Put in another way, man's consciousness, unlike that of the horse, is open to and geared to the pursuit of the *possible* that is latent in the *actual*. The human spirit has a divining power that can detect redemptive possibilities in a situation that would otherwise be crushing and destructive. Were Helen Keller a horse, born blind and deaf, it might have been best to shoot her. Being a person amid other persons, her exquisite possibilities could be and were realized.

Our suffering is human suffering and that means that it is suffering with possibilities. These possibilities may not always be realized, for though we be godly we are not gods. We experience limit. But still, the human capacity to transcend gives human suffering a qualitative distinctiveness.

There is no suggestion here that we return to the views of the past which gave suffering a *per se* value. Such a value suffering does not have, but rather assumes its meaning, value or disvalue, from the special circumstances of the sufferer. Christians see the crucifixion sufferings of Jesus as meaningful not because they have a sadistic love of crucifixions, but because the circumstances of this particular one lent it a special meaning. Only a sado-masochistic philosophy could see suffering as a value in itself. Of itself it is a disvalue to be alleviated if at all possible. Where no relief is possible, suffering at times can be made meaningfully redemptive through the creative spirit of the sufferer.

First of all, the suffering can be of benefit to the sufferer. As the British lawyer Norman St. John-Stevas put it:

> The final stage of an incurable illness can be a wasteland, but it need not be. It can be a vital period in a person's life, reconciling him to life and to death and giving him an interior peace. This is the experience of people who have looked after the dying.[34]

It should be noted, of course, that what is suggested here is something that *might* be achieved. It is also possible that it could not be and that a final agony will destroy peace rather than enhance it. In spite of all best efforts, the final stage of life may be a wasteland. It is then that the question of terminating that life takes on potential meaning, since death may be the only peace achievable.

There are possible ways also in which final suffering could be helpful to others. For one thing, the dying, while they still have sufficient consciousness, could help the living to come to a more realistic consciousness of death. Many of the dying have been doing this and Dr. Elizabeth Kübler-Ross has, in her writings, brought their teaching to a wide audience.[35]

Also, terminally ill persons should feel free to co-operate in experiments that might help future sufferers from the same disease.[36] We have noted earlier the suggestion of Mary Rose Barrington that a patient near the end of his life might arrange his death so as to permit an immediate transfer of a vital organ to a younger person. Given all the proper sensitivities of the medical profession about organ piracy or anything redolent thereof, it is not likely that this suggestion will get a hearing at this time. If the person to receive the vital organ were a relative or friend, the emotional effects of this generosity on the recipient could be anticipated to be such as to make the action morally unwise. There is also the medical problem of the value of the organs of a person dying of certain diseases. All the reality-revealing questions used in setting up the "moral object" would have to be focused on this case. It is not impossible, however, that all of the moral objections to such a procedure could be met in a particular case.

Aside from Barrington's suggestion of arranging death so as to make a vital organ available, there is also the possibility of donating a cornea or one of the other paired organs during a terminal illness. The operation for organ removal could be expected to hasten the dying process of the patient, but the benefits of the operation to someone else could easily be proportionate to the hastened death of the already dying donor. In fact, if a patient was anxious to bring on death sooner, the donation of an organ could be seen as a benevolent way of achieving this. The relevant moral questions would focus on medical feasibility, the mental state of the donor-patient, his relationship to the recipient, possible impact on the public acceptance of transplantation, etc.

Persons with a terminal illness who are still very alert of mind and imagination, or persons who have a serious illness such as kidney failure with a consequent need for dialysis, could see their illness as a platform from which to address the needs of their society. The sick could look for opportunities to help the well. With their unique credentials, and while their strength lasts, they could do more than they might realize. By working creatively with politicians and legislators, national health organizations, medical and legal societies, news media, writers, etc.—and in ways as yet unthought of which their healthy imaginations will bring forth—the lobby of the dying and the gravely ill could become a healing force in society. They could seek ways to address the sick priorities of our nation. They could call attention to the needs of the neglected poor of our land and of the third world. They could bear witness to the medical problems of the poor and to the need for better health insurance programs. They could educate legislators and others on the need for legislation to protect their right to die.

The words and feelings of those who stand at the brink of death have a special power. There is in literature a genre of "farewell addresses," real or imagined, but carefully preserved and attended to. The words of those who will soon leave us merit a natural and spontaneous esteem. We would have a healthier society if the dying found ways to speak to those who will survive them for a while.

While urging the positive possibilities of the suffering-dying, we cannot foreclose the sad possibility that a person's condition may be such that the value of terminating life might supersede all other values. There is such a thing as unbearable and undefeatable suffering of the sort that only death can end. In that event, it would be another mark of the distinctively human approach to death to procure the only relief imaginable. For the human person, unlike the horse, knows that he is going to die, knows that death can be a friend, and knows how to bring on death at a time when he can suffer no more. He has the capacity for death by choice; the horse does not.

KILLING FOR THE SAKE OF LIFE

Arthur J. Dyck of Harvard Divinity School opposes death by choice of the kind of which we have been speaking. He writes that "Any act, insofar as it is an act of taking a human life, is wrong, that is to say, taking a human life is a wrong-making characteristic of actions." This, however, does not make Dyck an absolute pacifist. Some killing is good killing. Here is how he justifies that:

> To say, however, that killing is *prima facie* wrong does not mean that an act of killing may never be justified. For example, a person's effort to prevent someone's death may lead to the death of the attacker. However, we can morally justify that act of intervention only because it is an act of saving a life, not because it is an act of taking a life. If it were simply an act of taking a life, it would be wrong.[37]

This particular argument of Dyck's has some basic weaknesses. First of all, most of the killing that is done in the self-defense situation of war, for example, is not done to save life in the physical sense of keeping someone alive. Most wars are fought to protect the quality of human life. They are fought because it is decided that a change in the quality of life is more important than submissive behavior that would probably let more people live but in conditions that are intolerable. Some wars, like the India-Pakistan war, can have the purported or even real purpose of ending an ongoing slaughter and therefore of "saving life." Other wars, such as wars of national independence, are waged for the same reason that tyrants are assassinated, to change the quality of life which had become intolerable under the reigning powers.

Obviously, war, tyrannicide, and killing in self-defense are different from death by choice in a medical context. In the latter case, however, the motive for imposing death is that the quality of this person's life, wracked as he may be by undefeatable and overwhelming pain, is intolerable. Obviously, in a narrow physical sense he is not "saving" his life by choosing to end it. He does, however, decide that he is saving himself by so choosing since the minimal requirements for personal existence have been obliterated by his condition. It would be sheer materialism to identify the patient's person and personal good with physical perdurance of life in any state.

Furthermore, as Dyck says, the mandate against killing derives from the perception that "no society can be indifferent about the taking of human life."[38] Ending the life of a person who wants it ended because of unsupportable agony is the very opposite of indifference to life. The respect for human life in this case leads to a respect for human death. Ultimately it is the experience of the value of the person that leads to the recognition of the value of death as well as the value of life.

It can also be said in response to Dyck's position that, although he is working out of a Christian perspective, he seems to ignore the Christian belief in an afterlife. It is Christian belief that death does not end life; it merely changes its condition. The ancient preface for the Mass of the Dead says that "life is changed, not taken away" in death. For a Christian and for anyone who believes in an afterlife, to "terminate life" is not to terminate life, but to move on to a new life. With such a faith, death is not nearly so drastic. It has lost its sting of finality. This would seem to make it easier for a Christian to see death as a friend, especially when he has, through his illness, lost all ability to respond and react to the invitation of his God to join him in the building up of this earth.[39]

A NATURAL DEATH

The term "natural death" or "death due to natural causes" means for most people that death occurred as a result of disease and not due to either an accident or human intervention. The implication therefore is that if one dies through positive human intervention, he has not died a natural death. This, then, would not be favorable to death by choice.

Show me your presuppositions and I will tell you what you are. The presuppositions of this linguistic approach are, to use a term that is not found in the dictionary, Ulpianesque. Ulpian was a Roman jurist who used the term "natural" to refer to that which was common to men and animals. The natural is "that which nature teaches to all animals."[40] To act naturally, then, is to conform to the rhythms of one's physical nature. With this kind of thinking, the biological and the physical become ethically normative. It was the influence of this kind of thinking and the whole stoic philosophy of nature that led many people to conclude that contraception was wrong. This exemplifies well what is wrong with what we have called Ulpianesque thinking. Thought of in this narrow physical way, sexuality was seen as geared to reproduction in men and beasts. Sexual exchange that blocks off the reproductive goal is therefore immoral and "unnatural." The error here arises from the failure to see that human sexuality is an ingredient of human *personal* nature. This puts it onto a plane where it has considerably more meaning than breeding people. Indeed, in human beings, the reproductive aspect of sex might often be quite secondary, or, at times, even contradict the human purposes and meaning of sexual expression and have to be suppressed.

Ulpianesque thinking (and poor Ulpian was not the only one to indulge in it) is described as "physicalist" and it is quite a mischievous approach to ethics. It can entirely short-circuit the discussion of the ethics of dying. If you start out with the physicalist presumption that only one's organic system can determine death in a way that is natural to man, the discussion is stopped in its tracks. If, however, you grant that it is *natural* for man to deliberate about alternative possibilities and to pursue that course which commends itself to his reason, then death by choice can be discussed. It could, in fact, be seen as quite natural to men whose distinctive dignity is their capacity for choice.

The Sense of Profanation

It might further be objected that there is something sacrosanct about a person's life, even his physical life. The proper attitude toward this life is awe, reverence, and support. Tampering with it, experimenting with it, or certainly ending it, is a profanation of the sacred. There is something jarring about the very idea. This, perhaps, is the reason why people have been so slow to accept the idea of mercy killing and why such killing is illegal in almost every land. This is a serious objection, based upon something (the sense of profanation) which I have presented as fundamental to good ethics.

In response, it can be said that the sense of profanation is a two-edged sword. It can, as I have mentioned, also be evoked by the sight of a person whose life is being agonizingly prolonged when truly personal living has become impossible because of unrelenting pain. In such a case, not to allow such a person the right to abbreviate his suffering could seem to subject this person to the dictates of his disease. Not being able to choose death when death is experienced as an essential benefit, could easily seem degrading and profaning of personhood. Why should the disease have all the say, and the patient none? By succumbing to such moral determinism, is not the sacred power of deliberation and choice profaned?

It must be remembered, too, that the sense of profanation does not of itself constitute an independent argument. Ethics is wholistic. All the questions must be asked and all the evaluational capacities of the human spirit tapped before moral judgment is pronounced. Moral discourse must operate with a system of checks and balances. No one activity or faculty, whether it be *Gemüt*, the sense of profanation, the use of principle, etc., must be allowed an unquestioned hegemony.

In the second part of this objection, it was suggested that maybe the negative stance of most law regarding mercy killing constitutes an argument (based on group experience) against mercy killing. To this, it must be said that law is rarely a pioneer which stakes out new vistas for moral freedom. Law normally has deep historical roots which can be either an illuminating asset or a recalcitrant drag on moral progress. Law has the weaknesses as well as the strengths of the past. On the positive side we must trust it as the fruit of much experience. On the negative side we must reject its myopia when we come to see an issue better. That is why law must be open to reform, or it becomes demonic.

Thomas Jefferson is an eloquent witness to the stranglehold of inadequate law. In 1816 he wrote:

> I know also that laws and institutions must go hand in hand with the progress of the human mind . . . As new discoveries are made, new truths disclosed, and manners and opinions change with the change of circumstances, institutions must advance also, and keep pace with the times. We might as well require a man to wear still the coat which fitted him when a boy, as civilized society to remain ever under the regimen of their barbarous ancestors.[41]

Before concluding that the voice of the law is the voice of God, it is well to look at the values and disvalues that the law has embodied in the past. Look how long law resisted the right of conscientious objection to war. With the greatest struggle and patience, the Quakers managed to win from government exemption to military service on conscientious grounds. And this was in 1802.[42] For centuries this right, now generally seen as sacred, was denied by law. Long denied too was the right of women to vote and of black persons to be free. For the reasons offered in this book and for reasons that others offer, I judge that current laws are denying a human right when they inhibit the individual's right to death by choice. In this case, law is a tabernacle of taboo, and not a beacon of light.

The Hippocratic Oath

Hippocrates lived in the fifth century B.C. In his time, medicine was terribly intertwined with superstition and decadent religiosity. Hippocrates is generally credited with instituting a revolution that desacralized medicine. Morris H. Saffron, the Archivist and Historian of the State Medical Society of New Jersey, says of Hippocrates: "To his majestic figure, subsequent generations of physicians turned as to a demigod, attributing to him many tracts written centuries after his death, so that the Hippocratic Corpus as it now stands, includes more than seventy works."[43] Of all the works attributed to Hippocrates, there is no part more influential than his famous oath, which has guided physicians for centuries. The key passage relevant to death by choice is this: "I will neither give a deadly drug to anybody, if asked for, nor will I make a suggestion to this effect."

This passage is thought to show the influence of Pythagorean philosophy on Hippocratic thought. Pythagoras denied the right of an individual to take his own life.[44] It is to these words of the oath that many people repair when contradicting the right to death by choice.

The prestige of this oath is enormous. Dr. H. Pitney van Dusen, former president of Union Theological Seminary, says that he does not think "there is any other profession that is wedded to such an ancient document, not even the clerical profession with its Ten Commandments."[45] Many physicians argue from this oath against death by choice as though they have an unwavering reliance on the self-sufficiency of this text that can only be compared to the attitude of a fundamentalist sectarian to his Bible. Undoubtedly, this attitude has been productive of much good, but it is again a one-rubric approach to the ethical issues involved and it has all the deficiencies that accrue to simplism in ethics.

In an effort to open the euthanasia issue to discussion, Joseph Fletcher has taken the tack of finding contradictions in the oath (a tactic also used against fundamentalist interpreters of the Bible). Fletcher notes that the oath promises two things: first, to relieve suffering, and, second, to prolong and protect life. Then he argues:

> When the patient is in the grip of an agonizing and fatal disease, these two promises are incompatible. Two duties come into conflict. To prolong life is to violate the promise to relieve pain. To relieve the pain is to violate the promise to prolong and protect life.[46]

More directly to the point, however, the oath has proved itself an invaluable encapsulation of some of the highest ideals in medical history. It is, however, not inspired by God, or by Apollo or Aesculapius, who are mentioned in the historical form of the oath. It is not a divine substitute for doing ethics. It is not oracular. Though it is good, it is perfectible. In fact, a modified form of the Hippocratic oath was adopted by the General Assembly of the World Medical Association meeting in Geneva in 1948. This form of the oath was also included in the International Code of Medical Ethics, which was adopted in 1949 and is used by physicians and medical schools. This version does not include the passage that swears against giving or counseling the use of something that would cause death. This omission did not constitute an endorsement of mercy killing in any form, but it does present a declaration that would admit of either a pro or con position on death by choice.

> Declaration of Geneva: I solemnly pledge myself to consecrate my life to the service of humanity. I will give to my teachers the respect and gratitude which is their due; I will practice my profession with conscience and dignity; the health of my patient will be my first consideration; I will respect the secrets which are confided in me; I will maintain by all means in my power the honor and noble traditions of the medical profession. My colleagues will be

my brothers; I will not permit considerations of religion, nationality, race, party politics, or social standing to intervene between my duty and my patient. I will maintain the utmost respect for human life from the time of conception; even under threat, I will not use my medical knowledge contrary to the laws of humanity. I make these promises solemnly, freely, and upon my honor.[47]

One could maintain "the utmost respect for human life" and observe the "laws of humanity" by recognizing that the inducement of death when death is good and befitting is a reasonable and good service to human persons. The decision to do this, of course, would not be the doctor's, since he does not have the moral authority to make these decisions for anyone. His expertise does not in any way equip him to make moral decisions for his patients. He may be asked to administer the injection that causes death. In that case his conscience must guide his own response. The decision to initiate is not his; the decision to co-operate is.

Of Laws and Insurance Companies

Objection: if morality is based on reality, one of the realities of life is the law. In the United States, for example, it is illegal to induce one's own death or to help someone to end his life. Therefore, if all the arguments of ethics point to the fact that a particular act of termination might be moral, the arguments fail by reason of the illegality. It is not moral to act in a way that puts you and others at odds with the law. On top of that, insurance companies take a dim view of this sort of thing and will probably claim exemption from liability for the death. Thus your insurance is wiped out, and how could that be rational or moral?

These are practical objections. To spin out a theory that detaches from such concrete realities as law and insurance is hardly acceptable. And, indeed, it would not only make bad sense but bad ethics. First of all, then, the objection is heavy with overtones of that pernicious confusion that identifies legality and morality. In reply let it be said (again) that what is illegal may be moral, even heroically so. Of this, we have said enough previously.

Secondly, it is not illegal to kill yourself in all states. And modern law does not punish you by stripping you of your estate. However, in some jurisdictions, self-killing is a crime and those who aid or abet a person normally incur responsibility before the law in any jurisdiction. We have alluded to the Texas case *Sanders* v. *State*, where it was judged that aiding a person to kill himself is not a crime since self-killing is not a crime. This case, however, was later overruled in Texas in *Aven* v. *State*, which held that one who furnishes poison to another, knowing that the purpose of the latter is to commit suicide, and who assists in administering the poison which is the cause of death, is guilty of murder.[48] Therefore, there can be no doubt about it. Death by choice does not enjoy the formal protection of the law. The tendency, as we have seen, is to treat these cases leniently, but this offers precarious promise at best. Anyone who attempts death by choice and succeeds obviously has little to fear from the law. Also, if he attempts and fails, he has little to fear even though in some states the attempt is an indictable offense. The hopes for leniency here are well founded. Assisting someone to die is, however, still legally perilous.

There are three options available in the face of this legal situation. Abstain from assisting in death by choice; assist and admit and hope for the best as Dr. Postma and Dr. Sander did; or assist clandestinely. The first course presents no legal problems. It could present moral problems if the patient's request for assistance is well considered and apparently justifiable. Then, it could be judged wrong not to give assistance such as making pills available. On the other hand, even if you felt that this person had a clear moral right to death by choice, it would be morally proper to weigh your consequent legal problems against his extended agony. Notice here again that omission is not an escape from moral choice. In such a case it is a moral choice and not necessarily a good one.

The second solution is the Postma-Sander solution. This requires considerable moral courage. Even though Dr. Postma escaped punishment in the form of a jail sentence, she must have been seriously punished by the trial and by the intense publicity visited upon her private sorrow.

Dr. Sander also had his ordeal even though he was found not guilty in the crowded, cheering courtroom. His right to practice medicine in New Hampshire was temporarily revoked and he was ousted by state and local medical societies. Reportedly, he was at one point reduced to plowing neighbors' fields for four dollars an hour.[49] No one could be morally bound to endure what might have to be endured for assisting someone to die by positive means . . . no matter how deserving the case. Normally, we are not morally bound to heroic acts. We are here in the realm of what some moralists call ultra-obligation. It could also, of course, be called the realm of moral opportunity.

Persons who do move ahead of the law here may, by their heroism, succeed in updating the law. Even within the conceptual inadequacies of the relevant American law, ingenious lawyers might be able to explore the possibility of defending this kind of action as being within the legitimate perimeters of religious freedom. Other defenses might also present themselves to the creative lawyer. The time might now be ripe for the development of precedents here.

The third course is the clandestine one. It has been suggested that there has been many an unrecorded use made of drugs such as bichloride of mercury, potassium, and some of the barbiturates.[50] This may be, but how would one judge it morally? All of the reality-revealing questions would have to be asked, especially the question of who was making the decision. Only then could this course of action be judged. This clandestine course is not *a priori* wrong. Conscientious objection in the form of both overt and clandestine action is a necessary corrective for those situations where reality demands what the law forbids. Thus assisting a consenting person to achieve death by choice would not be wrong on the sole count of illegality.

But what of insurance? Insurance companies may protect themselves from liability by a suicide clause, at least at the beginning of a policy. The term suicide would include all forms of self-killing, whether the person was well or dying, sane or mentally ill. So someone planning to abbreviate the process of dying in which he finds himself, has to weigh the possibility of loss of coverage. In proportional calculus this might outweigh the gains of an earlier death . . . or it might not. But what of the morality of a person surreptitiously hastening his death in a way that allows him to keep his insurance coverage intact? Insurance companies presume that death occurs without human intervention, even though they often pay in cases of self-killing if the person has been a policyholder for a reasonably long period.

As a moralist, I would suggest that insurance companies should make distinctions where there are differences in the area of self-killing. Motive and other circumstances are, after all, reality-constituting factors. If a man who is repentant over being a poor provider, takes out a policy to make his family beneficiaries, and then does himself in, in a way that makes his death look accidental, he is guilty of fraud. His generosity is at the expense of the company and other policyholders.

This is not the same as the case of a person who in extreme neurotic depression kills himself. In such a case, the darkness and terror of overwhelming emotions might plunge him into this act. This, it would seem, should be recognized as death from fatal illness. Uncontrollable depression can be fatal. It would seem wrong to punish this person posthumously by withholding payment on his policy. It can be said quite accurately that in such cases, death occurs because of illness. Normally, psychiatry will be able to attest to the active presence of serious illness preceding death in such a case. Obviously, if someone is emotionally ill when he takes out a policy, this should be revealed, since he has, by this reasoning, a potentially fatal illness. But if this kind of illness struck after the policy was taken out and while the policy is yet young, insurance coverage should not be lost any more than if the person had succumbed to rapidly developing cancer. To do otherwise reveals an archaic and cruel conception of mental illness.

There is also a difference between a person who, in ending his life, interrupts a healthy process and one who interrupts a dying process. A person dying of bone cancer who takes an overdose of barbiturates is not the same as the spurned lover who throws himself off a bridge. In the latter case, there might be good reasons to withhold payment on the policy. It may seem unromantic to suggest it, but this venal fact of life might be something of a deterrent to at least some frustrated lovers. Still, even here, such a desperate act is not calculated to be too frequent in our culture and insurance empires would not be likely to crumble if they covered such pathetic cases.

In the former case, involving the person dying of bone cancer, acceleration of this death should not in any way affect coverage. If it does, then the insurer is, in effect, punishing the insured for not holding the insurer's moral position on death by choice. There would seem to be something immoral and possibly unconstitutional about this. At any rate, the patient is, in this case, already in the dying process. The reasonable acceleration of that process should not be subject to financial punishment.

At this point, it should be clear that insurance people, doc-tors, nurses, lawyers, moralists, gravely ill persons, etc., should be in important conversations about this subject, for it is a subject that is utterly interdisciplinary in nature. Insurance com-panies would, I believe, find that death by choice represents a rare and reasonable event which will not revolutionize the in-surance business. Probably the prolongation of life by medical progress will make for more problems. As Bayless Manning comments:

> It is interesting to speculate too, upon the impact of the new technology on annuity premiums and other forms of insurance. The march of medical progress is apt to make life difficult indeed for actuaries and, one could even imagine, produce acute financial embarrassment for some annuity companies.[51]

The objections faced in this chapter were primarily taken as relevant to death by choice when one decides for one's self. As noted at the beginning, many of these arguments could also be lodged in different ways against the decision to end someone else's life. Without being repetitious we will allude to their relevance in the next chapter, where the special objections to deciding for someone else are treated. The division of these two chapters is due to the radical difference between the two kinds of decisions and to the fact that persons might easily conclude that they could defend the morality of a decision for self, but not the morality of a decision for others. So saying, we can turn to the objections against ending someone else's life without his consent, whether that someone else be a fetus, a deformed newborn infant, or an irreversibly comatose person.

FOOTNOTES—CHAPTER 6

1. Kutner, op. cit., p. 549.
2. Alexander, op. cit., p. 44.
3. *Time,* July 23, 1973.
4. In a book published in 1920 by Binding and Hoche, *Die Freigabe Der Vernichtung Lebensunwerten Lebens,* the notion of the destruction of life not worth living was exposed. This idea was popular with large segments of the German population. This book is cited by Helen Silving, op. cit., p. 356. Silving also notes that this idea was not new in influential German thought. Martin Luther, when seeing a twelve-year-old boy "who ate as much as four men who work in the fields, and did nothing other than eat and defecate," advised that the boy should be suffocated. When asked why, he replied that he considered the boy to be nothing more than a mass of flesh without a soul. 8 *Tischreden* no. 5207 (Clemen ed.).
5. Quoted by Yale Kamisar, "Euthanasia Legislation: Some Non-Religious Objections," in Downing, op. cit., p. 115.
6. While finding difficulty with the conclusions I allowed in my article "The Freedom to Die," Richard McCormick granted this point. "Maguire's rejection of the necessary connection of X, Y, and Z is theoretically true" ("Notes on Moral Theology," p. 73). But then he goes on to entertain practical doubts. Notice that his words do not so much imply an outright rejection but rather a question: "But practically, is it a realistic account of the many extremely important and delicate questions associated with direct termination of the terminally ill patient? Possibly not."
7. *Life or Death: Ethics and Options,* Edward Shils, Norman St. John-Stevas, Paul Ramsey, P. B. Medawar, Henry K. Beecher, Abraham Kaplan (Seattle and London: University of Washington Press, 1968), p. 139.
8. Ibid., p. 142.
9. Ibid., p. 143. These words are those of the authors of the experiment.
10. It might be countered that the ultimate goal of experimentation is a *good,* namely, better healing power, whereas the only result of death by choice is a *bad,* viz., the ending of a person's life with no consequent good resulting. There are two problems with this rejoinder: first, it presumes that death is in all circumstances a *bad.* This proceeds from a philosophy that cannot find a place for death despite its omnipresence and which, therefore, envisions death only as an enemy. Death can be a good. Secondly, it ignores the fact that the good envisioned in experimentation of the sort we discussed, is vitiated by the sacrifice of individual rights to the goal of medical progress. The yield of such experimentation is a moral

good only if you abstract from the rights of the patient. This is an enormous abstraction.

11. "The Principle of Euthanasia," in Downing, op. cit., p. 30.

12. There is also a kind of tutiorist bias in this objection (from the Latin *tutior*, meaning safer). Tutiorism implies an insistence on the safer and more rigorous course of moral action in spite of the fact that another more liberal position might be solidly probable.

13. Fletcher in *Morals and Medicine*, p. 192, quotes Koch-Preuss, *Handbook of Moral Theology* (St. Louis, 1925), n. 76, to the effect that euthanasia is the destruction of "the temple of God and a violation of the property rights of Jesus Christ."

14. *"Inter cetera autem rationalis creatura excellentiori quodam modo divinae providentiae subiacet, inquantum et ipsa fit providentiae particeps, sibi ipsi et aliis providens"* (*Summa Theologica* I II q. 91, a. 2).

15. "Social Aspects of the Prolongation of Life," 7 (1969), An Occasional Paper of the Russell Sage Foundation, quoted in Morris, op. cit., p. 241.

16. Joannes A. Sancto Thoma, *Cursus Theologicus*. In I, II, *De Donis Spiritus Sancti*, ed. Armand Mathieu and Herve Gagne (Quebec: University of Lavall, 1948), p. 77. See also Thomas Aquinas, *Summa Theologica* II II q. 124, a. 1 and 2.

17. *Summa Theologica* I II q. 94, a. 5. Also in *De Malo*, q. 15, a. 1, ad 8. And similarly, Hosea, too, going to a fornicating wife or an adulterous woman, did not commit adultery or fornication, because he went to a woman who was his by virtue of the command of God, who is the author of the institution of marriage. Thus also because of the authority of God himself, who is above the laws of marriage, that intercourse was not fornication which otherwise would have been fornication . . . See also *Summa Theologica* II II q. 66, a. 5, ad 1.

18. *Summa Theologica* I II q. 94, a. 5, ad 2.

19. See Milhaven, op. cit., on Thomas' realism as opposed to nominalism.

20. *Medical Ethics*, p. 149.

21. Job 7:15.

22. Job 42:16.

23. In Wolstenholme and O'Connor, op. cit., p. 129.

24. Lasagna, op. cit., p. 228.

25. Ibid., p. 229.

26. In Downing, op. cit., p. 37.

27. *The Patient as Person*, p. 149.

28. Morris, op. cit., p. 251, n. 30.

29. New York *Times*, July 3, 1973.

30. "The Duty of Using Artificial Means of Preserving Life," p. 203, n. 1.

31. Silving, op. cit., p. 351, n. 5.

32. Ibid., p. 352, n. 5.

33. Webster's New Twentieth-Century Dictionary, 2d ed. (1964).

34. Quoted in an editorial in *America*, May 2, 1970, p. 463. The words are from St. John-Stevas' Commons speech opposing the euthanasia bill.

35. *On Death and Dying* (New York: Macmillan Co.; London: Collier-Macmillan, 1969; Macmillan Paperback, 1970).

36. Dr. Henry K. Beecher opposes the use of dying persons for experiments even if they are mentally clear and willing. He argues that the person may die during the experiment from causes not related to the experiment. This would cast "an unmerited cloud over the investigator." In *Life or Death: Ethics and Options*, p. 137. Since, however, one does expect the dying to die, I do not think that the death need in any way discredit the investigator if there were true consent.

37. "An Alternative to the Ethic of Euthanasia" in Robert Williams, op. cit., p. 103.

38. Ibid.

39. Some heretical forms of Christianity have been so impressed with the value of death that they courted it and almost insisted on it. There is, however, a strong this-worldly emphasis in Christianity. The "reign of God" is a major part of the "good news." It means that God's promises to the children of this earth are being fulfilled and God asks his people to join with him in the ongoing drama of salvation that is taking place right now on this earth. Thus the accent is on living, not on dying. Still, the tragedy of death is relieved by the express hope of an afterlife.

40. See Heinrich A. Rommen, *The Natural Law* (St. Louis and London: B. Herder Book Co., 1947), p. 29. For some of the implications of Ulpian's thought in the area of sexual morality, see Charles E. Curran, *Catholic Moral Theology in Dialogue* (Notre Dame, Ind.: Fides Publishers, 1972), pp. 197–98.

41. Letter to S. Kercheval, 1816, in *Thomas Jefferson on Democracy*, ed. Saul K. Padover (New York: Mentor Book, New American Library, 1939), p. 67.

42. See Roland H. Bainton, *Christian Attitudes Toward War and Peace* (New York and Nashville: Abingdon Press, 1960), p. 161.

43. "Euthanasia in the Greek Tradition," in *Attitudes Toward Euthanasia*, a publication of the Euthanasia Educational Fund, Inc., New York, p. 5. This pamphlet comprises excerpts of speeches and discussions at the Third Euthanasia Conference of the Euthanasia Educational Fund, held in New York on December 5, 1970.

44. Ibid., p. 6.

45. See *The Right to Die with Dignity*, a publication of the Euthanasia Educational Fund, Inc., New York, 1971, p. 9.

46. *Morals and Medicine*, p. 172.

47. In Wolstenholme and O'Connor, op. cit., p. 222.

48. *American Jurisprudence*, at 585, n. 8.

49. Reported in an Associated Press story by Arthur Everet, the Milwaukee *Journal*, July 23, 1973.

50. Fletcher, *Morals and Medicine*, p. 206.

51. "Legal and Policy Issues" in Brim et al., op. cit., p. 269.

CHAPTER 7

Deciding for Others: The Objections

Ethical infallibility is one of the joys of blissful childhood. In a child's mind, the rights and wrongs are sharply delineated and only the faintest wisps of ambiguity becloud his moral consciousness. We miss this when we are struck by the pains of maturity. And one of the hardest pains of moral maturity is ambiguity. The mind eschews this pain instinctively, and would, if it could, retreat to earlier clarities. Wordsworth could have been speaking of this in his nostalgic recollections of early childhood:

> It is not now as it hath been of yore:
>> Turn wheresoe'er I may,
>>> By night or day,
> The things which I have seen I now can see no more.[1]

Nevertheless, as we have more experience and as we continually confront that experience in reflection, the paradoxical realization dawns on us that as knowledge grows, so too does the sense of ambiguity. Dean Swift reportedly once sat in a square watching a fishmonger prattling and selling through part of an afternoon. As he left the square, he mystified the poor lady by remarking that he wished he were as sure of one thing as she was of everything.

On the other hand, we cannot live or act without some certainties or near-certainties. We get to these certainties from various sources such as principles. This is why people cling to principles, at times indiscriminately, for they bring security, especially at times when ambiguity threatens like a barbarian force at the gates of the mind.[2] There are occasions, however, when ambiguity will not be dispelled. There is what some call "the borderline situation," where moral perception is gray. Speaking of this, Helmut Thielicke says: "The fact is that in the border-line situation we are confronted again and again with that which indeed does not add up. Every decision is inconclusive."[3]

The cases which this chapter considers are often of this sort. We are considering here situations where someone decides for a child or for an unconscious adult that life should be terminated by way of omission or commission. This is immensely more difficult than deciding for one's self. All the factors heretofore discussed take on greater weight when we decide for someone else that he should die. The possibilities of mistaken prognosis or suddenly available cure become more urgent, as does the calculation of the effects on society when people start decreeing death for other people. Indeed, every reality-revealing question may uncover important differences between deciding for self and deciding for another.

The Committee of the Person

Given the special problems involved in deciding on death for another, I shall begin here by availing myself of a suggestion which could easily bypass some of the special hazards of death by the choice for another. Professor Cyril C. Means, Jr., of the New York University Law School, calls our attention to an innovative act of the New York legislature in 1966.[4] A section was added to the Mental Hygiene Law. According to this provision, a person could designate a person (or persons) to be his Committee of the Person in the event that he becomes incompetent. This committee, which would be designated by the person and appointed by the court, would then be in a position to carry out the directions of the principal party as they understand them.

The main part of the amendment reads as follows.

Designation of person to act as committee in case of future incompetence. 1. Every person of the age of eighteen years or upwards and of sound mind may designate in writing a person or persons whom he desires to be appointed as the committee of his person, or as the committee of his property, or both, in the event that he shall be declared an incompetent pursuant to this article.

2. Such designation shall be executed and attested in the same manner in which a will shall be executed and attested.[5]

Professor Means points up the relevance of this for cases within our consideration:

It is quite obvious that medical treatment would be one of the subjects that would come under the jurisdiction of the *Committee of the Person*. I think that the option that is now opened in New York to leave a kind of will-like instrument whereby you can designate your own *Committee of the Person* is very useful because it makes it possible for a person who contemplates that he may be going to become unconscious, to designate someone other than his own next of kin who would normally be resorted to by the Court and the person he designates may very well have views on the course his medical treatment ought to take, more in keeping with the sufferer's own notions, than those of his next of kin.[6]

The New York law gives no indications that it is contemplating death by choice decided upon by the court-appointed Committee of the Person. However, the law is an instrument that could be used in this fashion were such an option legal. With this kind of structure, a person could instruct a person or persons whom he trusts completely concerning his view on death by choice. In so doing, he has the option of bypassing the next of kin so as to spare them the emotional onus of the final decision. This also could ease the problem that might obtain regarding the devolution of property when, for example, husband and wife are both fatally injured in an accident, and the will could be affected depending on who predeceases whom.[7] Matters such as this, and other legal matters related to time of death, could be provided for in the charges given at the time of the constitution of the committee.

The major advantage of the Committee of the Person is that the will of the patient can be known and carried out through the committee which he himself has informed and charged. His attitude on death by choice through omission or commission and his desire to donate organs could all be acted on in exact accordance with his wishes. In this case, the imposition of death would be his and no one else's decision and it would be made not under the stress of terminal illness, but in advance. The New York law also provides that a person may revoke, alter, or cancel his designation at any time. Thus, if someone made this designation at age eighteen, as is provided by the law, he could change it many times as his attitude on his dying and related matters changes.

For this kind of provision, of course, the meaning of "incompetent" would have to be spelled out clearly. The term could, of itself, cover everything from cerebral death to "mental illness." The same provisions regarding death or organ donation would not apply in all these varied states. Someone might prescribe the cessation of all nutriments and supportive measures in the event of irreversible coma. As to the possibility of a supervening mental illness, he might direct that if his condition is one of incurable psychosis, and if the judgment of incurability is sustained over a designated and long period of time, then all extraordinary measures to maintain his physical health should be discontinued and certain rather ordinary measures such as the use of antibiotics and various operations such as appendectomy should not be employed.[8]

Of course, the Committee of the Person idea could not be used for death by choice as long as death by choice remains illegal. Hopefully, however, it is a concept that legislators will employ when they move to reconsider man's natural moral rights over his dying. Until courts and legislators move in this direction, however, what of the objections against deciding for death for someone else?

WHO SHOULD DECIDE?

Objection: Who would dare arrogate to himself the decision to impose death on a child or unconscious person who is not in a position to assent or dissent to the action? What right does any person have to make decisions about life and death in any way that assumes absolute and ultimate authority over another human being? Could a doctor make such a decision? It would seem that he could not. His medical skills are one thing, the moral decision to end a life is another. How would a family feel who learned that a doctor had reached an independent decision to terminate their father's life?

Could the family make such a decision? It would seem not, for several good reasons. There might be a conflict of interest arising from avarice, spite, or impatience with the illness of the patient. And even if these things were not present, the family might be emotionally traumatized when their pain of loss is complicated by the recollection of their decision. Also, the family might constitute a split and therefore a hung jury. Then what?

Could a court-appointed committee of impartial persons make the decision? No, it would seem not. They would not only be impartial but also uninformed about the personal realities of the patient. The decision to terminate life requires a full and intimate knowledge of all the reality-constituting circumstances of the case. Strangers would not have this.

The conclusion, therefore, would seem inescapable that there is no moral way in which death could be imposed on a person who is incapable of consent because of youth or irreversible loss of consciousness.

This objection contains so much truth that my reply to it will contain much agreement as well as disagreement. To begin with, it should be noted that we are discussing not the legality but the morality of terminating life without the consent of the patient. Terminating life by a deliberate act of commission in the kinds of cases here discussed is illegal in this country. By an ongoing fiction of American law it would be classified as murder in the first degree. Terminating by calculated omission is murky at best and perilous at worst under current law. Therefore, it can be presumed that any conclusion we reach here will probably be illegal. This is a morally relevant fact; it is not to be presumed morally decisive, however, since there may be good moral grounds to assume the risk of illegality. As we have stated, morality and legality are not identical.

With this said, then, let us face up to the objection. There are two parts to my response. First, holding the question of *who should decide* in abeyance for the moment, I would suggest that there are cases where, if that difficult question could be satisfactorily answered, it would seem to be a morally good option (among other morally good options) to terminate a life. In other words, there are cases where the termination of a life could be defended as a moral good if the proper authority for making the decision could be located. Of course, if the objections raised against all those who could decide are decisive, then this otherwise morally desirable act would be immoral by reason of improper agency.

There are cases where it would appear to be arguably moral to take the necessary action (or to make the necessary omission) to end a life. Dr. Ruth Russell tells this story:

> I used to annually take a class of senior students in abnormal psychology to visit the hospital ward in a training school for medical defectives. There was a little boy about 4 years old the first time we visited him in the hospital. He was a hydrocephalic with a head so immensely large that he had never been able to raise it off the pillow and he never would. He had a tiny little body with this huge head and it was very difficult to keep him from developing sores. The students asked, "Why do we keep a child like that alive?"
>
> The next year we went back with another class. This year the child's hands had been padded to keep him from hitting his head. Again the students asked, "Why do we do this?" The third year we went back and visited the same child. Now the nurses explained that he had been hitting his head so hard that in spite of the padding he was injuring it severely and they had tied his arms down to the sides of his crib.[9]

What are the defensible moral options in this kind of case? One might be to keep the child alive in the way that was being done. This might show a great reverence for life and re-enforce society's commitment to weak and defective human life. It may indeed be the hallmark of advancing civilization that continuing care would be taken of this child. Termination of this child's life by omission or commission might set us on the slippery slope that has led other societies to the mass murder of physically and mentally defective persons.

All of this is possibly true but it is by no means self-evidently true to the point that other alternatives are apodictically excluded. This case is a singularly drastic one. Given its special qualities, action to end life here is not necessarily going to precipitate the killing of persons in distinguishably different circumstances.

Furthermore, keeping this child alive might exemplify the materialistic error of interpreting the sanctity of life in merely physical terms. This interpretation, of course, is a stark oversimplification. It is just as wrong as the other side of the simplistic coin, which would say that life has no value until it attains a capacity for distinctively personal acts such as intellectual knowledge, love, and imagination. A fetus, while not yet capable of intellectual and other distinctively personal activity, is on a trajectory towards personhood and already shares in the sanctity of human life. (This does not mean that it may never be terminated when other sacred values outweigh its claim to life in a conflict situation.)

The sanctity of life is a generic notion that does not yield a precisely spelled-out code of ethics. Deciding what the sanctity of life requires in conflict situations such as the case of the hydrocephalic child described by Dr. Russell, may lead persons to contradictory judgments. To say that the sanctity of life requires keeping that child alive regardless of his condition and that all other alternatives impeach the perception of life as sacred, is both arrogant and epistemologically unsound. In this case, maintaining this child in this condition might be incompatible with its sacred human dignity. It might not meet the minimal needs of human physical existence. In different terms, the sanctity of death might here take precedence over a physicalist interpretation of the sanctity of life. There is a time when human death befits human life, when nothing is more germane to the person's current needs. This conclusion appears defensible in the case of the hydrocephalic boy.

Also, to keep this child alive to manifest and maintain society's respect for life appears to be an unacceptable reduction of this child to the status of means. Society should be able to admit the value of death in this case and still maintain its respect for life. Our reverence for life should not be dependent on this sort of martyrdom.

The decision, therefore, that it is morally desirable to bring on this boy's death is a defensible conclusion from the facts and prognosis of this case. (We are still holding in abeyance the question of who should make that decision.) There are two courses of action that could flow from that decision. The decision could be made to stop all special medication and treatment and limit care to nourishment, or the decision could be made in the light of all circumstances to take more direct action to induce death.[10]

There is another case, a famous one to which we have already alluded, where the life of a radically deformed child was ended. This is the tragic case of Corinne van de Put, who was a victim of thalidomide, a drug that interfered with the limb buds between the sixth and eighth weeks of pregnancy. Corinne was born on May 22, 1962, with no arms or shoulder structure and with deformed feet. It would not even be possible to fit the child with artificial limbs since there was no shoulder structure, but only cartilage. Some experts said the chances for survival were one in ten and a Dr. Hoet, a professor of pathological embryology at the Catholic University of Louvain, was of the opinion that the child had only a year or two to live. Eight days after the baby was born, the mother, Madame Suzanne van de Put, mixed barbiturates with water and honey in the baby's bottle and thus killed her daughter.

During the trial, Madame van de Put was asked why she had not followed the gynecologist's advice to put the child in a home. "I did not want it," she replied. "Absolutely not. For me, as an egoist, I could have been rid of her. But it wouldn't have given her back her arms." The president of the court pointed out that the child appeared to be mentally normal. "That was only worse," said Madame van de Put. "If she had grown up to realize the state she was in, she would never have forgiven me for letting her live."[11]

Is Madame van de Put's decision to be seen as one of the several morally defensible options available in this case? I think that it is. Again, this does not say that other solutions have no

moral probability. As Norman St. John-Stevas points out in his
discussion of this case, there are individuals who, though terribly
disadvantaged, live fruitful and apparently happy lives. He
speaks of Arthur Kavanagh, who was born in 1831 without limbs.
No mechanical mechanism could be devised to help him. According to St. John-Stevas, however, Kavanagh managed to
achieve some mystifying successes.

> Yet throughout his life he rode and drove, traveled widely, shot
> and fished. From 1868 until 1880 he sat as Member for Carlow
> and spoke in the Commons. In addition, he was a magistrate, a
> grand juror, a poor-law guardian, and he organized a body to de-
> fend the rights of landlords.[12]

St. John-Stevas, however, does admit that "Not everyone can
be an Arthur Kavanagh . . ." Neither could everyone be a Helen
Keller. The problem is that no one knows this when these decisions are made. The option to let the person live and find out
is not necessarily safe. The person may not have the resources
of a Kavanagh or a Keller and may rue both the day of his birth
and the decision to let him live. As Madame van de Put said,
Corinne may "never have forgiven me for letting her live." The
decision to let live is not inherently safe. It may be a decision
for a personal disaster. There are persons living who have found
their lives a horror, who do not think they have the moral freedom to end their lives, and who ardently wish someone had
ended life for them before they reached consciousness. It is
little consolation to these people to be told that they were let
live on the chance that they might have been a Beethoven. The
presumption that the decision to let live will have a happy moral
ending is gratuitous and is not a pat solution to the moral
quandary presented by such cases.

Interestingly, in the Van de Put case, the defense counsel
told the jury that he did not think Madame van de Put's solution was the only one, but that it was not possible to condemn
her for having chosen it.[13] It could have been moral also to
muster all possible resources of imagination and affection and
give Corinne the ability to transcend her considerable impair-
ments and achieve fullness of life. In this very unclear situation,

this could have been a defensible option. It was not, however, one without risks. It could have proved itself wrong.

The decision to end Corinne's life was also arguably moral, though, again, not without risks. It could not be called immoral on the grounds that it is better to live than not to live regardless of the meaning of that life. This is again a physicalist interpretation of the sanctity of life. It also could not be called immoral on the grounds that this kind of killing is likely to spill over and be used against unwanted children, etc., since this case has its own distinguishing characteristics which make it quite exceptional.[14] It could not be called immoral because it is direct killing since, as I have argued, the issue is not directness or indirectness, but whether there is proportionate reason.

In this case, then, as in the case of the hydrocephalic boy, we have a situation where the imposition of death could seem a moral good, prescinding still from the question of who should decide. There could be other cases, too, where death could be seen as a good. Suppose someone suffers severe cerebral damage in an accident but due to continuing brainstem activity can be kept alive almost indefinitely through tubal nourishing and other supportive measures. Would it not seem a clear good if a decision could be made to withdraw support and allow death to have its final say? The spectacle of living with the breathing but depersonalized remains of a loved one, could make death seem a needed blessing. In conclusion, then, there are cases where the imposition of death would seem a good. It was logically indicated to state that conclusion before going to the main thrust of the objection, the question of who could decide when the person in question can give no consent.

THE DOCTOR?

The objection stated that the doctor had no right to decide, and I concur. And, indeed, since the illusory rights of the doctor in this and other matters are so commonly presumed, I would offer further reasons why the decision is not the doctor's except in an utterly unique situation where there is no one else who can decide.

There are, I believe, at least seven reasons why doctors should not have the onus of deciding who should die and who should live. The first reason is that doctors are victims of a bad myth. According to this myth, the doctor in our society wears a mantle of priestliness. He is a sacred figure. This sacral character of the physician is, of course, not without roots in both the nature of the medical enterprise and in the history of professional healing. As we have mentioned, the character of sacredness readily attaches to man's experience of ultimates, such as birth and death. The doctor presides over both of these. Thus, historically, it should not be surprising to find the role of the doctor often intertwined with theurgy, witchcraft, and various forms of religiosity. We remember that Hippocrates was credited with liberating medicine from the constraints of superstitious religion.

Doctors today should bring the same reverence to this part of the Hippocratic revolution that they bring to the Hippocratic oath. For the ties have not all been cut. The high priestly character of the physician shows up in some frivolous but significant ways such as the insistence on the use of titles, which is characteristic of the priestly caste, the reverent courtesies from law-enforcement officers, and in the use of vestments, which, however practical, are richly symbolic. (Professors also sin by priestliness, but their pretensions have been shaken by the revolutions of the sixties.)

In less frivolous ways, the doctor as high priest is a fact of modern hospital life. The doctor's sacred rights and privileges seem paramount in the hospital, to the point where one could sometimes almost wonder whether the good of the doctor or the good of the patient is the primary meaning of the institution. All of this can be said without detracting from the heroic service that many doctors have traditionally given their patients. Indeed, this history of service only serves to enhance and consolidate the sacerdotal status of the physician.

When we come to the question of deciding on death, however, the priestliness asserts itself in an unacceptable way. Consider the unfortunate title of a fine essay by theologian Helmut Thielicke: "The Doctor as Judge of Who Shall Live and Who

Shall Die."[15] The doctor is not the judge on this issue. He is a person skilled in medical technology. His technical advice on the state of a disease and the prospects of its course are indispensable. His counsel on how to achieve death by choice if that is decided upon is also indispensable. His assistance in achieving death, if he agrees, could also be necessary or helpful. But the choice for death is not his. It is a moral choice involving personal, non-medical factors and values over which the doctor has no special competence . . . unless, of course, he is presumed to have some oracular gifts of a preter-scientific nature.

Doctors should recognize that bad myths may have certain gains but are more likely to have greater burdens. If the doctor is thought of in too sacral a way, too much will be expected of him and he shall be asked to bear a weight that is not his by the nature of his profession. He will, for example, hear Glanville Williams, the British jurist, propose this as a law

> It shall be lawful for a physician, after consultation with another physician, to accelerate by any merciful means the death of a patient who is seriously ill, unless it is proved that the act was not done in good faith with the consent of the patient and for the purpose of saving him from severe pain in an illness believed to be of an incurable and fatal character.[16]

Williams, of course, is not giving sovereign powers to the physician. At least, he does not intend to. "Under the present suggestion, no patient would have a right to euthanasia: it would be in the discretion of his doctor to agree or to decline."[17] It is his intention to leave it up to the patient to pick a doctor who is or is not disposed to perform euthanasia. "Some may wish to be satisfied that their physician will never in any circumstances administer euthanasia; others may feel that the knowledge that euthanasia is open to them is a reassurance."[18] Still, the wording of his proposal gives dangerous judicial powers to the doctor, in consultation with, of all things, another doctor. I see in Williams' suggestion a misunderstanding of the doctor's proper role as a practitioner of medical science. If we demythologize the doctor's role, doctors will find themselves relieved of an onerous prestige.

The second reason why doctors should not decide for death is that it may compromise their profession. Dr. Weerts, the gynecologist of Madame van de Put, said at the trial in Liege: "I am a doctor. I cannot kill. I must let live. The day doctors start killing I shall change my profession."[19] There is something true and something excessive in what the doctor said. The physician's role would, I think, be compromised if he were to decide for death. It does not follow, however, that his role would be betrayed if the decision were made by someone else and he assisted in carrying out that decision. The fact that he could not and would not decide, would keep alive the expectation of patients that doctors will persistently apply the art of healing. The goal of medicine would still be healing and preserving life. The physician would adhere to that goal, *except* when a decision has been made by the patient, by the patient's Committee of the Person, or by someone deemed to have moral authority over the patient's dying. If this decision were made when the healing art could do no more, then co-operation in the imposition of a good death would not contradict the art of healing. Again, the decision to co-operate in administering death is the doctor's; the decision for death is not. The fact that doctors never decide for death should be enough to fulfill the expectations of their clientele.

The third reason why doctors should not decide, relates to the current trend toward specialization in the field. A study of the class of 1915 at the University of Buffalo, showed that only 3.8 per cent were full-time specialists six years after graduation. By 1950, however, this percentage had increased to 53.8.[20] This trend is quite general. Thus, among medical school graduates during the first twenty-five years of this century, 47 per cent entered general practice. This declined steadily, so that during the period from 1955 through 1964, only 19 per cent chose this traditional medical career.[21]

The result of this is that the more specialized doctors become, the less qualified they are to attempt to make a decision for death. The old family doctor could at least offer some likely arguments for decision-making power. He was likely to know the family personally as well as medically and to be familiar with many of the other value-problems they might have. His could be more of an integrated view of the case. The specialist brought in for the final illness would not have this view.

The trend toward specialization is being moderated with the current stress on family-centered medical care. Even if this develops, the other arguments against the physician's right to decide for death still hold. But as long as specialization remains a prominent fact of life, this too constitutes an argument against the doctor's right to decide for death.

A fourth argument relates to the trend toward experimentation already discussed. Investigatory medicine has a bias and a deep-seated potential for conflict of interest. The individual patient may easily be seen as a *datum* among *data*. The need to prove something from the special handling of his malady can supersede the patient's good. This can be as dangerous to the individual as it may be promising to the species.[22]

The presence of a strong experimental bias in the medical schools, the possibility for career advancement as a result of experimental achievement, and the preoccupation with research results conspire to disqualify the doctor as judge of who should live and who should die.

Fifthly, some studies indicate that the judgment of doctors on issues such as death by choice do not derive from medical training or expertise, but rather are the product of the philosophical and religious upbringing of the physician. As Dr. Earl R. Babbie writes in his study of the attitudes of medical educators:

> A very religious Catholic physician and a very religious Catholic plumber are both likely to oppose infanticide as immoral. The source of their opposition is to be found in their shared religious perspective, however, not in medicine or in plumbing.[23]

In consigning the decision over death to a physician, therefore, you are actually adopting his particular religious or philosophical bias as determinative of wisdom and morality in this case.

Sixth, as Dr. Louis Lasagna says: "Doctors must deal repeatedly with the most complicated kinds of ethical, life-and-death decision, ranging from abortion to euthanasia, but during their years in medical school there is almost no serious discussion of these matters."[24] I would disagree with Lasagna's implication that these decisions are the doctor's, but I underline his statement that the training of doctors involves "almost no serious discussion of these matters." These are decisions for which doctors are not trained. A survey of twenty-two medical schools in the New York area showed that only two out of the nineteen responding institutions had courses on death and dying.[25]

Aside from the lack of training on the various non-technical aspects of the dying process, doctors seem to display a marked aversion to the fact of death. This would clearly further disqualify them from having the definitive say on death. One observer of the medical scene puts it this way:

> The doctor should know more about dying and death than any other man. The greater part of his life is spent with people who consider death, or its herald, pain, pressing enough to seek the doctor's help. Yet, I am not impressed with either the volume or profundity of medical thought concerning death or dying people. It is as if this one certainty of life were to be avoided not only by vigorous positive thought and action, but also by giving it, as an event, no more attention than one gives to a period at the end of a moving, impressive novel.[26]

Dr. Herman Feifel, who has written much on this subject, submits that some physicians have an aversive reaction to the dying patient because of their own latent fears about dying. He also alludes to the "wounded narcissism of the physician" when he faces a patient whose impending death is a denial of the doctor's essential skills.[27]

The reasons why doctors have an uneasy or even squeamish attitude toward death do not have to be determined here. The point is that neither by training nor by disposition do most doctors have the comfortable attitude toward the human fact of death that would make for good judgment on when death is a friend.

The seventh and final reason why doctors should not decide, derives from the delicate subject of medical incompetence and malpractice. The Judicial Council of the American Medical Association in 1965 made what is a rather extraordinary and alarming observation:

> Medicine has not continued its efforts after the discharge of the licensing function. All too seldom are licensed physicians called to task by boards, societies, or colleagues. The Council would hope that greater emphasis be given to ensuring competence and observance of law and ethics after licensure.[28]

Very few doctors have their licenses revoked each year in the United States, and when they do it is usually not for medical errors, but for abuse of the narcotic license, addiction, alcoholism, income tax evasion, and the like. Could there be so few serious errors, and how would we know? Bernard Shaw has Sir Patrick say in *The Doctor's Dilemma:* "All professions are conspiracies against the laity." The conspiracy charge does seem less than farfetched regarding the cover-up of malpractice. It is a conspiracy of the caste, where brother does not betray brother.[29] The words of Lindsay F. Beaton, Vice Chairman of the Council on Mental Health of the American Medical Association, put it bluntly: "The honest truth is that only the doctor in the medical college or the large hospital (usually university-connected) or the major urban clinic, associated with teaching and research as well as with patient care, can truly be considered modern."[30] Most doctors do not avail themselves of serious continuing education programs. Many learn of new drugs from salesmen for the drug companies. The pharmaceutical industry is making capital out of medicine's failure to provide for continuing education in a field where progress races on. (The term thalidomide comes to mind.) Doctors who are barred from one hospital for some form of malpractice can usually find another hospital. Suggestions that the right to practice should hinge on taking recurrent licensure examinations have fallen on arid soil. (No profession is likely to punish itself with such risky requisites. Only sufficient pressure from without could effect this.) The layman, therefore, must suspect that serious malpractice is not as rare as we would fain think it to be.

This, then, is another reason why doctors should not be

judges in matters of death by choice. It might give them a way of burying their mistakes. If we have no guarantee that they are up-to-date in their own area of competence, if only 25 per cent of practicing physicians take advantage of further medical school courses,[31] then large percentages of doctors are not up-to-date. This gives added reason not to entrust them with responsibilities outside their reputed field of competence.

SHOULD THE NURSE DECIDE?

Sadly enough, this is not even considered a question by most people. In a true way it can be said, show me your questions and I will tell you what you are. If it is never asked whether a nurse should decide, it is because of the presuppositions about what a nurse is. Suppose Glanville Williams' suggested law were to say that a doctor should only accelerate the death of a patient after consultation with a nurse. His proposal would have been looked on as quite absurd. Yet a nurse probably has better qualifications to make this kind of moral decision than a doctor. The nurse enters into the patient's drama not only at the professional medical level, but also in a more personal way. She provides a personal context that the intermittent appearances of the doctor cannot. She can hardly avoid knowing the personal dimensions of the patient's drama of illness. She might also come to know the family problems that affect the dying person. She is, therefore, more equipped for a moral judgment than is the doctor.

There are many sad reasons why she is not even considered a potential judge in matters such as this, or even as a potential member of a committee which might decide the case. The nurse, normally, is a woman, and, myth-wise, that is a problem in our prejudiced cultural environment. She is also associated with those kinds of patient care which are not esteemed in the doctor-heavy atmosphere of the medical profession. She is, further, a victim of non-processual thinking which fails to see that her role should have evolved into something greater as medicine advanced. As a result of all these things, she is looked down upon (much as librarians often are by professors) and her unique capabilities are not realized.

With all of this said, however, the nurse normally should not be the judge of life and death either, for many of the reasons offered above regarding doctors. If in cases of emergency, she or a doctor should have to participate in such a decision, it would be as *persons* who, in a situation of last resort, happen to be the ones best suited to judge the whole moral reality of a patient's need for death. Their strictly professional skills would in that case merely provide the relevant medical data. The judgment for death would be the product of their personhood, not their technical abilities, in situations where emergency makes them equivalently the next of kin.

SHOULD A COMMITTEE OF HOSPITAL ADMINISTRATIVE PERSONS DECIDE?

It might seem attractive to some to have non-medical personnel of a hospital form a committee to decide for death when there are no close relatives to make the decision. This possibility is rife with problems. Barring an extreme emergency, it is a bad idea. They are too far removed from the patient in his personal reality. They might see the patient as an administrative problem, rather than as a person. This is not to imply that administrators are not personalistic but only to acknowledge one possible debit that could affect their perspective. There is, in effect, nothing that particularly qualifies them for making this decisive judgment for a person they do not know.

There is another difficulty that arises in considering this possibility. Some hospitals are affiliated with a particular religion and thus might have a particular religious position on death by choice. This also could disqualify them from making a choice for a patient since it would involve the imposition of one's religious views on another, who cannot consent to them.

If, however, death by choice were made legal, what would be the rights of a patient in a private hospital in this regard? Suppose, for example, it were a Catholic hospital where the administration might be firmly opposed to all positive intervention in the dying process. It would seem that not only should such a hospital not make the decision for death, but it should also not make the decision against it if it has been decided upon by the patient or those qualified to speak for the patient, and if it were legal. A doctor asked to participate in death by choice, has a right to refuse if he considers it immoral. The institution of a hospital is not the same as a person. Private hospitals have to recognize that they appear to have a split personality. While fund-raising or petitioning for new building permits or parking facilities over the objections of local residents, they perhaps wear one face. They would then present themselves as a public service facility which responds to the needs of the community. When, however, it comes to issues which they as a religious group hold to be immoral, they are not public, but quite sectarian.

I would submit that on moral issues where there is what I will call respectable debate, private hospitals in a pluralistic society should allow for all respectably debated issues to be acted on. Let us take abortion as an example of this at the present time in the United States. Though there is no single monolithic Catholic theological position on abortion, the hierarchical magisterium of the Church subscribes to an absolutist position against abortion. In the bishops' directives for Catholic hospitals, this position is taught in no uncertain terms. Should a patient in a Catholic hospital be able to have an abortion if she believes that it is morally indicated, if a doctor is willing to perform it, and if it is legal? Or could the administration ban all abortions because of its religiously grounded objections to all abortions? This question becomes particularly acute when a Catholic hospital is the only medical facility for a community.

The moral correctness of some abortions is widely granted in pluralistic America, even among Catholics. On the other hand, many people feel that abortion is always immoral. This I would describe as an issue of respectable debate. What makes this debate "respectable"? A moral option comes within respectable debate if it is supported by serious reasons which commend themselves to many people, and if it has been endorsed by a number of authorities in the field of ethics, and if it has been approved by reputable religious or other humanitarian bodies.[32] Some kinds of abortion meet all of these requirements and therefore Catholic hospitals serving a morally pluralistic community should allow abortions for the same reason that a hospital run by Jehovah's Witnesses should permit blood transfusions. If a Catholic hospital does not do this, and no other hospital service is reasonably convenient for a patient, then the hospital is effectively imposing a sectarian view on the pluralistic public it serves. (Also, if a hospital only accepts medical personnel who subscribe to its viewpoint on a respectably debated issue, it again may not present itself as serving the needs of a morally pluralistic community.)

Abortion on demand, however, is not an issue of respectable moral debate. The term implies indiscriminate abortion or abortion on whim at any time during the pregnancy. I believe a hospital would be within its rights to appoint a morally pluralistic committee to judge whether a particular abortion comes within the generally accepted rationale for moral abortion or not. Such a committee should, I believe, have a majority of women since women legitimately complain that too often laws and decisions on abortion are made by the inseminators not by the bearers, and that this has a prejudicial effect.

This may seem to some an infringement of the individual's right to moral decision, but I would judge it a reasonable curtailment of freedom to ensure that innocent life is not frivolously destroyed within a medical environment. It also reflects the *de facto* moral climate in which abortion on demand (or indiscriminate abortion) has not won "respectable" support, but certain abortions in conflict situations have. It also helps to forestall the domino objection against allowing any abortions at all.

SHOULD A COURT-APPOINTED COMMITTEE DECIDE?

If by a court-appointed committee is meant a committee of strangers who do this sort of thing on a regular basis, the idea is unacceptable by reason of their distance from the individualized, personal situation. If the committee were a Committee of the Person previously assigned by the patient, this would be ideal. If the committee consisted of members of the family who were given official status by the court, which could then check them out for possible conflict of interest, such a committee could be acceptable. And this brings us to the last question.

Should the Family Decide?

Normally, the family has the most to lose when a loved one dies. They have a primary relationship with the patient; they have intimacy with him, and are most likely to know his mind well enough to interpret what he would want done in these circumstances. I am referring here, of course, to the decision to terminate the life of an adult who is irreversibly unconscious. In the case of a child, the parents would have a natural right to decide. In so saying, I am presuming that there is a strong case for the moral desirability of death in this instance. Given that strong case, the family should decide. This precludes any compromising of the medical profession and also blocks government intervention in this essentially private decision. The persons being decided for in this case are incapable of decision and therefore the best that the supportive human community could do is to interpret and to act as a stand-in for the incompetent person.

Obviously, if the unconsciousness of an adult is not irreversible, the decision remains that of the patient when he regains it. That should not even be a question. If the child, like the hydrocephalic boy we considered, will never have a capacity for consent, his case is like that of the irreversibly comatose. If, however, as in the case of Corinne van de Put, the child will presumably grow to consciousness, the case is more difficult. It is not obvious that the best solution is to let the child grow up and decide for herself, as parents might do regarding a child's choice of religion. Madame van de Put seemed to feel that she did not have the personal resources or any desire to bring the child up with that decision before her. Indeed, although in the abstract it sounds more noble to let people decide for themselves, that decision, in the concrete, might be a simple evasion. It is distinctly possible that the child will grow up and see that it would have been good for the parents to have decided for her, but that the decision, however desirable, is much too difficult to carry out later on. The child might wish that the case had been settled when it was morally more simple and when she was totally dependent on persons who could weigh the competing values with more strength. No answer here is clear. On that point, Madame van de Put would probably be the first to agree.

There is, of course, danger that the family will act out of self-serving motives. The mercy of mercy killing is often for the killing, not the killed. The experience of protracted illness can create a desire for death in those attending the patient before such a desire arises in the patient. For this reason, if this action were to be taken, morality would require that weariness with the patient or avarice or other unworthy motive not be decisive. All other alternatives, such as nursing homes, should be explored before the decision is made. If this kind of death were made legal, provision could be made to make sure that the death is good for the patient and not just for the family. That is good ethics and would be good law.

THE SACRIFICE OF THE PATIENT TO ABSTRACTIONS

An argument against deciding for someone else could be structured in this way: one of the dangers that ethics must always be on guard against is the sacrifice of the concrete to the abstract. Camus, in stating that he valued his mother before justice, was the master ethicist, for his mother was concrete, and justice is abstract, a plaything of the mind. In the name of abstractions, such as national interest, freedom, democracy, revolution, and communism, persons are slain every day. And consciences, seduced by abstractions, stand mute at the slaughter. The same thing could happen in medicine. A patient could be dispatched in the name of the unspecified (and therefore unconcretized) needs of other patients, in the name of unclarified notions of compassion, or right reason, or progress, or something as abstract as "the new morality." All of these terms are perilously abstract. None of them are flesh that can be met and cared for and touched. They are, therefore, never to be preferred to that about which we can be really clear, the actual embodied person.

I pose this objection not to brush it aside, but to see it as a danger of which we must be reminded. It is not such a danger that it forecloses all moral options regarding the administration of death. The danger can be met, but only if it is acknowledged. The weakness of the objection, however, is that it is a two-way street. A person can also be kept alive in obedience to abstractions that do not encompass that person's good. Taboo and untested assumptions about God's will are for many completely determinative of morality in these difficult cases. It may be attention to the concrete that shows the value of imposing death. When a cerebrally dead "person" is kept alive without reason for a long period after all hope is gone, abstractions may be presumed to be taking precedence over the meaning of the concrete facts.

FAILURES IN PROGNOSIS

A four-year-old boy had a cardiac arrest while in surgery. After returning to intensive care the child remained unresponsive. Each day there was increased evidence of cerebral irritation, which progressed until the physicians involved were certain that there was "no possibility of his being anything other than a vegetable." It was their decision that only "supportive means" were to be continued. The mother remained with the child almost constantly. There was no improvement that anyone could document for a period of over three weeks, with the exception of one time that the mother thought there may have been a slight movement of his one eye as she called his name. When reported, this was considered to be a reflex response, or "mother's imagination." However, a few days later a movement of his one little finger was noted. Each day after that there were additional responses. Six months later the only apparent residual was a slight limp. Speech had been regained, alertness and awareness restored, and no apparent mental regression.

A seven-year-old girl was admitted with apparent encephalitis. For nearly four months there was no response, after that only fleeting moments of recognition. The parents were encouraged to consider nursing home arrangements, to realize that the girl was "near vegetable status," to forget the child and return to "a normal family life." The parents, however, continued confident that their child would recover. They decided to keep the child at home after discharge in spite of recommendations to do otherwise. Two months passed and the girl was still being maintained on feedings via a gastric tube and showed no increase of responsiveness beyond sporadic moments. One evening as the family was gathered around her bed she recognized her brothers and sisters and home environment. Within a week she was eating and speaking, and four months from that date she resumed classes and school activities.

A twenty-nine-year-old man, father of five, was admitted with a diagnosis of confusion and dizziness. Within twenty-four hours he was comatose, convulsing, with a temperature of 105. The diagnosis of encephalitis was made and all measures to control symptoms and treat the condition were instituted. Within two days his temperature returned to normal but he continued to convulse and remained unresponsive to any stimuli. After five days with no improvement the physician decided that "medically, there was nothing left to do . . . No need to provide extra nursing coverage, he'll probably die in a day or two." That directive was countered, however, by the nursing personnel, at which time they arranged nursing coverage to provide the specialized care he needed. They also requested that the physician provide an order for fluid maintenance. The man did recover after two weeks, was discharged in one month, and did return to his former employment and family with no apparent residual effects.

Each of these cases is an actual case described for me by members of the medical teams involved. Each occurred in a large modern hospital located in a metropolitan center of the United States. Each of them is a stern reminder of the fallibility of medical judgment and the need for reverence in the face of the mysterious recuperative powers of our physical nature. These cases could also be presented as an objection to deciding for another. This, however, would, I think, be an attempt to prove too much. From the fact that mistakes are often made in diagnosis and prognosis, the conclusion should be that ever greater care should be taken to prevent such things. The conclusion is not that when massive evidence which has been corroborated in various ways indicates that there is an irreversible loss of consciousness, we must always stand by passively awaiting a miraculous course of events. Prognosis, though fallible, can achieve very firm certainties in many cases.

KILLING THE SENILE

Senile dementia is a brain disease of aged persons in which there is a progressive impairment or loss of intellectual functions. This problem is coming more to the fore as more people survive into old age. The problems of senility are considerable. Take the case of a person who is "completely senile." He no longer recognizes anyone, and because of loss of control of urine and feces, he has to be treated like a child. He may indeed be much more difficult to care for than a child since he may have greater strength and habitual patterns of movement which make him hard to constrain. Should he not be considered on a par with the irreversibly comatose patient since he is beyond consent and death would be a blessing for him? Would he not then be a good candidate for death by omission or commission with the decision made by those nearest to him?

I would judge that this does not appear to be a moral option. This case is quite different from the case of the irreversibly comatose patient and different moral judgments seem indicated. First of all, the condition of the senile person is not coma. He is, rather, like a child, capable of gratitude, simple pleasure, and affection. There is a distinguishable personal consciousness here, however drastically impaired. Furthermore, this condition is somewhat susceptible to remission and there can be more or less lucid moments with many of these persons. Senility has varied causes, but neglect and loss of appropriate stimulation are sometimes aggravating factors if not causes, and this can be corrected. For all these reasons, at the level of *what* we are talking about, the senile person is not to be equated with either the comatose or the hydrocephalic child we discussed.

Secondly, the effects of killing senile persons by positive and direct means seem too harmful to be justified by any competing value. Senility is a gradual disease, one in which a person could sense that he is slipping into. It is not difficult to imagine the kind of panic it could add to the problems of the aged if they sensed that they were by this fact becoming eligible for extinction through a decision in which they have no part. Psychologically, I think the domino theory could have legitimate critical application in this instance. The effects on society of terminating non-consenting persons who are, to all appearances, enjoying a kind of twilight consciousness of a still personal sort, are too formidable.

Also, if the care of such persons becomes too much for those relatives who have charge of them, alternatives can be thought of. Government assistance should focus on these cases and good nursing homes where these persons can be given a lot of attention and care should be available. Needless to say, putting such persons into a home where they will be left to sit or mill with little care or attention would be more immoral than terminating their lives directly.

In these cases, the moral distinction between omission and commission can be seen. If it becomes clear that the senile state is progressive and irreversible, the decision could be morally made to suspend treatments that would cure such maladies as pneumonia or diabetes. In these cases, the persons should be made as comfortable as possible and, after assessing all of the circumstances, it might be judged moral to let the disease take its course.

If senile dementia reaches the point where the person is reduced to vegetable status, it would then seem that the situation is equivalent to other cases involving irretrievable loss of consciousness. In such cases, even the twilight of senile personal consciousness would have turned into darkness, and direct or indirect means to end such a life would be arguably moral.

There is another possibility in these cases, however. If a person has a Committee of the Person, he might instruct them while still of sound mind and body that direct means should be used to terminate his life if he passes into a state of senile dementia which blots out his ability to recognize friends or relatives and which appears clearly to be an irreversible and progressive condition. The deleterious effects that could easily follow from decisions to end the lives of others in this condition would not seem likely to ensue if the person has decided on this for himself.

FOOTNOTES–CHAPTER 7

1. William Wordsworth, *Ode: Intimations of Immortality* from *Recollections of Early Childhood*. Unfortunately, early moral consciousness was not Wordsworth's preoccupation in this ode.

2. Throughout these pages, I have attempted to stress the two sides of principles, their generalizable wisdom content and their limits. An ethician should, I believe, be equally at home with both these aspects of principles. The exceptional case which seems to contradict the principle should not be seen as an interloper seeking naturalization in the land of ethics. Excessive confidence in principles, and excessive defensiveness, in the face of cases to which they do not apply, reveal an attitude of untenable faith in the power of generalization.

3. "The Doctor as Judge of Who Shall Live and Who Shall Die," in Vaux, op. cit., p. 172.

4. See *Dilemmas of Euthanasia*, a pamphlet containing excerpts, papers, and discussions from the Fourth Euthanasia Conference, held in New York on December 4, 1971; this is a publication of the Euthanasia Educational Council, Inc., New York, pp. 11–12.

5. *Laws of New York*, 1966, Chapter 244, Section 1, #101-a.

6. *Dilemmas of Euthanasia*, p. 11.

7. "The time or order of deaths also may have important substantive effects upon the devolution of property. It may be quite important to know when close relatives such as husband and wife die. If both husband and wife are fatally injured in the same accident and the husband dies first, the wife would usually inherit his property for the short time before her own death, and such property would ultimately pass to her relatives or to persons entitled under her will. If the wife dies first, here property will usually descend, through the counterpart process, to the husband's side of the family. The order in which the parents die may determine whether the bulk of the estate is subjected to death taxes once or twice (usually with some credit for property previously taxed)." Lasagna, op. cit., pp. 227–28.

8. As I mentioned in the discussion of ordinary and extraordinary means in

Chapter 5, means can be considered extraordinary if they do not imply a reasonable hope of a return to health. In the case of incurable mental illness (and that is a matter for clinical determination), means such as antibiotics and normal surgery could be seen as not giving hope of a return to personal health. This, obviously, expands the notion of health since a deeply psychotic person could have excellent physical health.

9. *Dilemmas of Euthanasia,* p. 35.

10. Moralists have traditionally spoken of moral opinions as being probable, more probable, or most probable. In this case, I would see the inducement of death, in whatever fashion, as most suitable in the concrete circumstances and as being more probably moral than the decision to let the child go on living. This judgment would be based on those facts reported by Dr. Russell. This, of course, is a *prima facie* judgment which could be overturned by factors not revealed by Dr. Russell. This proviso must be entered in all cases where the full moral object has not been presented. Even the *prima facie* judgment has usefulness in an argument as long as its limits are acknowledged.

11. For an account of this case and a negative judgment on Madame van de Put's action, see Norman St. John-Stevas, *The Right to Life* (New York, Chicago, San Francisco: Holt, Rinehart & Winston, 1964), pp. 3–24.

12. Ibid., p. 16.

13. Ibid., pp. 7–8.

14. See our discussion of the domino theory in Chapter 6.

15. Vaux, op. cit., pp. 146–86.

16. Williams, op. cit., p. 345.

17. Ibid., p. 346.

18. Ibid.

19. Quoted in St. John-Stevas, op. cit., p. 6.

20. Milton Terris and Mary Monk, "Changes in Physicians' Careers: Relation of Time After Graduation to Specialization," in Jaco, *Patients, Physicians and Illness,* p. 363, quoted in Babbie, op. cit., p. 4.

21. Aura E. Severinghaus, "Distribution of Graduates of Medical Schools in the United States and Canada According to Specialities, 1900 to 1964," *Journal of Medical Education* 40, no. 8 (August 1965): 733, quoted in Babbie, op. cit., p. 4.

22. On some aspects of this question, see Paul Ramsey, "The Ethics of a Cottage Industry in an Age of Community and Research Medicine," *New England Journal of Medicine* 284 (April 1, 1971): 700–6.

23. Babbie, op. cit., p. 169.

24. Lasagna, op. cit., p. 23.

25. *Attitudes Toward Euthanasia,* p. 21.

26. August M. Kasper, "The Doctor and Death," in Feifel, op. cit., p. 261.

27. "Attitudes Toward Death," in Feifel, op. cit., p. 122.

28. Quoted in Lasagna, op. cit., p. 60.

29. The small number of women doctors in this country makes the term "brother" quite literally descriptive in the profession. Another argument could be constructed against the life/death decision-making authority of doctors based on the distorting effect of segregating women out of the councils of medicine. This is bound to be an influence on "the mind of the medical profession," since the bisexual nature of the race has psychological and cognitive significance too, especially in the area of morals. An ethicist, however, should be slow to level charges here since his colleagues in professional ethics also constitute a very closed male club.

30. Quoted in Lasagna, op. cit., p. 63.

31. Reported by Lasagna, op. cit., p. 64.

32. Students of moral theology will recognize here the influence of the principle of probabilism. Of probabilism, Henry Davis, S.J., writes: "In its ultimate

analysis, Probabilism is common sense; it is a system used in practical doubt by the majority of mankind. People rightly say: I am not going to debate all day before acting in doubtful matters; there must be some very obvious way of making up my mind. At all events, if I cannot make up my mind for myself, I will act as some good people act, though many other good people might disapprove. That practical solution of doubt is common sense, and it is Probabilism." *Moral and Pastoral Theology*, Vol. I, p. 93. Probabilism recognized moral ambiguity and allowed the individual to take any side of what I call a respectable debate. It became the predominant viewpoint in Catholicism. Alexander VIII condemned in 1690 what is known as absolute tutiorism, which held that you could not follow an opinion that was probable because of the authorities who supported it or because of its own apparent merits. Tutiorism insisted on the most rigorous position in any doubtful discussion. What I am suggesting to Catholic hospitals is that they are practicing absolute tutiorism if they do not recognize the probability of conflicting views on abortion, sterilization, and other debated issues within the Catholic and greater community.

CHAPTER 8

From Abortion to War:
The Gamut of Legal Killing

The law of the land—any land—always allows for many forms of death by choice. No society functions without the recognition that life may be terminated for good reasons. Usually the laws mirror the mores of the populace in this regard, though at times they run ahead, and at times they lag behind. The kinds of killing indulged by American law provide a specimen of some traditional and some not so traditional attitudes toward acceptable killing.

Americans are permitted by law to terminate life in four kinds of situations: abortion (because of the Supreme Court decision of January 22, 1973); capital punishment (though the Supreme Court struck down the death penalty laws of thirty-nine states in *Furman* v. *Georgia,* nineteen states, not yet ready to fire the hangman, have restored the penalty); war (declared and undeclared); and, in some jurisdictions, suicide. What this indicates is that in some cases, such as war and abortion (if one follows the Court in discounting the claims of the fetus in the first six months of its uterine life), man's moral dominion over death has been exaggerated. In other cases, such as death by choice in a medical context, moral dominion is minimized. Particularly in war, the tolerance for killing is virtually unlimited. Long and destructive wars can be waged by this country without the usual constitutional formalities such as declaration by the Congress. The rights of a President to wage war have swollen malignantly. Dubious precedents are adduced to justify military crusades without giving the people a real chance to judge.

The worm, however, is turning. The Indochina war showed that it had become necessary to hide the facts of war from the people and the Congress in order to wage it. Protest from within and without the armed forces and from non-involved nations reached an historic high point in this debacle of a war. Demonic abstractions such as national security and containment of communism have been exposed to cleansing light. World conditions generally are also serving to alter the popular esteem for war as policy. The need for natural resources has made former enemies friends of necessity. Commonly perceived threats to the environment have also helped to dispossess us of a lot of long-tenured devils. Kill-power is yielding to the neglected art of diplomacy as warriors ungird and sit down to study peace. The mores, in a word, are less tolerant of war now than are the legal structures.

Also not reflected in the law is a major shift in attitude on the subject of mercy killing. In a Gallup Poll the change of opinion since 1950 is remarkable. The question asked both in 1950 and in 1973 was:

> When a person has a disease that cannot be cured, do you think doctors should be allowed by law to end the patient's life by some painless means if the patient and his family request it?

In 1950, only 36 per cent said yes to this question. In 1973, 53 per cent replied in the affirmative. The breakdown of statistics also is striking. Among adults under thirty years of age, the approval figure is 67 per cent. Noteworthy too is the fact that only 46 per cent of the Catholics interviewed said they disapproved; 48 per cent approved and 6 per cent were unsure, meaning that not even a majority of Catholics voiced disapprobation of mercy killing. It is worth saying, too, that the poll was not taken without a context. Two stories were being highly publicized at this time, that of Dr. Montemarano, who was charged with giving a fatal injection to a patient, and that of a young man who shot his brother who had been paralyzed in a motorcycle accident and who had pleaded for death.

Thus there are shifts occurring in general moral outlook on killing. Inasmuch as those shifts reflect a recognition that we have overestimated our moral right to kill in a military setting and underestimated it in some medical and private situations, I believe the shifts are in the right ethical direction. In this chapter, I propose to look at the four classes of legal killing and bring the theory of this book to bear on them in a necessarily brief but specific way. First, to

ABORTION

The moral discussion of abortion is plagued by the wrong questions. Though the wrong questions might accidentally lead to some right answers, they are more likely to befoul discussion. This has happened in the abortion debate. The first potentially bad question is, "Is the fetus a person?" The question is pernicious if it implies that if the fetus is not a person, it has no claims to reverence. Not only fetuses are threatened by the presupposition of this question; infants are too. For if personhood and the distinctive affective, imaginative, and intellectual activities thereof are the foundation of respect for fetal and infant life, fetuses and infants are in trouble.

Joseph Fletcher has written a somewhat unfortunate article entitled "Indicators of Humanhood: A Tentative Profile of Man."[1] I say "somewhat" unfortunate because the attempt to delineate personal human qualities is an attempt to explain the *what* and that is always a gainful ethical endeavor. I say "unfortunate" because there are threatening implications in the air when Fletcher says that "mere biological life . . . is without personal status."[2] That is potentially dangerous language because it implies too strongly that fetuses and comatose persons lacking humanhood in Fletcher's sense of the term, lack a claim to life or are reduced to merely animal or object status.

Fletcher equates "humanhood" and personhood. He lists the positive qualities that are the marks of personal being. They are: minimal intelligence (anyone below the IQ mark of forty is probably not a person), self-awareness, self-control, a sense of time, of futurity, and of the past; concern for others, communication, control of existence, curiosity, changeability and creativity, a balance of rationality and feeling, distinctiveness, and neocortical functioning.[3]

Applying these criteria of personhood to the fetus, it is clear that the fetus is not a person. But what conclusion would be drawn from that? Is it mere tissue or a negligible maternal growth? Could it be plucked like a flower for little or no reason? Is the question of personhood, in other words, ethically decisive? The question "Is the fetus a person?" sometimes implies this. It is then a bad question.

By way of correction, I would say that the fetus is not a person, but that does not answer the question about whether it is moral to abort it. The conceptus from the very beginning is a human reality. From the first moment of its existence it is in a process toward personhood. And from that first moment, too, it is a miracle (a term that can be used religiously or non-religiously) deserving of an awe-filled reverence. In a situation of value conflict, there may be proportionate reason to terminate fetal life, but not because this fetal life is valueless or worthless. Rather, it is valuable but not so absolutely valuable that no other value could ever outweigh it in the unavoidable and sometimes tragic calculus of ethics. But in this calculus, the determinative issue is not personhood or non-personhood. Neither should this calculus proceed under the assumption that the sanctity of life does not extend to the marvelous subtle beginnings of the human personal drama.

The question "Is the fetus human?" can be a bad question too. First of all, it can mean the same thing as the person question and be rife with the same objectionable implications. Otherwise the answer to this question is yes. The fetus, from its beginnings, is a human development, a human being. This is important in knowing *what* we are talking about. Again, however, this does not substitute for the moral analysis that must search among the competing values and disvalues and then issue forth in a moral judgment that hopefully yields more value than disvalue. Knowing that we are dealing with a human being which is on a trajectory to personhood, gives our considerations great seriousness. In any moral analysis that may lead to an abortion, conscience must recognize that one of the values striving not to be negated is an incipient human life. In the final decision, it may have to be negated, but not until its claim has been

sensitively heard could this negation have the possibility of
being moral.

WHAT DIFFERENCE DOES THE TIME MAKE?

This bad question appears in arguments that say that it does
not make a difference. If abortion is wrong, it is wrong at any
time. What difference does it make if the fetus is two, ten, or
twenty-two weeks old?

It does make a difference, a real difference that indicates cor-
respondingly real differences in the potential moral meaning
of the act. The expulsion of a minute conceptus before im-
plantation in the uterus is one thing. The removal of a fetus
old enough to cry is another. Anyone who heard the cry would
know the difference. In terms of the moral object, the *when*
here is significant. There are differences, too, at the level of the
what, the alternatives, and the effects.

At the level of *what*, it is clear that the age of the fetus makes
a critical difference. A newly fertilized ovum is a microscopic
speck. Of course, it already contains its own genetic code and
thus has its genetic individuality and its own innate potentiality.
Nevertheless, it is at this point largely potentiality. It has not
yet been able to interact with its environment and become more
of what it can be. When, by around the fortieth day, it has developed the basic structure of a typically human cerebral cortex,
it obviously *is* something significantly more. And when it has
developed all of its organs and systems and is near viability,
(the ability to live outside the womb), it is something else again.
At a certain point in a pregnancy, abortion becomes very like
infanticide. And that is a difference.

The difference in the reality to be judged can also be revealed
by reference to the new alternatives that emerge as the process
unfolds. The closer a fetus gets to viability, the more alternatives
there are to abortion. If the abortion is contemplated because
of the mother's poor health, which is judged to be threatened
by the pregnancy, the further the mother has gone in the pregnancy the greater the possibility there *may* be that she could
be brought to term. If abortion was desired because the child

was conceived through rape, and the experience of the pregnancy is traumatizing the mother, alternatives may begin to emerge as the pregnancy advances. With counseling and support, the mother might be helped to bring the child to the point where it could be born and offered for adoption. And so it is with otherwise motivated abortion prospects.

Also the effects of an early or late abortion on the mother, on society, on those who assist could all be different. It has been truly said that there is no more defenseless form of human life than a fetus. The experience of removing a somewhat developed fetus which has come a long way in its struggle to look like and to be one of us, and which is painfully eloquent in its manifest helplessness, can be a morally traumatizing experience. The potential effects of this experience may argue strongly against effecting it.

Indeed, the question might be, what could justify the destruction of fetal life? The answer to this shows again that the age of the fetus makes a critical difference. We have seen that the principle of proportionality is a master rubric of ethical calculation in conflict situations. It applies very directly here. Because of the growth in the reality and potentiality of the fetus, because of the gradual emergence of alternatives to abortion, and because of the mounting debits in the area of effects, a proportionately greater reason for abortion is needed with each passing day of the fetus' life. As the fetus nears viability, it becomes virtually impossible (though not absolutely impossible) to imagine a reason that could justify extinguishing its life.[4]

In summary, then, the ethical consideration of abortion must be prejudiced in favor of the fetus. He is mute, and the other competing values are loud and articulate. They also might, at times, have a better claim, but his case must be pleaded forcefully in each contest of values with the recognition that his case grows stronger each day. The unborn sends a message to the born to strain their imagination in any conflict situation to find a way for his life, which is silently and ingeniously pressing on, to be welcomed by us into the extrauterine world.

CAPITAL PUNISHMENT

Capital punishment is, in a way, a species of killing the incurable. A judgment is made that the person who has committed certain kinds of crimes is, morally, a terminal case and so he is killed. Of course, no supporter of capital punishment explains it in this way. A variety of other explanations are offered—self-defense on the part of society, deterrence of crime, redressing injustice, etc.—but none of these make any sense, as we shall see. They need not make sense, however, since capital punishment has needed little defense. Throughout the years, it has enjoyed enthusiastic popular support or, at the least, an imperturbable tolerance. It has also been spared acute and persistent moral criticism. The question of why capital punishment has been so well received is an intriguing one. Yet the fact remains that only war has won greater popularity.

In recent years, the zest for capital punishment has receded. Executions are no longer festive public events. This development, however, is shockingly recent. For example, it was not until 1868 that executions ceased being public in England.[5] A. Alvarez, the author of *The Savage God*, feels that capital punishment, on the European scene, was a surrogate for the gladiatorial games.

> In Christian Europe, executions replaced the Roman circuses. Criminals were beheaded publicly; they were hanged, their intestines drawn out and their bodies quartered; they were guillotined and elaborately tortured in front of festive crowds; their severed heads were exposed on pikes, their bodies hung in chains from gibbets . . . The execution was like a fun fair, and for the more spectacular occasions even apprentices got the day off.[6]

No strained arguments about deterrence will account for the long and wide acceptance of penal killing. The roots are deeper than logic and are traceable to our primitive past.

Capital punishment can, I submit, be easily shown to be incompatible with minimal respect for life and consequently immoral. In support of that contention, I would offer these arguments:

1. Capital punishment is suspect in its origins. Nicolas Berdyaev, the Russian philosopher, writes: "Capital punishment is rooted in the ancient instinct of blood vengeance and human sacrifice, though it has assumed a civilized and legal form."[7] He sees it as blood-vengeance transferred to the state, and he suggests that "Vengeance is the chief moral emotion of ancient humanity."[8] Primitive tribes often believed that only by the shedding of blood could the debt incurred by certain crimes be satisfied. This was the meaning of the Jewish *go'el* or the *tar* of the Arabs. The rule was simply this: "The blood of a kinsman must be avenged by the death of the one who shed it, or, failing him, by the blood of one of his family."[9] "An eye for an eye and a tooth for a tooth" was a lived-out maxim for a good number of our barbaric ancestors. In some societies this notion was heavy with superstitious content, so that the spirit of a dead man who died violently would roam tortured and discontented until the blood of his assailant was shed. This primitive notion was purely vindictive punishment which had no interest in correcting or redeeming the malefactor. He was, rather, to be obliterated.[10]

The history of warfare also shows some of these barbaric elements of pure vindictiveness. The Roman assault on Carthage was one example of this, as was the practice of *herem* of the ancient Hebrews. The application of *herem* is described in the Book of Deuteronomy:

> . . . you must kill all the inhabitants of that town without giving any quarter; you must lay it under ban, the town and all it contains. You must gather all the wealth of it in the public square, and set fire to the town and all its goods, offering it all to Yahweh your God. It shall be a ruin for all time, never to be built again.[11]

This kind of genocidal war was mitigated by the thinking that eventually became enshrined in the just war theory. It became recognized that war should redress wrongs without going to the extent of annihilation. This represented a limitation of force and a move away from the barbaric thirst for the complete obliteration of the enemy.

Capital punishment represents a perdurance of the primitive lust for liquidating the malfeasant or enemy. It is untainted with the more civilized notions of constraining the criminal or even converting him. On this count alone it is worthy of moral reprobation. But there are other arguments against it.

2. Capital punishment does not work. The story is told that at one point in British history, pickpocketing became such an epidemic that public execution of pickpockets was decided upon as a deterrence. This certainly would seem likely to have a chastening effect on those who were disposed to indulge in this kind of thievery. As it turned out, the hangings were immensely popular and everyone including the still thriving pickpockets attended. What ensued, however, was that this best layed plan went astray. Consumed with interest in the event, people were inclined to be more than usually careless about their pockets. As a result, few pockets went unpicked. Even in the presence of the gallows, the temptation was too great for the malintentioned deft of hand. The deterrent did not deter.

As one study of the effectiveness of the death penalty puts it:

> Whether the death penalty is used or not, and whether executions are frequent or not, both death-penalty states and abolition states show rates which suggest that these rates are conditioned by other factors than the death penalty.[12]

Murder is often the result of fright or other passion. It usually is not accompanied by a cool estimate of the possible consequences. Also, it is done by those who have no intention of being caught and having to put up with the legal consequences. Small wonder that Justices Brennan and Marshall pointed out on the occasion of *Furman* v. *Georgia* that capital punishment is unnecessary for the protection of the public.

Most people assume that the deterrence argument is a solid argument for penal killing. It is not. Yet even if the deterrent deterred, there are moral problems with using this means to that good end. There is, first of all, the obvious problem of killing someone to impress others. This seems an unacceptable, ex-

ploitative reduction of a person to the level of means. Furthermore, to use such a drastic deterrent without using other
potentially more effective deterrents is likewise a grave moral
defect. If nothing deterred like execution, that would be one
thing. But if better deterrents are neglected, executions become
all the more gross in their immorality. More and more efficient
courts of justice, prison reform, firm jail sentences for certain
heinous crimes performed without extenuating circumstances,
better anti-poverty programs, greater attention to health, education, and welfare in lower income areas, etc., are all more
likely to prevent serious crimes than the killing of guilty prisoners. The neglect of alternatives is a neglect of reality, and
that is bad sense and bad ethics.

3. Capital punishment is not a form of self-defense. It is sometimes alleged that the death penalty is society's way of defending itself from aggressors. What the death penalty compares to,
however, is not self-defense, but the shooting of prisoners. The
condemned man was presumably an aggressor against some part
of society. At the moment of his execution he is an unarmed
prisoner. Killing unarmed and unresisting prisoners is immoral.
Even killing in self-defense is immoral if there are alternative
modes of defense available.

4. Capital punishment is unevenly used. In recent years in
the United States, only about one out of ten men convicted of
capital murder was sentenced to die, leading Justice Stewart to
conclude that the death penalty is "wantonly" and "freakishly"
imposed."[13]

5. Capital punishment presumes the infallibility of juries and
judges. It leaves no room for correction of a miscarriage of
justice. The fallibility of judges and juries, however, is a scream-
ing fact of history. Juries, at best, provide a cross section of the
wisdom, foibles, myths, and prejudices of a society. No matter
how sequestered, they are impressed with public expectations.
They can be duped and befuddled by the double-talk of the
law. They can be overly generous or blindly cruel. And if they
err, the error, in the case of execution, is incorrigible.

6. Those condemned to capital punishment have not lost
their right to life. Whatever they did, even if it was murder, does

not take away the right of the murderer to life after his apprehension. It does take away his right to freedom and maybe
quite a few other rights. But it is simply gratuitous and un-
meaningful to say that he has lost his right to live. Here again,
the primitive origins of this custom assert themselves. The ancient practice of blood vengeance is back, bedecked in the language of rights. An assailant bent on murder may be said to
have lost his right to live if there is nothing short of his death
that can prevent his murderous action. An incarcerated prisoner
is not a threat and therefore has a moral right to life.

7. Capital punishment is immoral in the light of its effects.
The direct experience of capital punishment is demoralizing. A
prison chaplain with much experience wrote:

> An execution is a moral shock of such a nature that it is impos-
> sible to say what may be its ultimate effects on mind and body.
> . . . No one can leave the slaughter-shed without a deep sense of
> humiliation, horror and shame.[14]

When an execution occurs, it is not just the immediate execu-
tioner who kills; society kills. The hangman is our legate. There
is a collective character to criminal justice. Perhaps this justice
would be abandoned if the people actually had to do the killing
as in olden times. In ancient Israel, for example, the condemned
person was taken out of the town. The witnesses for the
prosecution cast the first stones and then all the people joined
in the stoning until death occurred. As Professor Roland de
Vaux puts it, "The collective character of communal justice was
thus expressed to the end."[15] A society that kills its prisoners
can only be brutalized by the practice.

8. Capital punishment bespeaks an absolute and demonic
conception of the state. This is an argument which is pressed
vigorously by Nicolas Berdyaev. He finds Western, non-
Russian societies uncivilized in their tolerance of capital punishment.

> Tolstoy . . . was shocked by capital punishment, as were Do-
> stoyevsky, Turgeniev and Soloviev and as all the best Russians
> were. The Western peoples are not shocked, and capital punish-
> ment arouses no doubts in their minds; they even see in it the

outcome of social instinct. We, on the other hand, have not been so socialized, thank God![16]

He sees this institution as a concession to "the supremacy of the State, to its absolutism, to its encroachment upon the spiritual freedom of man, to its will to power."[17] To the West, this may be acceptable but it is not "the Russian idea." "To us it is man who is the important thing; to them it is society, civilization."[18]

Whatever may be the facts of the Russian purity of soul in this regard, I believe Berdyaev is making a realistic criticism. If the state undertakes to kill persons in its custody when those persons have ceased to be a threat to society, the state is acting as if it had an absolute dominion over life. It is presuming that it could sacrifice one man's life to influence the behavior of other men. In essence, this action is arbitrary, despotic, and replete with pretension to a false sovereignty.

9. Finally, capital punishment should be repugnant to such influential religions as Christianity. It is amazing to see the support that reputed Christians have so glibly given to this institution when they should have seen it as thoroughly inimical to their faith. Christians hope to convert the sinner, not kill him. That alone should have made them suspicious of penal death. It repudiates the Christian hope for moral resurrection.

Christian and other religious and non-religious persons should also have sensed the idolatrous character of capital punishment. The act assumes a kind of divine authority. As sociologist Peter Berger says, the act of execution "takes on the quality of divine intervention."

> It is in this fog of sanctified delusion that hangmen will shake the hand of their victim to the last moment of the atrocity, that officials presiding over all this will afterward shake their heads and say, "I hated to do it!"—and that there will even be people who sympathize with them.[19]

In other words no paltry human emotions are involved here. The state's hangman is rather a man on a mission of the Lord. This is not an act of primitive barbarism, vengefulness, or retaliation. It is an act of God. It is "playing God" in the most

objectionable sense. This hypocrisy, too, should have turned
religious and non-religious folk away from what Berger aptly
calls an atrocity.

WAR

War is an enterprise which seeks to resolve conflict of interest
by violence. It is a form of death by choice which decides to
kill those who do not wish to be killed. It is generally accepted
that war can at times be justified. There are few absolute
pacifists. The problem is that we are so habituated to wars and
rumors of wars, that we have justified war too facilely. We have,
in fact, tragically overestimated our moral right to wage war.

I have urged that the beginning of ethics is the question *what?*
By analyzing what war is, I propose to show that it is not easy
to justify war morally. Because of their nature, wars are to be
presumed guilty until proven innocent. John Fitzgerald Kennedy once said that there will always be wars until the status
of the conscientious objector is as honored as that of the warrior. I would add that everyone should be a conscientious
objector to every war until overwhelming evidence makes him a
warrior. The burden of proof is on the war-maker, not the objector. That is a hard saying for a martial society to hear. Let
me offer analytical proof for it.

In general, my position is that it is difficult for violence to
do more good than harm. It is not impossible that violence
could do more good than harm. But it is unlikely. The reasons
underlying that assertion are:

1. Violence makes community building and harmony hard to
achieve in the post-violence period. One of the slowly civilizing
insights of slowly civilizing man is the realization that the force
of war must not blot out the opportunities of post-war peace.
The force expended should be limited to the achievement of
the goals of the war. This civilizing insight is difficult if not impossible to maintain in the heat of battle. Successful violence
requires abstraction. The violent must abstract from the concrete fleshy individuality of the enemy or the cutting edge of his

violence will be blunted. That abstraction is achieved either by distancing one's self from the enemy, as does the pilot of a modern bomber who never sees the enemy, or by hatred. Hatred is an abstractive force. Hatred, to sustain itself, must distort. As J. Glenn Gray says in his reflective book *The Warriors,*

> In a sense, hatred is nearly always abstract to some degree, since as a passion it is unable to view anyone or anything in entirety. The hatred that arises for the enemy in wartime . . . is peculiarly one-sided, for it is a fear-filled image. The enemy is not an individual man or woman, but a hostile power intent upon destroying our people and our lives. Our unreflective response is normally total enmity for the image of evil that possesses our imagination.[20]

Violence, therefore, is rarely a happy prelude to peace. In war, the enemy must be swallowed up in abstractions such as freedom, national security, and making the world safe for democracy, or he must be experienced as subhuman and depraved. Otherwise the unambiguous vigor that violence requires cannot be mobilized or unleashed.

Harmonious peace is not the natural sequel of such an experience. Resentments that burn as long as the eternal flames that honor the killing heroes are the normal product of war. Georgia remembers Sherman. The weird anomaly of pursuing peace with the sword was noted by Augustine. The Middle East, Southeast Asia, Northern Ireland are all destined to be further pathetic exhibits to make the case for the almost inevitable counter-productivity of violence. Like a man struggling in quicksand, the more violence these lands engage in, the further they are from the good life that all reasonable human activity seeks. As the violence proceeds, the possibilities for harmony, which is the indispensable ingredient of the good life, are being pulled out by the roots.

2. Violence is addictive. It affects the people who rely on it with the ecstasy of the "quick fix." It brings relief from the frustrations of patient and imaginative struggle. Impatient cultures are most liable to become fixated at the level of violent power. Take a society that is hyperactive, task-oriented, little given to the admiring contemplation of the slow rhythms of

nature—I speak of the United States—such a society will be drawn by the promise of immediate relief that violence offers. Like heroin, violence can give a temporary sense of well-being, of achievement, of change where change is needed. Something is getting done where something ought to get done. There is an addictive exhilaration in that. And there is the tendency to believe, quite irrationally and compulsively, as addicts will, that more and more of the same will make things right.

Most tragically, this addictive reliance on violence, this unimaginative equating of violence with power, is not an atmosphere in which the neglected art of diplomacy will be enhanced. Diplomacy is primarily a work of patience and imagination, of sensitivity, tact, delicacy, and ingenuity. Diplomacy learns where the doors are and learns which will open and which will not. The true diplomat views the other protagonists in the international drama in their cultural concreteness. With discerning eye he dissipates myths that becloud the reality of the other. Diplomacy at its best is the supreme act of statecraft.[21] The violent are not likely to believe this. Fingers grown rough with bludgeoning are unlikely candidates for doing needlepoint.

3. Violence limits creativity by inducing a situation of limited options. Alternatives are part of reality. Where alternatives are unperceived, reality-contact is impaired. Man is blessed among the animals because he is inventive and can discover the possible beyond the given. I have referred to creative imagination as the prime moral faculty. Man can burst free from the confines of the actual, imagine what is not, and make it be.

In violence, this glory is lost. At an early stage in an altercation, many solutions are possible. As violence mounts, fewer options remain and the dispositions of the subjects are less open to whatever options there may be. As violence progresses, the goal of violence exercises a reverse telescopic effect. In the contracting power of violence, reality is shrunken, focus narrowed, vision fixated. Imagination, tender though promising shoot that it is, is the first casualty in the storm which is violence.

4. Violence minimizes the conditions for rationality. By its nature, it is alien to nuance. For violence to be successfully

mounted, there must be clear distinctions between right and wrong such as the real world does not afford. Warriors must see war as either a crusade or a crime. Their war is the crusade; the enemy's, a crime. Is it not significant that the just war theory presumes one side right and the other side wrong, even though, in point of historical fact, such a clean division of merit has never obtained.

Simplism, which is the bane of sensitive reasoning, would seem to be of the essence of violent power. Without simplism, violent force is immobilized. Violence thus does violence to reason and because of this it is unlikely to be the work of moral man or moral society.

Let it be clear that I am not saying that for a war to be justified, it must be pure with no admixture of evil. Such a requirement for a justified war is absurd and unrealistic. War will always do harm, a lot of harm. It may be justified if it does more good than harm, and if there was no other way to do that good, and if the good is at least proportionate to the harm. There will be disvalues mixed with the values even in a justified war. What I am saying here is that it is difficult for the values to outweigh the disvalues. The abolition of the conditions for rationality is prominent among the disvalues.

5. Violence is inherently escalatory. A harsh word leads to a shove and then a push and thence to fisticuffs. At the beginning of World War II, Hitler's bombing of population centers provoked expressions of shock from England and the United States. As the momentum of the war increased, however, the shock gave way to imitation. The Western Allies soon swallowed their moral indignation and determined that civilian morale and private property were legitimate targets of war. The British Foreign Secretary, Mr. Eden, wrote to the British Air Chiefs in the spring of 1942:

> I wish to recommend therefore that in the selection of targets in Germany the claims of smaller towns of under 150 thousand inhabitants which are not too heavily defended should be considered, even though those towns contain only targets of secondary importance.[22]

A Member of Parliament voiced his approval with enthusiasm. He declared himself to be "all for the bombing of working-class areas in German cities. I am Cromwellian—I believe in 'slaying in the name of the Lord.'" To this, the Secretary of State for Air, Sir Archibald Sinclair, replied that he was "delighted to find that you and I are in complete agreement about . . . bombing policy generally."[23] These were not mere words. On the night raid on Hamburg of July 27–28, 1943, phosphorus incendiaries and the techniques of the "bomber stream" produced within thirty minutes a fire storm, several miles wide, which burned or asphyxiated from forty-two to a hundred thousand people. Fire-bombing and attacks on civilians also became American policy against Japan. In the March 9–10, 1945, raid on Tokyo, 83,800 persons are reported to have died. Then, of course, followed Hiroshima and Nagasaki, and American consciences had grown so at ease with slaughter of populations that these unjustifiable attacks were borne with complacency. Such is the way of war. Here the domino theory does seem to be a telling argument against the possibility of a moral war. In unleashing violence, we unleash a force that has a power to possess its perpetrators. The escalatory thrust of violence is not easily contained within the ridges of right reason.

6. Violence tends to bypass the need for social and cultural restructuring such as would truly correct the aggravation at issue. With regard to social reform, violence can be superficial. When the storms of violence have passed, the myths, structures, and problems that precipitated the violence may still stand tall against the sky. Violence may change the *dramatis personae* only to discover that it is the same old show—or nearly so. Symbolically and really you may trade the Czar for Joseph Stalin.

It is the beginning of political wisdom to realize that all of our social problems have deep and tangled roots in history, economics, and in the scarcely known regions of social psychology. Social problems are processes that do not so much admit of cure as redirection. They must be addressed with patience and a sense of intricacy. More often than not, violence pulls off the leaves of the offending weeds while allowing the roots to prosper. States too easily descend to the logic of a bully who believes that differences are best settled with a punch in the mouth.

This aspect of violence relates to the escalatory thrust of violence. As the warriors begin to sense that the violence is not a panacea, and may indeed be making things worse rather than better, there develops a frantic urgency to increase the violence as though more and more of the unavailing medicine will somehow work the cure.

7. The violence of war represents a reversion to the primitive notion of collective responsibility. The term "collective responsibility" can mean something quite realistic and something that is ever modern and in need of appreciation. I refer to the fact that peoples are responsible for the misdeeds and culpable nondeeds of their nations, at least because of their mute apathy which allows the ruling powers to sally forth into moral crimes on the international scene.

The term "collective responsibility" here is used to describe the primitive notion that if one member of a tribe offends you, the whole tribe of the offender is guilty. Anthropologist Robert Lowie gives examples of this:

> The sibless Hupa were content to kill any member of a murderer's family in order to punish the crime; among the Crow if a Fox had disgraced himself and his society by taking back an abducted wife, the rival Lumpwoods had the right to cut up the blankets of all the Foxes; and in the same tribe the grief of the parents mourning the death of a son slain by the Dakota was at once assuaged when vengeance had been wreaked on any member of the hostile people.[24]

It is Lowie's judgment that this primitive conception is still operative in modern societies. "Though this is an archaic notion," he writes," it persists to the present day in the warfare of civilized nations, which summarily shelves the practice of determining individual guilt or innocence."[25] Lowie is both right and wrong here. I do believe the primitive myth persists in modern war, but the determination of guilt is not a question that is dismissed "summarily," as Lowie says. Efforts have been made traditionally in the just war theory to apply the principle of discrimination. Originally, when war was simpler, this principle was translatable as the principle of non-combatant immunity. Kill-power had to be focused on other potential killers only. In modern war a complicated lip service is still paid to the principle of discrimination. In theory, an effort is made in "conventional" wars to be discriminatory in the infliction of war deaths. In practice, there are Coventry and Dresden and Hamburg and Mylai. In theory, fire-power is to be directed only at militarily strategic targets. In practice, many civilians are killed or maimed or dislocated. The theory accounts for civilian deaths with such clinical terms as indirect killing, of which we have spoken, and "collateral damage." If, in going after a legitimate target, some civilians are *indirectly* killed, this is justified if there is proportionate reason to allow the "collateral damage." This rule paints with a broad brush. It does not turn out to be very discriminating in application. In practice, Lowie is right. Risks are taken with the lives of civilians that would not be taken if they were not implicitly swept under the archaic shadow of collective responsibility. Police would not go after a gang of criminals in New York City the way that we have gone after "the enemy" in Vietnam, Cambodia, and Laos. Care for civilian life would be a paramount concern in New York. It has not regularly been such in Southeast Asia, where even civilian life is tainted. This taint is evinced in the callously loose application of the principle of discrimination.

Of course, with regard to nuclear war, only a notion of collective responsibility in the primitive sense could justify the total war of nuclear weapons. Because of its inexorably indiscriminate effects, nuclear war was condemned in strong language in the Second Vatican Council.

> Any act of war aimed indiscriminately at the destruction of entire cities or of extensive areas along with their population is a crime against God and man himself. It merits unequivocal and unhesitating condemnation.[26]

All of these considerations seem to give us a well-grounded bias against violent power as a politically and morally acceptable means toward social ends. Normally, violence will do more harm than good. We cannot, however, exclude the possibility that, at times, violence might do more good than harm. But, in such a case, all of the negative elements we have brought to bear must be shown to have been outweighed by countervailing benefits. It seems to be suggested by the arguments offered here that this is true of far fewer cases than we have been culturally conditioned to expect. It also seems true that moralists have all too facilely provided abstruse and uncritical rationalizations to justify the barbaric instinct for war which lingers unredeemed in human consciousness.

SUICIDE

If suicide is allowed then everything is allowed. If anything is not allowed then suicide is not allowed. This throws a light on the nature of ethics, for suicide is, so to speak, the elementary sin.

Ludwig Wittgenstein[27]

Suicide is a vocation.

Jacques Rigaut[28]

Whatever it is, suicide is a common fact of life. About a thousand persons a day abandon life on this planet by way of suicide. In the United States alone the estimate is from eighty to a hundred suicides a day. And all estimates are probably low since many suicides are disguised or mistaken for accidents. Whether pro or con, persons react strongly to suicide, and many explanations have been offered to explain this unique tragedy. Forbes Winslow, a surgeon, wrote in 1840, with confidence, that the increase of suicide in that day was due to the appearance of "socialism." There was, he noted, a sudden increase in suicides following upon the publication of Tom Paine's *Age of Reason*. Not unaware of the complexity of the phenomenon, however, he went on to cite other causative factors such as "atmospherical moisture" and "masturbation." He saw masturbation as "a certain secret vice which, we are afraid, is practised to an enormous extent in our public schools."[29]

Cold showers and laxatives were seen as cures for the suicidal urge. It was popular to believe that suicide was primarily the act of young lovers, although the facts are that young lovers are not the most successful of suicides. Others see it as a national habit which overtakes some peoples like a plague, and President Eisenhower opined that the high Swedish rate of suicide was an example of what too much social welfare can do.

Spinoza said quite simply that "all persons who kill themselves are impotent in mind."[30] And Aristotle, in his *Ethics*, described suicide as a failure in courage. "To run away from trouble is a form of cowardice and, while it is true that the suicide braves death, he does it not for some noble object but to escape some ill."[31]

Harvard Professor Edwin S. Schneidman sees suicidal purpose involved not only in some deaths but in most deaths:

> The most important death category—the one that I believe may be characteristic of a majority of deaths—is the *subintentioned* death, in which the decedent plays some covert or unconscious role in hastening his own demise.[32]

As evidence of this he sees a variety of behavioral patterns such as poor judgment, excessive risk taking, neglect of self, disregard of medical regimen, and the abuse of alcohol and other drugs. He notes too that "There is a notion that the speed at which some malignancies grow may be related to deep inner psychological variables."[33]

Suicide of a sort may also take place in large numbers through what some psychologists call "victim-precipitated homicide," i.e. homicide where persons have acted in such a way as to make their own death almost certain.[34] In the same vein, Robert Lowell once remarked that if there were some little switch in the arm which one could press in order to die immediately and without pain, then everyone would sooner or later undertake suicide. If some or all of this is true, then self-killing is statistically normal. Our question is, may it be moral?

To begin with, I am speaking of suicide in a non-medical context. Death by choice in a medical context is a different reality to the point where it must be treated and judged separately. My position is that, with suicide as with war, there are massive presumptions against its moral rightness. Those presumptions may at times be overridden by other value considerations. At such times, suicide, like war, could be a morally good action. I am, of course, speaking of objective morality, as ethics should. I am not judging the subjective dispositions of those who perform suicide or implying that those who do so are in any way depraved. Thus, following the lead of Anthony Flew, I do not say "commit" suicide. That would imply guilt. As Flew puts it:

> . . . if you believe, as I do, that suicide is not always and as such wrong, it is inappropriate to speak of "committing suicide"; just as correspondingly if you believe, as I do not, that (private) profit is wrong, it becomes apt to talk of those who "commit a profit."[35]

Now to the reasons which militate against a positive judgment on the morality of suicide. First to the basic ethical question *what?* One must be careful in answering that question. The word suicide covers a multitude of realities. As Oliver Wendell Holmes once said, a word is not like "a crystal, transparent and unchanged." Rather, it is "the skin of a living thought." In a certain sense, no two suicides are alike, but, at the same time, no two are completely dissimilar. Nevertheless, there are strong indications that suicide springs from isolation and loneliness. A. Alvarez, who himself attempted suicide, speaks of "that total loneliness which is the precondition of all suicidal depression."[36] He says, too, that the suicide is "overwhelmed by his obscure and obscuring sense of inner chaos and worthlessness."[37]

The Professors Lester, in their book *Suicide: The Gamble with Death* write:

> Suicide is far less likely for a person who has lasting, satisfactory, unambivalent relationships with other people than it is for the social isolate or for the person whose closest relationships are permeated with resentment. Loss of close relationships, whether by accident or by deliberate withdrawal, may serve as a signal to a person's friends that the danger of suicide is increasing. Suicidal behavior does not occur without warning, and one of the most accurate warnings is found in the social relations of the potential suicide.[38]

The very loneliness of the suicide constitutes a moral objection to his suicide. We are social beings intrinsically and essentially. That does not just mean that we are together; it means that we are by being together. Our selves are the counterparts of other selves and action to be human must reflect that firm fact of our nature. The decision of the suicide is lonely, and that is a moral debit. It does not reflect his communitarian nature. On that count alone, it is likely to be a bad decision. His decision is, of course, related to people. Thus the suicide note and thus the finding of studies that suicide is almost always signaled in advance to someone.[39] But the decision does not proceed from the interpersonal context which is the natural humus from which personal decision, especially serious ones, should emerge. The good work that is being done by suicide prevention centers is trying to meet this need. Even telephone contact with a center counselor gives a context to many which enables them to overcome the crisis and opt for life.

At the level of *what*, it might also be noted that the person inclined to suicide suffers from vision dimmed by pain. When we are in pain, our perception of other realities is minimal. We notice little of what is going on around us. Partial vision leads to bad moral decisions. The fruitful lives of many persons who gave life another chance or who attempted suicide and failed and later rejoiced in their failure, indicates that the suicidal decision is, by its nature, not bathed in clear light.

Secondly, suicide may be morally indictable by reason of its *why*. Here the danger of generalization is even more dangerous than in our first consideration. Many are the motives of those who die by their own hand. But in assessing the potential moral meaning of suicide it is well to note that there is some evidence that suicide is often an act of aggression against others.[40] Suicide notes give evidence of this. These notes, in ways that vary from bluntness to subtlety, sometimes show that the death is being used to inflict pain and guilt on the survivors. "Mary, I hope you're satisfied. Bill."[41] This is a short example of a not uncommon theme. It would seem calculated to vitiate the morality of the act in several ways. First, it totally subordinates one's life to an irrational need for spite. Also, it is, to say the least, cruel and unusual punishment.

Suicide also can be wrong at the level of *foreseeable effects*. First, there are the effects on the bereaved. Studies are now showing that bereavement can be a fatal disease. One must have extraordinary reason, therefore, to inflict it on others. Dr. Dewi Rees and Sylvia Lutkins did a study of bereaved persons in Llanidloes, Wales, over a six-year period. During the first year of bereavement, they found that nearly 5 per cent of the bereaved died, whereas the figure in a comparable group of non-bereaved persons was less than 1 per cent.[42] The death rate among widowers and widows during the first year after death was 12 per cent, as compared to 1.2 per cent of their non-bereaved counterparts. If a spouse or child died suddenly outside the home or hospital, the death rate of the bereaved went up by a factor of five, due undoubtedly to the suddenness of the shock.

Dr. Arthur Schmale considered a number of women who were suspected of having cancer of the cervix. While they were in the hospital for a biopsy, Schmale and his colleagues interviewed these women, looking for two factors: had they suffered a serious break in significant social relationships, and had they reacted to it with feelings of hopelessness and depression? If both of these were present, Schmale predicted that the woman would have cancer. He was correct in 75 per cent of his predictions, both positive and negative. About one hundred women were interviewed.[43]

Other studies have shown that such symptoms as insomnia, trembling, and a variety of physical and psychiatric disorders may come upon the bereaved.[44] Again, the more sudden the death, the more likely it is that these disorders will occur.

These are factors to be weighed by one contemplating suicide. Good moral decisions are ones where the values outweigh the disvalues. Death may seem an important relief for persons in great distress, but the question is, does the relief of death compensate for the problems that death will cause?

Also, in the area of effects, any suicide may have an exemplary effect. That is, it may encourage other suffering persons to do likewise even though they could have overcome their problem with more time and support. All actions are imitable, especially dramatic ones like suicide. Each suicide may be an inducement to others to end their lives prematurely with much possibility unspent.

Finally, suicide is most likely a wrong decision because of the presence of alternatives. The human spirit can create and transform and, because of this, it should be slow, very slow, to admit despair. Man is a self-transcending animal and he has a native ability to transcend even the forces that move him toward suicide. The suicidal mood, of course, does not give ready entrance to alternatives, and that brings us back to our first point. The suicidal decision should not be made alone. Only the hardness of other persons can drive persons to the brink of suicide; only compassion and company can bring them back.

Having said all this, however, I must concede, "in a mournful mood," to use Augustine's phrase, that suicide may at times be moral. Even then, like war, it will be tragic; but it can like war be moral. Generally, I judge, persons perform suicide because they have been stripped of the essential ingredients of human life—hope and love. It would be naïve to think that human perfidy is not capable of depriving some of its members of these ingredients so that they can do no more and must depart. There may indeed be cases where all of the disvalues of suicide can be outweighed by ineffable pain and aloneness. In those cases, it is the survivors who are to be morally indicted, not the victim, who seizes the only remaining relief.

Life is *the* good thing and the precondition of all good things. Any decision to end it in any context, for self or for another, must be slow, deliberate, and reverential. But the life that is good, also bears the mark of the tragic. There are times when the ending of life is the best that life offers. Moral man will see this, and then, more than ever, he will know the full price of freedom.

FOOTNOTES—CHAPTER 8

1. *The Hastings Center Report* 2, no. 5 (November 1972): 1–4.
2. Ibid., p. 1.
3. Ibid., pp. 1–3. He also lists five negative criteria: man is not artificial, but rather characterized by technique, he is not essentially parental, nor sexual. Neither is he a "bundle of rights" or a worshiper, pp. 3–4.
4. Although I have always stressed the claims of the fetus, and joined other theologians in a public protest of the Supreme Court's fetus-slighting decision on abortion, I have recently felt in my Gemüt the rights of the fetus in a new way due to personal experience. The experience was the birth of my firstborn. His appearance proclaimed to me the marvel of that fetal community from which he just graduated. Thus the dedication of this book to him is not mere ceremonial affection. It is also gratitude. He has already been my teacher.
5. See A. Alvarez, *The Savage God* (New York: Random House, 1970), p. 53.
6. Ibid., pp. 53–54.
7. *The Destiny of Man* (New York and Evanston: Harper Torchbook, Harper & Row, Publishers, 1960), p. 205.
8. Ibid., p. 60. Berdyaev might have been on better ground here if he had said that vengeance is a prominent rather than "the chief" moral emotion of primitive man. Primitive societies had many manifestations, not all of them barbaric by any means. Indeed they often had more civilized modes of conflict resolution than we. See Robert H. Lowie, *Primitive Society* (New York: Liveright Publishing Corporation, 1947), pp. 397–426, on the systems of primitive justice.
9. Roland de Vaux, *Ancient Israel* (New York, Toronto: McGraw-Hill Book Co., 1965), Vol. 1, p. 11.
10. Primitive societies also had processes of medicinal punishment, but it seems fair to say that the vindictive character was usually paramount. See Lowie, op. cit.
11. Deuteronomy 13:16–18. The translation is from *The Jerusalem Bible* (Garden City: Doubleday & Company, Inc., 1966).
12. The quotation is from the report of the Royal Commission on Capital Punishment, cited in St. John-Stevas, op. cit., p. 96.
13. On the state of capital punishment in the United States, see Michael Meltsner, "Capital Punishment," *The New Republic* 169, no. 3 (July 21, 1973): pp. 12–13. See also, Meltsner's book *Cruel and Unusual: The Supreme Court and Capital Punishment* (New York: Random House, 1973).
14. Quoted in St. John-Stevas, op. cit., p. 90.
15. Vaux, op. cit., Vol. 1, p. 159. To see this practice, see 1 Kings 21:10, 13; Leviticus 24:14; Numbers 15:36. Other candidates for stoning in ancient Israel were idolaters, blasphemers, a woman who concealed the fact that she was not a virgin at the time of her marriage, a rebellious son, or someone who profaned the Sabbath. In not such ancient times in England, it was a capital offense to consort with gypsies, damage a fish pond (imagine what this would mean today to, say, the Board of Directors of General Motors or some other polluting industry), poach, and forge. As society progresses from greater to lesser barbarism, capital punishment diminishes.

16. *The Russian Idea* (Boston: Beacon Press, 1962), p. 152.

17. Ibid.

18. Ibid., p. 110. Berdyaev allows, of course, that the mentality of capital punishment has seeped into Russia, but he sees it as alien to the Russian spirit. Only those whose statism is absolutized can support such a practice.

19. *The Precarious Vision: A Sociologist Looks at Social Fictions and Christian Faith* (Garden City: Doubleday & Company, Inc., 1961), p. 115.

20. Gray, op. cit., p. 135. Significantly, Gray dedicates his book to "Ursula, My Wife, Formerly one of 'The Enemy.' "

21. Had Henry Kissinger been party to a more human and imaginative administration, there is every likelihood, I believe, that he would have given the art of diplomacy a new lift. Indeed, he has done so to a degree in spite of the deficiencies of his "superiors." Kissinger misspoke himself when he wrote: "Power has never been greater; it has also never been less useful" (*The Troubled Partnership* [New York, London, Toronto: McGraw-Hill Book Co., 1965], p. 18). He was falling into the same trap that made Lyndon Johnson complain that he had more power than any man in history, but that he could not use it. The error here confuses power with kill-power. There are other forms of power. Diplomacy is one of them. Kissinger, if he sorted his concepts out, would know that this is power of a still useful sort.

22. Sir Charles Webster and Noel Frankland, *The Strategic Air Offensive Against Germany 1939–45* (London: Her Majesty's Stationery Office, 1962), quoted in Edmund Stillman and William Pfaff, *The Politics of Hysteria* (New York, Evanston, and London: Harper & Row, Publishers, 1964), p. 33.

23. Ibid.

24. Lowie, op. cit., p. 399.

25. Ibid.

26. *The Documents of Vatican II*, ed. Walter M. Abbott, S.J. (New York: Herder and Herder, Association Press, 1966), "Pastoral Constitution on the Church in the Modern World, #80, p. 294. For related condemnations by the popes, cf. Pius XII, Allocution of September 30, 1954, AAS 46 (1954), p. 589; radio message of December 24, 1954, AAS 47 (1955), pp. 15 ff; John XXIII, encyclical letter "Pacem in Terris," AAS 47 (1963), pp. 286–91.

27. Ludwig Wittgenstein, *Notebooks, 1914–16*, ed. Anscombe, Rhees, and Von Wright (Oxford and New York, 1961), p. 91e. Entry dated 10.1.17; quoted in Alvarez, op. cit., p. 220.

28. Quoted in Alvarez, op. cit., p. 231.

29. Quoted in Alvarez, op. cit., p. 212.

30. Benedict de Spinoza, *Ethics* (New York: Hafner Publishing Co., 1957), p. 202.

31. *The Ethics of Aristotle* (Hammondsworth, Eng.: Penguin Books, 1953), p. 97.

32. Schneidman, op. cit., p. 41.

33. Ibid.

34. See Richard H. Seiden, "We're Driving Young Blacks to Suicide," *Psychology Today* 4, no. 3 (August 1970): 24–28.

35. In Downing, op. cit., p. 46.

36. Alvarez, op. cit., p. 111.

37. Ibid., p. 107.

38. Gene Lester and David Lester, *Suicide: The Gamble With Death* (Englewood Cliffs, N.J.: Prentice-Hall, 1971), p. 72.

39. Ibid., p. 3 et passim.

40. See Norman Farberow and T. McEvoy, "Suicide Among Patients with Diagnoses of Anxiety Reaction or Depressive Reaction in General Medical or

Surgical Hospitals," *Journal of Abnormal Psychology* 71, pp. 287–99; see also Lester and Lester, op. cit., pp. 52–55.

41. Lester and Lester, op. cit., p. 79; cf. also pp. 74–81, 42, and 106.

42. "Morality of Bereavement," *British Medical Journal,* October 1967.

43. Reported in *Death Education: Preparation for Living,* ed. Betty R. Green and Donald P. Irish (Cambridge, Mass.: Schenkman Publishing Company, 1971), p. 20.

44. See Hendin, op. cit., pp. 164–84 and Diana Crane, "Dying and Its Dilemmas as a Field of Research," in Brim et al., op. cit., pp. 319–21.